BRIDGES TO RETIREMENT

Older Workers in a Changing Labor Market

Peter B. Doeringer, Editor

ILR Press
School of Industrial and Labor Relations   Cornell University

Cover design by Kat Dalton

Library of Congress Cataloging-in-Publication Data

Bridges to retirement : older workers in a changing labor market /
    Peter B. Doeringer, editor.
        p.   cm.
    Includes bibliographical references.
    ISBN 0-87546-159-X.—ISBN 0-87546-160-3 (pbk.)
    1. Age and employment—United States. 2. Aged—Employment—United
States. 3. Career changes—United States. I. Doeringer, Peter B.
    HD6280.B73 1990   89-26789
    331.3'98'0973—dc20   CIP

Copies may be ordered through bookstores or directly from
ILR Press
School of Industrial and Labor Relations
Cornell University
Ithaca, NY 14851–0952

Printed on acid-free paper in the United States of America
5   4   3   2   1

CONTENTS

TABLES AND FIGURES

ACKNOWLEDGMENTS

THIS VOLUME HAD ITS origins in the work of the Commonwealth of Massachusetts Older Workers Task Force, appointed by the Executive Office of Economic Affairs in 1983 to develop an employment and training policy for older workers under the Job Training Partnership Act. As chair of the task force, I conducted a review of the labor market experiences of older workers in Massachusetts to determine their training needs. Although ample statistical materials were available to describe the employment and unemployment of older workers, most of the analytical studies focused on retirement rather than on jobs. Yet jobs, and access to jobs, were critical to the economic well-being of the aging work force.

With the encouragement of task force member Katherine Villers, a number of foundations were approached with a proposal to examine the changing job prospects for older workers. In 1984 a favorable response was received from the Florence V. Burden Foundation for a grant to study expanding employment opportunities for older workers. Subsequent funds were provided in 1987 by the Commonwealth Fund, under the auspices of the Commonwealth Fund Commission on Elderly People Living Alone, for an in-depth examination of the employment patterns and workplace experiences of older workers. The support from these foundations is greatly appreciated. In all cases, however, the statements made and the views expressed are those of the authors and do not reflect those of the Commonwealth Fund, the commission, or the Florence V. Burden Foundation.

Resources for research are, of course, only a small part of what it takes to complete a project such as this. David Nee (previously the executive director of the Florence V. Burden Foundation), Karen Davis (director of the Commonwealth Fund Commission on Elderly People Living Alone), Barbara Lyons of the commission staff, and

Thomas Moloney (senior vice president of the Commonwealth Fund) helped keep the project on track. Katherine Villers of the Villers Foundation and Pamela Wescott of the Massachusetts Department of Employment and Training provided frequent opportunities for us to review our findings with practitioners concerned with issues affecting older workers. Charlene Arzigian managed the research projects and the preparation of the manuscript with her usual aplomb, and the editorial staff at ILR Press helped smooth out the manuscript's rough edges. Others, too numerous to name, contributed to the research findings and otherwise helped advance the study. On behalf of the research team, I express our thanks.

———— INTRODUCTION ————

1

ECONOMIC SECURITY, LABOR MARKET FLEXIBILITY, AND BRIDGES TO RETIREMENT

Peter B. Doeringer

THE PROPORTION OF SENIOR citizens in the population has increased markedly in recent years as the elderly live longer and as birth rates decline. In the last two decades, the population aged 55 and older has grown by about 40 percent, roughly twice the rate of the rest of the population, and another 15 percent growth is anticipated by the year 2000. This population shift is coupled with a startling decrease in labor force participation rates among older workers. In 1967, almost half the population 55 and over spent some time in the labor market. By 1986, this figure had fallen to about one-third, a drop of 25 percent (see chapter 3).

This reduction in labor market activity has affected all groups of older workers, but it has been particularly acute for males and the poorly educated. The decline has also been persistent, even during periods of growth in the demand for labor, and is expected to continue for most segments of the older population to the year 2000 and beyond.

A worrisome consequence of these trends is that the balance between those who work and those who do not is tipping. The earnings base of the older population and the opportunities it provides for the accumulation of resources for retirement are shrinking at the same time that life expectancy is increasing.

Much of the debate over what to do about this decline in employment among older workers has focused on the financial solvency of the Social Security and Medicare systems in meeting the economic needs of the elderly, but it is also important to explore whether employment and earned income can play a greater role in meeting these needs in the future. A critical issue is the extent to which work incentives can be restructured so as to increase the labor force participation and earnings of the elderly.

What little we know about this issue comes indirectly from studies of the supply side of the labor market. Research on the labor market for older workers has traditionally focused on disincentives to employment—principally on how Social Security and pensions affect the labor supply through their impact on the timing of individual retirement decisions (see chapter 2; Lazear 1986; Fields and Mitchell 1984; Burkhauser 1979; Boskin 1977; Boskin and Hurd 1984; Pellechio 1979; Rosen 1980; Barzel 1973).

This literature underscores the importance of economic incentives in controlling how and when older persons wind down their working lives (see chapter 2). Contrary to widespread perceptions, Social Security has been found to have a relatively minor net effect on labor supply, and its influence is likely to be further diminished by recent legislative reforms. This is not true, however, for private sector pensions with "defined benefit" plans that contain significant disincentives to work. Poor health and mandatory retirement, the other major obstacles to work that have been studied, play a secondary role to economic considerations in the retirement decisions of most workers.

These findings, however, largely reflect the pension and retirement experience of white males. There have been few investigations of the patterns of work and retirement of women and ethnic minorities, whose work, health, and pension experiences are likely to differ substantially from those of white males. This neglect of women and minorities is particularly unfortunate because these are the high-growth groups in the older population that will account for most of the net growth in the labor force in the next decade or so (see chapter 3). They are also the groups that encounter the most serious economic problems with aging (see chapter 4; Commonwealth Fund Commission on Elderly People Living Alone n.d.).

Whatever the limitations of research on pensions and labor supply, however, the truly critical gap in the literature on older workers is in the demand side of the labor market. Pension incentives are only half of the labor supply equation. Equally important are the quality and availability of jobs.

Bridges to Retirement:
Finding the Right Model

Almost nothing is known about the structure of job opportunities that older workers face in choosing whether to work or retire. The typical image held by most economists in discussing older workers and the retirement decision is that of the worker (usually a white male) who is employed in a career job until he becomes eligible for pension or Social Security income. The structure of pay and job opportunities available to the older worker is taken as given, and access to pension income is seen as the variable that triggers the decision to retire.

There is mounting evidence, however, that this model does not adequately characterize the labor market situation for increasing numbers of older workers. For example, there are substantial shifts in the composition of employment by industrial sector as older cohorts age in the labor market (see chapter 3). This evidence suggests that many older workers take some sort of postcareer employment before they retire. Whether this job changing is voluntary or forced and its effects on the retirement decision have been largely unexplored. Equally little is known about the work incentives provided by career jobs, postcareer jobs, or the part-time or casual jobs that are often a source of income for partially retired workers.

Traditionally it has been assumed that workers can adjust their working time to suit their preferences for earned income, pension income, and retirement. Survey research, however, suggests that older workers may want more work or a different mix of hours than are available to them in the labor market (see chapter 3; Louis Harris and Associates 1981).

Some industries seem to accommodate a larger number of part-time older workers than others (Kahne 1985), but we understand little about what controls the mix of part-time and full-time work or the access older workers have to such jobs. How do employers' practices on the demand side of the labor market—job design, recruitment, retention, and compensation—affect the employment opportunities and work incentives of older workers? Do employers and unions encourage the retention or the retirement of older workers? Is the labor market becoming more or less hospitable to the job preferences of older workers?

Without answers to these questions it is difficult to determine the prospects for older workers in the labor market or to evaluate the potential effectiveness of various policies directed at the older worker labor market. To date, public policy has concentrated almost exclusively on the supply side of the labor market through reforms in the Social Security and pension systems designed to reduce work disincentives. Such policy intervention as has occurred has also been mainly on the supply side, through training programs to increase the employability of older workers. Very few programs have been directed at restructuring labor demand and improving employment opportunities for older workers.

This volume seeks to redress this imbalance in research and policy by focusing broadly on the preretirement labor market experience of older workers, rather than emphasizing their retirement behavior per se. It assesses the impact on the economic well-being of older workers of two important developments in the economy—changes in the employment structure of older workers, including women and minorities, and the dramatic increase in flexible employment practices at the workplace. It looks both at overall trends and patterns in the market for older workers, including women and minorities, and at developments in the workplace that directly affect the employment prospects of older workers.

In particular, the book explores the significance of "bridge jobs"— the jobs that follow career employment and precede permanent retirement. As Christopher J. Ruhm discusses in chapter 4, bridges to retirement are more varied than had previously been thought. Some workers move directly from career jobs to permanent retirement. For a majority of older workers, however, career jobs end early and are exchanged for other types of work.

The postcareer period of bridge employment before retirement can be lengthy. For example, about one-third of all career jobs end by age 55 and almost half by age 60. Yet less than one in nine workers has retired by the latter age (see chapter 5).

For some, bridge employment involves a period of partial retirement with part-time work or a return to part-time employment after a spell of retirement. For many, however, full-time employment remains an important part of the bridging process. Although the majority of these full-time workers hold one postcareer job, some hold a succession of full-time bridge jobs, most of which involve a change in work setting. There is no evidence of pervasive opportunities for flexible retirement within the same firm or even the same industry.

Few systematic data are available about bridge jobs or how they are evolving. Nevertheless, there is considerable evidence that the labor market seriously penalizes older workers who change jobs and that many bridge jobs are a step down in pay and status.

For example, three-quarters of all bridge jobs for older male workers involve a change in occupation or industry, and almost half involve both. Bridge jobs are typically of lower status than the career jobs they replace, and over half involve pay cuts of 25 percent or more (see chapter 5). Bridge jobs are likely to be found in small and medium-sized firms (see chapters 3 and 8) in which employment can be erratic and fringe benefits such as pensions and health insurance tend to be inferior to those of larger companies (National Federation of Independent Business 1985).

The following section briefly highlights the major findings of the empirical research. It reveals the need for "fine-grained" analysis of the labor market for older workers concentrating on the long-term experience of at-risk groups in the elderly population and placing these risks in the context of the changing structures of the workplace and the labor market. Current labor market programs are evaluated in light of these findings, and in the final section of this chapter, new directions for policy are outlined.

The Economic Security Package: Successes and Failures

The economic security package—full employment, Social Security and private pensions, job-based health insurance, and promotion and lay-off protections based on seniority—that emerged in postwar America was supposed to give the older worker a secure position in the economy. With aging would come seniority protection, higher-paying jobs, and steady employment. These would be followed by the opportunity to retire from a career job with at least a minimally sufficient pension income.

The data confirm that the majority of today's older workers, born in the 1920s and the early years of the Great Depression and employed under these postwar arrangements, have secured the benefits of career employment, stable earnings, and adequate pensions (see chapters 4 and 5). On average, elderly individuals (55 and over) occupy a relatively favored position in the economy. Seniority and accumulated work experience place many older workers high on their career ladders and insulate them from much of the economic uncertainty and job restructuring that have affected the job security and earnings of younger workers.

As a result, older workers have been spared much of the job displacement and work disruption associated with recent structural changes in the American economy. They have long had the lowest unemployment rates of any group of workers, and they are one of the few groups in the society whose real income has improved in the last fifteen years.

The advantages of age, experience, and seniority, however, are not evenly spread throughout the older population. White males, for example, have been the most successful in obtaining well-paying career jobs (mainly in larger companies) and have the most adequate pension and Social Security coverage. But even white males are now being displaced from such work, and other groups of older persons participate only minimally in the nation's public and private systems of economic security (see chapter 4).

AT-RISK GROUPS

The statistical analyses in chapters 4 and 5 reveal troubling developments affecting the labor market circumstances of older workers. Although no group of older persons is exempt from employment problems, four groups experience the most severe difficulties—ethnic minorities, women living alone, the working poor, and displaced workers. Unfortunately, these vulnerable groups are the most rapidly growing segments of the older population.

Ethnic Minorities. The most rapid growth within the elderly population under 70 is among ethnic minorities, particularly Hispanics and Asians, as pointed out in chapter 3. Minorities are roughly twice as vulnerable to unemployment, involuntary part-time employment, and discouragement as are white workers. The population growth rates and special disadvantages of these groups have often been ignored in the debates over policies regarding older workers.

Women Living Alone. It is well established that a large fraction of the elderly poor are women living by themselves. Most of these women are widows or divorced, do not work, and have no recent preparation for entry into the labor market. By the time they find themselves in poverty, it is often too late for the labor market to provide solutions to their income inadequacy. Women who are particularly at risk of living alone in poverty will need to be identified at an age when their employment needs, and those of their husbands, can be anticipated.

Women whose husbands are not working because of ill health or disability are particularly vulnerable to early widowhood. In 1987 there were about 1.3 million women married to older men (over 55) in this category (see chapter 4). Even among the younger husbands in this group, those aged 55 to 59, mortality rates are three to four times higher than for their counterparts without health problems.

Moreover, three out of four of these wives were not in the labor force, often because of the need to care for family members. While participation in the labor force among such at-risk females is rising, greater efforts to bring them into the employment system are critical to alleviating poverty during widowhood (see chapter 4; Commonwealth Commission on Elderly People Living Alone n.d.).

The Working Poor. Job loss, unemployment, lack of preparation for employment, and discouragement are not the only causes of poverty among older workers. A significant number of the elderly remain poor despite having some employment. For example, over one-third of the poor aged 55 to 59 and over one-fourth of those aged 60 to 62 were employed at some time during 1987 (see chapter 4). Among the working poor over age 55, about one-third worked full time throughout the year; two-thirds of them were males. The presence of this group of fully employed but nonetheless impoverished older workers means that problems of earnings potential must be addressed as well as problems of employability.

Displaced Workers. Even for white male workers with established careers, labor market displacement is an increasing problem. The result of displacement is often unemployment or bridge employment at lower pay (see chapter 5). The data reveal that these problems are not rooted in the period immediately surrounding the retirement decision, as much previous research has implied. Instead, the labor market problems of older workers arise from long-standing inadequacies in their preparation for employment, from structural problems of job access, and from the premature termination of career jobs before retirement. Thus the focus of labor market solutions to the economic needs of older persons must begin long before workers reach retirement age.

COMPOUNDING THE PROBLEMS

Approximately 6 percent of the age group 55 and over (and 11 percent of those between 55 and 60) suffer from one or more severe labor market disabilities—unemployment, involuntary part-time work, discouragement from lack of work, or low-wage employment—

that leave many of them poor or near poor (see chapter 4). Blacks and Hispanics are two and one-half times more likely to have these problems than are whites, and high school dropouts are twice as likely as college graduates to be in this category. One-half of all such disadvantaged workers are numbered among the working poor.

Job Access and Career Employment

Factors such as gender, ethnicity, occupation, and marital status are typical correlates of poverty and labor market difficulty, but the problems of employment disadvantage can also be measured by the types of jobs to which older workers have access. For example, the earnings, employment security, and fringe benefits of older workers in large corporations are generally superior to those available in smaller firms or in casual or temporary work. Moreover, the older worker who changes jobs or who decides to enter the labor market after a long spell of not working is likely to be disadvantaged compared to those who remain in established career settings (see chapter 5). Older workers who are displaced from career employment can be expected to experience great difficulty in finding comparable replacement jobs, and older workers reentering the labor market after a long absence are likely to end up in relatively low-paying, dead-end work.

Career employment often has been elusive for many women workers, minorities, and the educationally disadvantaged. It is widely believed, however, to characterize the typical employment pattern of the white male work force and to be the direction in which other groups of workers are moving. But recent developments in the economy—the substantial contraction of employment in large firms, the growth of service sector employment, the shift from permanent to contingent employment relationships, and the decline in the coverage of union-based job security arrangements—are reducing the chances that workers will hold career jobs.

The shrinking perimeter of career employment may now be threatening older workers whose career employment heretofore has been relatively secure. Even the employment systems of large corporations, once designed to move workers in a secure and orderly way from entry-level jobs to retirement, are affected. With the merger and downsizing of many large corporations, workers are being encouraged to retire at a younger age and displacement of older workers has been common in some industries hard hit by competition.

There is evidence that career jobs for workers in their fifties and sixties are ending before such workers are ready to retire. When their career jobs end, these workers experience substantial job changing, lost earnings, and reduced job status. Instead of retirement at the end of a career job, there is an extended period of work in the twilight zone of bridge jobs between career jobs and retirement (see chapter 5).

FLEXIBLE EMPLOYMENT—SOLUTION OR PROBLEM?

Not only is employment contracting in the large corporations that have been the source of much career employment, but the jobs that remain are becoming more flexible and contingent (see chapters 6, 7, and 9). Coincident with these changes in large corporations has been a growth in small and medium-sized firms (Loveman, Piore, and Sengenberger 1990) and in services. Together, these trends should result in a net increase in the availability of part-time, part-year, or other flexible employment opportunities (see chapter 8).

In principle, this rise in flexible employment should be an asset for older workers because it expands the stock of potential bridge jobs that can be tailored to the preferences of older workers for part-time or part-year work. The downside of contingent jobs, however, is that they often pay less than the permanent jobs they replace, and many of the new flexible jobs in the service sector pay relatively low wages.

Older workers are often a labor pool of choice in lower-wage bridge jobs, and there are few barriers to their employment (see chapters 6 and 8). Nevertheless, even as flexible bridge jobs are on the increase, it appears that older workers may not be assured their proportional share of such jobs (see chapter 6). In the labor market for flexible jobs, older workers can and do lose out to competing groups—women with children, young workers, and immigrant workers.

Even when older workers can compete successfully for bridge jobs in the flexible or contingent labor markets, many of these jobs may not adequately match the economic needs and job preferences of older workers, who may reject or resent these jobs if they entail a loss of status as well as pay (see chapter 9). They may, therefore, offer inadequate economic incentives to entice substantial numbers of older persons with pension or Social Security income back into the labor market, and they may not pay enough to raise out of poverty those older workers not yet eligible for retirement income.

There are, however, optimistic developments in the bridge job sector that may improve the employment prospects of older workers. Trade unions, for example, may provide one antidote to the economic limitations of contingent work. Many trade unions once resisted the development of both part-time and contingent work, but some are now seeking to represent contingent and part-time workers more aggressively and to upgrade the wages and conditions of such work (see chapter 7). To date, however, these policies have been directed more at the needs of female workers than older workers.

A second source of better-quality bridge jobs is the flexible retirement programs offered by a handful of progressive, large corporations (American Association of Retired Persons 1986; ICF 1988). These programs extend career job options for older workers by providing new bridges to retirement in their own firms.

These flexible retirement programs, however, have limitations. They are available only to incumbent employees, not to older workers generally. Moreover, such programs have usually been conceived as experiments in corporate social responsibility rather than arising out of "business necessity" (Paul 1983) and may have a limited potential for expansion in the corporate sector. Most large firms continue to have career promotion structures, severance pay, and pension programs that encourage their employees to retire completely from employment with the firm.

A more significant, yet often overlooked, source of higher-quality bridge jobs is in the informal arrangements to retain skilled and experienced workers beyond normal retirement age devised by non-bureaucratic small and medium-sized firms (see chapter 8; Gibbons and Perotta 1981). These bridge jobs are often customized to the needs of individual workers. They provide the flexibility, economic benefits, and status that make bridge employment an attractive option to both career jobs and permanent retirement. Such bridge jobs are of particular significance in that they are the result of business necessity, not corporate conscience.

Approaches to Policy

Statistical analysis places the earnings and employment needs of at-risk groups of older workers squarely in the domain of developments in the preretirement labor market for such workers. It also shows that emerging trends in the structure of employment are not likely to reverse the risk of income inadequacy facing many of the elderly unless there are effective policy interventions in the labor market.

Two developments—the above-average increase in the numbers of difficult-to-employ older workers and changes in the job and career structure of the American economy—pose a difficult challenge to employment and training policy. Labor market policy has historically neglected older workers. Moreover, the record of employment and training programs implemented to meet the most critical needs of older workers, such as those operating under the current Job Training Partnership Act (JTPA) legislation, has not been strong.

Promoting access to good-quality career jobs for women, ethnic minorities, and the poorly educated of any age has been an elusive goal, and programs for the working poor have been among the most difficult to design and implement. Both prior policy experience and the recent trends in economic and demographic structure suggest that the redirection of employment policy concerning older workers must occur as part of a more general rethinking about how the job market works for Americans of all ages.

Curing the employment problems of older workers must involve both traditional approaches of human resource programs and nontraditional programs targeted at changing employment practices in ways that lead to a better fit between jobs and the employment needs of older workers.

CAREER JOBS AND BRIDGE JOBS

The findings about the prevalence of bridge jobs have a number of important policy implications. First, that a large number of career jobs end before retirement indicates that even relatively stable work attachments do not mean lifetime employment. Lifelong education and training, long considered a luxury, will become a necessity as workers begin career jobs later and end them earlier and as more and more workers spend ten or twenty years in bridge employment before retirement.

Because of job changing, postcareer employment will frequently be punctuated by periods of not working. When new work is obtained, it is frequently in a different industry or occupation and earnings are often reduced. The prevalence of job changing and earnings loss raises important questions about the causes and consequences of labor turnover among this group. Many of those who take bridge jobs will need to be retrained because bridge employment is far different from career employment. Currently, fewer workers are aware of this prospect and even fewer are prepared for it.

Finally, nonwhites and females spend fewer years in career jobs and their career jobs end at a younger age. Preventive policies are needed to help such groups find stable career employment earlier in their working lives so they can avoid difficulties in the labor market in their older years.

PARTIAL RETIREMENT AND
FLEXIBLE EMPLOYMENT

Partial retirement is both more common and longer lasting than generally believed. For example, 50 to 55 percent of workers consider themselves partially retired during some part of their working lives, and more than 20 percent of 65- and 67-year-old workers are partially retired at a given time (see chapter 5). The average duration of partial retirement slightly exceeds five years, and a fifth of partially retired workers remain in the labor force, in some capacity, for more than eight years following the start of partial retirement.

Part-time employment is twice as common among older workers as it is among the general population, but it remains a relatively underused job option (see chapter 3). Full-time work is still the predominant form of employment among older workers, and part-year employment is contracting. Part-time jobs are becoming increasingly important, however, for those between ages 62 and 65. Recent trends toward greater use of part-time and contingent labor by employers may encourage more flexible employment options that will be attractive for older workers, particularly those on the verge of retirement, but there is evidence of considerable competition for such jobs among other groups in the economy.

Relatively few workers are able to retire partially on their career jobs. To the extent that switching to bridge employment renders useless the firm- and sector-specific skills that have been acquired during a lifetime of work, mechanisms that permit greater flexibility on the career job are likely to yield benefits such as higher incomes and increased labor force participation for older workers and the retention of motivated and productive employees by their firms.

Individual companies have experimented with a number of programs targeted toward older workers—flextime, job sharing, phased retirement, and trial retirement. Information on successful experiences has not been widely distributed, however, and efforts to provide legislative reform that encourages further experimentation and implementation are needed.

More generally, programs will be required to provide greater flexibility for workers who wish gradually to reduce their labor force attachment while remaining on their career jobs before ultimately retiring; for those who wish to return to work on a part-time or part-year basis; and for firms desiring to use the expertise of highly experienced older workers in nontraditional employment relationships.

TRAINING AND SUBSIDIZED JOBS

Current labor market policies measure up rather poorly when compared to the interventions suggested above. Training policy has focused on the existing job structure, job creation has done little to change the employment structure, and the working poor have been neglected.

The principal arm of labor market policy for older workers is the Job Training Partnership Act, a federally funded program of employment and training assistance administered at the state and local levels. Older workers who are economically disadvantaged can receive assistance under the general provisions of the act (Title IIA programs), under a special set-aside of 3 percent of the general training funds for programs targeted at older workers, or under programs for assisting dislocated workers (Title III programs). Little attention has been paid to the possibility of using training funds as an incentive to restructure work or to the mechanisms for doing so.

With a few exceptions, JTPA programs for older workers have concentrated on the traditional approaches of recruiting and placing unemployed, job-ready older workers and of providing training and work orientation to facilitate job placement. Moreover, the national experience under JTPA suggests that it has not been able to reach a significant fraction of those in need, particularly the working members of the older disadvantaged population. In program year 1985, for example, only about sixty-four thousand workers (or 5 percent of the total JTPA participants) were 55 or older. They made up less than one-twentieth of unemployed older workers (55 to 64) eligible for such programs.

Policies toward employment structure have largely been confined to the creation of part-time, low-wage employment in public and non-profit settings. These are typically the same bridge jobs that are already available to older workers and do little to alter the quality of their job opportunities. Moreover, the resources appropriated for such jobs are trivial. The main work experience program available for older persons, the Senior Community Service Employment Program (SCSEP), provides jobs for only one hundred thousand persons.

Because of these limited resources and the patterns of labor force participation and discouragement among the economically disadvantaged, it would seem most useful to target JTPA funds toward workers between 55 and 62 and to reserve the SCSEP funds for part-time job seekers aged 63 to 70. But limited training funds are only part of the problem, and the targeting of available resources is only part of the solution. Much more central is the need to address a series of structural problems that have been neglected by JTPA and SCSEP.

Both JTPA and SCSEP jobs need to be used more aggressively to promote upgrading. JTPA has not substantially upgraded the types of jobs for which participants are eligible. SCSEP has rarely included a training component, and little attention is paid to integrating public employment more generally into a comprehensive labor market strategy for older workers that includes the transition to unsubsidized work. There is considerable room for better use of such programs by tailoring the work more closely to the employment needs of discouraged workers and by improving the linkages of such programs to both training and placement in unsubsidized jobs.

Neither program has successfully reached the groups most difficult to serve—the working poor, the "hidden unemployed," Hispanics, and Asians. Large numbers of older persons are barred from participation in such programs because they fail to meet strict income eligibility requirements, and little has been done to anticipate the needs of at-risk groups such as the wives of the working poor or those with ill or disabled husbands. Attacking these problems will require more resources and a substantial reorientation of policy toward hard-to-serve groups and toward changes in the structure of job opportunities for older workers.

EXTENDING WORK LIFE
THROUGH PENSION REFORM

Pension reform is the major policy now affecting the employment of older workers. It, too, focuses on labor supply, leaving the structure of employment opportunities unchanged. There is a substantial literature suggesting that the Social Security system and private pensions have lessened the attachment of older persons to the labor market. Although the evidence of diminishing attachment is clear, the link to pensions is much less certain.

Despite an enormous body of research examining the effects of Social Security incentives on the labor supply behavior of the elderly, it is not evident whether the system promotes or retards retirement. It is clear, however, that proposed changes in the system will have only small effects on retirement behavior. For example, elimination of the Social Security "earnings test" would enable employed Social Security beneficiaries to work substantially more hours, but, because so few recipients work, will only slightly change total labor supply.

Private pension plans often encourage early retirement because the actuarial value of benefits usually peaks before age 65. Evidence that workers respond to these economic incentives suggests that changes in private pension structures might have a significant impact on the work behavior of persons in their late fifties and early sixties. This is likely to be particularly effective for individuals covered by "defined benefit" plans with large increases in value occurring at particular ages or years of service (see chapter 2).

These pension effects are likely to be strongest for white males and other persons who have had a substantial attachment to well-paid employment. They are less likely to increase the falling participation rates of minorities and the economically disadvantaged, whose work and retirement decisions are less strongly subject to the influences of private pension incentives.

FULL EMPLOYMENT

It is sometimes argued that full employment and growth will substantially affect the employment prospects of older workers. There is, for example, some evidence of cyclical sensitivity in unemployment rates and involuntary part-time unemployment for older workers, both of which have been rising in recent years when compared to the tight labor markets of the late 1960s and early 1970s.

It is more difficult, however, to determine exactly how much of the underemployment problem is tied to the macroeconomic situation. Overall rates of labor market discouragement have been relatively stable over the business cycle (although there are signs of increasing underemployment among older workers with no postsecondary schooling and among older minorities). The potential for a more buoyant economy reducing underemployment is likely to be only modest if the experience in Massachusetts (where the unemployment rate has been consistently below 4 percent for several years) is any guide.

Massachusetts data suggest that full employment would have its greatest impact on the participation rates of 55- to 64-year-old workers. For this group, labor force participation is about 7 percentage points higher than the national average, whereas there is no difference in participation among those 65 and older. Extending this experience to national data suggests that a more buoyant economy would principally affect those older workers seeking full-time employment and would probably fail to remedy the structural problems of job quality and job access.

As the recent political debates over pension reform, health insurance, minimum wages, and plant closing legislation show, policies to effect structural change in the labor market do not come easily. Because the structural disintegration of the American labor market is no longer limited to workers displaced by foreign competition, or to minorities and the disadvantaged, or to workers nearing retirement, the overall need for such changes will be heightened in the next decade and the prospects for change will be much improved.

Plan of the Book

A combination of approaches is taken in examining these developments. Indeed, the major strength of this volume is the complementarity between the quantitative analysis of the changing position of older workers in the economy and the case studies exploring, at the micro level, the sources of these aggregate trends and their likely consequences for the workplace and the older worker.

Part I provides a quantitative examination of the changing labor market for older workers. A brief literature review in chapter 2 establishes the research baseline upon which the subsequent chapters build. Chapters 3, 4, and 5 develop statistical profiles of the labor market for older workers and discuss the significance of bridge jobs.

In chapters 3 and 4, two decades of data on a cross section of the population are analyzed to determine which groups of older workers have benefited from the postwar economic security package and which have been left behind. In chapter 5, a rich source of panel data is used to trace the work histories of a cohort of older workers as they pass from career employment into retirement.

The statistical studies in part I are complemented by the chapters in part II, which look at how employment opportunities are changing at the workplace under pressures for more flexible employment arrangements. These include studies of corporate initiatives for flexible staffing, union responses to flexible employment practices, and the informal staffing arrangements for older workers adopted by small and medium-sized firms. These studies provide additional information about the character of bridge employment and the prospects that such jobs offer to older workers.

Part III reports the results of a series of interviews with older persons whose working lives are in transition as a result of economic change. Through the "voices" of workers we learn about other dimensions of bridge jobs and about what economic change means in human terms.

PART I

*The Labor Market for
Older Workers*

2

DETERMINANTS OF THE TIMING OF RETIREMENT

Christopher J. Ruhm

RESEARCH EXAMINING THE LABOR force behavior of older w
ers has proliferated during the last decade. The principal con
of these studies has been to address the problem of how the eld
will be supported in the coming years as the size of this popula
cohort grows and its rate of labor force participation declines. S
there are questions about the extent to which the younger wor
population is able or willing to finance future payments, attentior
naturally turned to issues of work and retirement.

The bulk of this study has concentrated on the circumstance
mediately surrounding the retirement decision, principally tho
health and of the work disincentives in Social Security and pr
pensions. This chapter briefly reviews this recent research. It ou
the broad conclusions of previous studies in order to establish a
line for the statistical analyses that follow, rather than to prov
comprehensive survey of the field. The review covers six top
health, mandatory retirement, Social Security, private pensions,
ings and wealth, and partial retirement.[1]

Health

Some older persons undoubtedly leave the labor force because
health deteriorates to the point that they can no longer work. I
theless, it is increasingly evident that voluntary responses to cha

---

1. This chapter draws heavily on material previously presented in Ruhm 1!

23

economic incentives and possibly increased desire for leisure, rather than deterioration in health, are primarily responsible for the declining labor force participation rates of the elderly. The most obvious indication of this trend is that labor force participation rates of persons over 65 in the United States have drastically declined over the last forty years at the same time that their health and life expectancy have markedly improved.[2] The same patterns of improving health and declining labor force participation are evident for virtually all European countries. Evidence also indicates that most individuals retire for reasons other than poor health. Gary Fields and Olivia Mitchell (1984) find that only 12 percent of men cite poor health as the primary reason for leaving their main job, and Ruhm (1988b) suggests that a wide array of health variables can explain only 3 percent of the variance in labor force participation probabilities for middle-aged and older women.

Although changes in health status cannot account for the declining propensity of the elderly to work, virtually all studies find that the probability of retirement increases as self-assessed health status declines (see Quinn 1977; Boskin and Hurd 1978; Gordon and Blinder 1980; Burkhauser and Quinn 1983; Hanoch and Honig 1983; Burtless and Moffitt 1984, 1985; Diamond and Hausman 1984; and Burtless 1986). Generally, the impact of self-reported ill health is quite large. Men who report that their health is poor typically retire an average of 1.1 years earlier than those who state that their health is average or above average (Burtless 1986).

Unfortunately, there is also considerable reason to believe that self-assessments of health are systematically biased in ways that overstate its actual impact on labor force patterns. Poor health is a more socially acceptable reason for retirement than is the preference for leisure, and health disabilities are a prerequisite for enrollment in some government transfer programs. When "objective" and self-assessed measures of health status are compared, the latter are found to be more strongly associated with withdrawal from the labor force than the former (see Parsons 1982; Program Analysis Staff 1982; Burkhauser 1980; Anderson and Burkhauser 1985; Bazzoli 1985; Butler et al. 1987).

Nonetheless, declining health does appear to cause small reductions in labor force participation, even when objective health measures are used. Richard Burkhauser (1980) finds that a 10 percent decrease in

---

2. For example, the life expectancy of men aged 65 has increased from 12.8 years in 1950 to 14.2 years in 1980; the corresponding increase for women is even larger— from 15.0 to 18.5 years (Poterba and Summers 1987:21).

number of weeks worked as a result of ill health is associated with a 0.6 percent increase in the probability of taking early retirement. Further, the objective measures almost certainly underestimate the importance of health because they do not capture all changes in health. For example, when future mortality rates are used as indicators of health status, physical limitations that do not affect life expectancies (such as arthritis) are ignored.

Mandatory Retirement

Mandatory retirement provisions constitute a second noneconomic factor that might force early departure from the labor force. The minimum age at which firms could impose mandatory retirement was raised from 65 to 70 in 1978 and has recently been eliminated altogether for most workers. Even before these changes occurred, however, mandatory retirement had little effect on aggregate labor force statistics.

Between one-third and one-half of older men were employed in jobs with mandatory retirement provisions in the late 1960s and early 1970s. The majority, however, left these jobs by choice at or before the age of required retirement and so were not constrained by the provisions. As a result, a maximum of 10 percent of older workers were forced to retire as a result of mandatory retirement during this period (Halpern 1978), around 5 percent during the mid-1970s (Parnes and Nestle 1975), and 2 to 3 percent in the early 1980s (Fields and Mitchell 1986). Burkhauser and Joseph Quinn (1983) estimate that the elimination of early retirement would have raised labor force participation rates of 64- and 65-year-olds in the early 1970s from 38 to only 40 percent.

Social Security

Economists interested in the labor force behavior of older workers have most commonly focused their research on the effects of the Social Security system. This interest is motivated by the importance of Social Security as a source of financial support for the elderly, the implications of changing labor force patterns for financing the Social Security system, and the somewhat peculiar incentives implicit in the system.

Social Security is the primary source of income for most older persons. Approximately 90 percent of retired persons receive a portion of their incomes from Social Security, compared to only 66 percent from assets and 35 percent from private pensions (Upp 1983). Further, Social Security payments account for between 40 and 53 percent of those incomes, versus 22 percent from assets and 10 to 14 percent from private pensions. The percentage of total retirement income accounted for by Social Security has also been rising over time (Kotlikoff and Smith 1983; Upp 1983).

To understand how potential changes in the Social Security system might affect the behavior of older workers, it is important to have some knowledge of the structure of the system. Men first received the option to obtain reduced Social Security benefits at age 62 in 1962. For every month past that age that benefits are not initiated, future payments are adjusted upward at the rate of five-ninths of 1 percent. If benefits are not taken past age 65, a delayed retirement credit is granted. The size of the credit was 1 percent for every year of delay through 1977, 3 percent per year after 1981 (with a transition period in the interim), and will gradually rise to 8 percent between 1990 and 2009. The resulting system will be approximately actuarially fair.[3] Current workers, however, are significantly penalized for delaying acceptance of Social Security past age 65, and relatively few do so. Between 1961 and 1982, the percentage of men less than 65 who filed for Social Security rose from 5 to 58 percent (Fields and Mitchell 1986).

There are no employment restrictions on Social Security recipients over the age of 70. Younger beneficiaries are allowed to keep their entire benefit for annual earnings up to a ceiling amount (slightly over eight thousand dollars at present). Above this ceiling, they lose fifty cents in benefits for every dollar of earnings.[4] The age at which workers become eligible for full Social Security is being raised from 65 to 67, in gradual steps, starting in the year 2000, and the benefits available at given ages of early retirement are being correspondingly reduced. Finally, real Social Security benefits have risen dramatically since the 1960s, with the most important increase being a more than 30 percent jump between 1969 and 1973. In addition, benefits are now indexed for inflation.

Virtually all studies agree that Social Security incentives cause a moderate jump in the probability of retirement at age 62 (when workers first become eligible for benefits) and a much larger spike at 65

---

3. In an actuarially fair system, the expected discounted value of lifetime benefits is unchanged, regardless of the age at which benefits are first taken.

4. Before 1973, earnings in excess of a second higher amount were taxed at 100 percent. In 1990, the implicit earnings tax will be reduced from 50 to 33 percent for individuals above the normal retirement age.

(after which the actuarial value of benefits declines). For instance, annual retirement rates gradually increase from 1.0 to 5.8 percent between ages 57 and 61, jump to 15.3 percent at 62, rise still further to 25.4 percent at 65, and then decline to less than 1 percent by age 69 (Burtless and Moffitt 1985).

Surprisingly, it is not obvious whether Social Security raises or lowers average retirement ages. Most early studies and a few later ones have found that retirement occurs significantly earlier for those with Social Security eligibility than for those without it (Boskin 1977; Quinn 1977; Boskin and Hurd 1978, 1984; Diamond and Hausman 1984; Bazzoli 1985). Other researchers, however, argue that retirement is delayed (Burkhauser 1980; Blinder, Gordon, and Wise 1980; Gordon and Blinder 1980), and careful recent studies (i.e., Mitchell and Fields 1984; Burtless 1986; Slade 1987) typically indicate that Social Security causes very small decreases in retirement age but significant bunching of withdrawal from the labor force around ages 62 and 65.

Although the total impact of Social Security on the labor market behavior of older workers continues to be debated, it is clear that moderate changes in the system's incentives will have minuscule effects. For example, Gary Burtless and Robert Moffitt (1984) estimate that eliminating the implicit earnings tax would increase average post-retirement work hours from only 3.2 to 4.2 hours per week.[5] Similarly, Fields and Mitchell (1986) argue that reducing monthly benefits obtained from retiring at age 62 from 80 to 55 percent of those received if Social Security is first taken at 65 increases retirement ages by just three months. Raising the late retirement credit by 10 percent (for working until 68) has an even smaller effect, lifting retirement ages by an average of only one week. Similarly, Burtless (1986) estimates that the 20 percent (unanticipated) increase in Social Security benefits, which was granted in the early 1970s, reduced expected retirement ages by only two months (from 64.6 to 64.4 years).

Even relatively large changes in the system would have fairly small effects. For example, Burtless and Moffitt (1985) calculate that an across-the-board 20 percent cut in Social Security benefits would increase average retirement ages from 64.40 to 64.58 years and raise expected postretirement hours of work from 3.1 to 4.7 hours per week. Increasing the normal retirement age from 65 to 68 or raising the delayed retirement credit to actuarially fair levels would delay retirement to ages 64.75 and 64.79 respectively.

As these results indicate, changes in the Social Security system which

---

5. The impact is so small because only about 10 percent of recipients work at all.

are in the process of being implemented or have recently been considered will have little impact on the labor force patterns of older Americans. That is, to increase significantly the labor force participation rates of older Americans would require extremely large alterations in the system's incentives and would significantly affect the financial well-being of senior citizens. A combination of modest changes in Social Security and restructured incentives in other areas such as private pensions, however, could have a more important influence on labor market behavior.

Private Pensions

Private pensions have become an important source of retirement income in the last twenty years and have received increasing attention by economists. An actuarially fair pension system would be expected to cause slight reductions in the labor supply of the elderly, to the extent that pensions increase total wealth. Conversely, if pensions represent deferred wage payments, there is no a priori reason to expect any effect. Private pensions, however, are rarely actuarially fair. Instead, the net present value of most pension plans reaches a maximum well before "normal" retirement ages, giving workers strong incentives to leave career jobs (and possibly the labor force) early.

For persons currently approaching retirement age, actuarially unfair pension plans are the rule rather than the exception, and the incentives for early retirement are frequently very strong. Laurence Kotlikoff and Daniel Smith (1983) estimate that fully half of civilian employees can retire at age 62 and as many as 15 percent by 55 with no actuarial reduction in pension benefits. Mitchell and Fields (1984) surveyed, in detail, ten pension plans and found that the average retirement age at which lifetime pension benefits are maximized is 62. In five of the plans benefits are maximized at age 60 or before, in four of the ten at 62, and in only one plan later than the normal retirement age of 65. The changes in pension incentives at varying ages and length of service can be astonishing. In Kotlikoff and David Wise's (1989) study of a single firm, the extra lifetime pension accrual for remaining one extra year with the company is $72,527 for 54-year-old managers with twenty-five years of service but *negative* $14,936 for their 65-year-old counterparts with thirty years of seniority.

Given these strong incentives, it is not surprising to find that pension systems, as currently structured, encourage early retirement. Most early research, although lacking much detail on the characteristics of pension plans, finds that pension eligibility is associated with earlier retirement (Gordon and Blinder 1980; Bazzoli 1985). The studies also indicate the importance of the structure of the pension plan. For instance, Burkhauser (1979) estimates that when an extra year of work results in a 10 percent loss in lifetime pension benefits, the probability of accepting a pension in the next year increases by 6.5 percent.

Recent work, with more comprehensive pension plan information, indicates that profile-neutral increases in pension wealth have very small effects on retirement behavior but that changes in the pension profile are much more important. Thus whereas Mitchell and Fields (1984) find that an actuarially neutral 10 percent increase in pension wealth reduces average retirement ages by only one month and Burkhauser and Quinn (1983) uncover similarly small pure wealth effects, the benefits of early retirement found in Kotlikoff and Wise's (1989) case study are estimated to increase retirements occurring between the ages of 55 and 60 by 30 percentage points (from 14 to 44 percent). Kotlikoff and Wise also argue that the combination of pension and early Social Security benefits is particularly important for workers who are fully vested in the pension plan.

Earnings and Wealth

Virtually all studies find that higher wages are associated with later retirement (for example, Boskin 1977; Boskin and Hurd 1978; Burkhauser 1979, 1980; Gordon and Blinder 1980; Burkhauser and Quinn 1983; Diamond and Hausman 1984; Mitchell and Fields 1984; Bazzoli 1985). Whereas some research predicts a relatively small impact on earnings (Quinn 1977; Burtless and Moffitt 1985), the consensus of most work is that the wage effect is important. Burkhauser (1979, 1980) and Mitchell and Fields (1984), for example, find that earnings are the most important factor in determining whether workers retire before age 65.[6]

Accurate data on asset holdings are much harder to obtain than is information on earnings. As a result, the impact of wealth on the labor supply of elderly workers has been estimated less frequently. The research that has been done indicates an inverse relationship between wealth and retirement ages (Boskin 1977; Burkhauser 1980; Burtless and Moffitt 1984). Giora Hanoch and Marjorie Honig (1983) also

---

6. Burkhauser (1979) estimates that a 10 percent increase in earnings reduces the probability of early pension acceptance by 18.5 percent.

provide some indication that the effects of wealth are stronger for women than for men.

Although it is clear that increases in incomes and wealth have been one factor encouraging the trend toward reduced labor force participation among the elderly, no estimates are available indicating the relative importance of these factors as compared to changes in pensions, Social Security regulations, and preferences for leisure. Nor is there any indication of how the stagnation of earnings over the last fifteen years will affect future patterns.

Partial Retirement

Until now, this review has ignored partial retirement. This neglect follows most of the economics literature, which classifies individuals (frequently according to arbitrary criteria) as either "working" or "retired."[7] This section discusses the phenomenon of partial retirement. Because previous work is sketchy, only tentative conclusions can be reached.

Partial retirement is relatively common. Honig and Hanoch (1985) estimate that between 14 and 20 percent of 62- to 67-year-old men were partially retired in 1973 (depending on the definition of partial retirement). Honig (1985) finds roughly similar numbers for women. Similarly, Alan Gustman and Thomas Steinmeier (1984) forecast that at least one-third of white males partially retire at some point in their lives, although most are forced to change jobs to do so.[8] Furthermore, many reenter the labor force following retirement. For instance, Burtless and Moffitt (1984) estimate that 18 percent of men hold part-time jobs two years after retirement, and Peter Diamond and Jerry Hausman (1984) find somewhat smaller reentry rates, ranging from 10.3 percent for 55- to 59-year-olds to 9.0 percent for persons over 65.

Higher preretirement wages reduce the probability of partial retirement by raising the likelihood of remaining in the labor force full time; eligibility for pensions and self-reported poor health also reduce the probability of partial retirement, but in these cases because they promote complete withdrawal from the work force (Gustman and Steinmeier 1984; Burtless and Moffitt 1985; Honig and Hanoch 1985;

---

7. One reason for this categorization is that conventional econometric techniques are unable to handle a three-stage classification of "retired," "not retired," or "partially retired," especially when the third group includes individuals who work varying numbers of hours.

8. Our current work suggests that this is an underestimate (see chapter 5).

Honig 1985). Higher potential Social Security benefits raise partial retirement probabilities in some studies (Boskin and Hurd 1978; Gustman and Steinmeier 1984) and lower them in others (Honig and Hanoch 1985; Honig 1985). Mandatory retirement has ambiguous effects on partial retirement, and the latter is frequently associated with movement into self-employment.

We know very little about the transition from full-time work in career jobs to complete retirement. This is an important area for future research. We would benefit from learning what barriers prevent workers from partially retiring on career jobs, why some individuals reenter the labor force after retiring, and what patterns typify partial retirement (e.g., full- or part-time work, full- or part-year jobs, a sequence of short jobs, or a single position of considerable duration). Understanding this transition process has important implications for policy.

Conclusions

This survey of recent research on the labor force patterns of older workers suggests five main conclusions. First, most workers choose when to retire and respond to economic incentives that change the preferred timing of retirement. Although a minority of persons leave the labor force because of health limitations or (previous) mandatory retirement provisions, these are exceptions rather than the rule. Seen in this light, the efforts to increase the labor force participation rates of older workers must be structured carefully so as to ensure that their economic well-being is not sacrificed.

Second, current Social Security provisions encourage early retirement and limit the work hours of those continuing to be employed after beginning to receive benefits. These effects are relatively minor, however, and revisions to the Social Security system which are being phased in between 1990 and 2029 will eliminate or reduce many of the disincentives. The remaining disincentives will be negligible, and significant changes in labor force behavior would result only from very large changes in the system (i.e., eliminating eligibility for early retirement altogether).

Third, most defined benefit pension plans encourage early withdrawal from the labor force by penalizing workers who stay on career jobs past their early sixties. To some extent, the switch from defined benefit to defined contribution plans will reduce these disincentives. Several changes could be considered, however, to increase the participation rates of 60- to 65-year-olds. For example, firms could be required to allow workers the option of partial retirement (at reduced rates of pay) without suffering actuarial reductions in pension benefits. Similarly, the tax laws could be further restructured to increase the incentives to adopt defined contribution plans.

Fourth, additional examination is needed of the labor force patterns of older workers after the conclusion of their career jobs. Preliminary work suggests that these positions frequently end well before retirement, and little is known about the structure of postcareer bridge jobs. We also have a poor understanding of why some workers choose to retire partially while others do not, why reentry into the labor force is relatively common following retirement, and what the major barriers are preventing older persons from accepting part- or full-time work.

Finally, the existing literature on older workers concentrates disproportionately on white males. We therefore need to examine whether there are important differences in the retirement patterns of nonwhites and females and particularly how the effects of pensions, Social Security, and health status vary across demographic groups. For example, pension disincentives are likely to be less important for females than males because women have relatively small average accruals. Conversely, transfer programs, such as Medicaid and Supplemental Security Income, targeted toward low-income individuals, may have a more critical influence on the labor force behavior of elderly nonwhites and women, who, on average, are less well off than white males.

PROFILE OF THE LABOR MARKET FOR OLDER WORKERS

Andrew M. Sum and W. Neal Fogg

OLDER WORKERS ARE NEITHER a homogeneous nor an unchanging pool of individuals. Demographic developments and changes in the labor force participation behavior of key subgroups of this population have fundamentally altered their characteristics over the past few decades and will continue to do so over the remainder of this century. At the same time, the ongoing transformation of the industrial structure of the American economy, technological changes in the production process, and accompanying shifts in the occupational distribution of employment have altered the labor market in which older workers operate. The role and character of bridge jobs for older workers are critically influenced by these changes in the labor force and in the structure of available employment opportunities.

This chapter examines and assesses trends in the demographic characteristics, labor force behavior, and employment patterns of Americans aged 55 and older. This is the age group defined as "older workers." Most of the analysis is based on data obtained from the Current Population Survey (CPS) over the past two decades. This survey, conducted monthly by the U.S. Bureau of the Census for the Bureau of Labor Statistics, is currently based on a representative sample of approximately fifty-seven thousand households.[1] In addition

---

1. The size of the household sample for whom interviews are completed has varied over time, expanding and contracting in response to budgetary allocations. In the late 1960s, the beginning period of our analysis, 48,000 households were interviewed each

to capturing information on the labor force status and employment characteristics of respondents at the time of the survey, the March CPS interview contains a work experience supplement that is used to generate more detailed data on working-age individuals and their households during the preceding calendar year (U.S. Bureau of the Census 1987b). March CPS public-use tapes thus provide opportunities to examine the labor force behavior, employment patterns, and labor market problems of older persons at a particular time, during an entire calendar year, and over time.

Recent Trends in Population and Demographic Characteristics

During the past two decades, the number of persons aged 55 and over in the civilian noninstitutional population of the United States increased by 39 percent (see table 3.1),[2] from 35.8 million[3] in March 1968 to nearly 50 million in March 1987. This growth rate exceeded that of the total civilian population over this time period. As a consequence, the share of the total civilian noninstitutional population represented by older persons increased from 18.0 percent in 1967 to 20.8 percent in 1986 (see table 3.2).

From a labor market perspective, a more relevant measure is the relative share of the U.S. working-age population (16 and over) represented by older persons. A rise in this figure could create a labor supply squeeze that might either reduce the relative wages of older persons or raise their relative rate of unemployment. Previous research has indicated that cohort size significantly influences the economic and social behavior of a group (Easterlin 1980). The older persons' share of the working-age population, however, was fairly stable over this time period (see table 3.2). The coming of age of the postwar baby boom generation sufficiently boosted the growth rate

---

month. The sample size fell to 45,000 in the early 1970s, increased to 62,000 in the 1980–81 period, and fell to 57,000 from 1985 to the present (U.S. Department of Labor 1988c).

2. The estimates of the number of older persons in the civilian noninstitutional population are based on the March CPS public-use tapes for each year in the table. The March 1980 total appearing in table 3.1 was later revised upward by 1.1 million on the basis of new population estimates generated by the 1980 census. For a review of these revised civilian noninstitutional population totals, see U.S. Department of Labor 1982b.

3. These population estimates exclude older persons living in institutions such as nursing homes, long-term hospitals, and correctional institutions, whose numbers are approximately equal to 3 percent of the total number of older persons in the civilian noninstitutional population.

of the population of 16- to 54-year-olds over this period to make it essentially identical to that of older persons.

In contrast, the demographic composition of the nation's older population has changed somewhat by age, sex, race and ethnic origin, and formal educational attainment (see table 3.1 and figures 3.1 and 3.2). Both the absolute and relative number of persons over 65 increased more rapidly than the 55 to 64 age cohort over the past two decades. As a result, the share of persons over 65 in the older population has increased and is projected to continue to do so throughout the remainder of this century (Fullerton 1987).

Over the past two decades, the share of women in the older population has risen slightly, from 54.7 percent in 1968 to 56.2 percent in 1987. No further increase is expected over the remainder of the century. In fact, the share of males is expected to rise somewhat.[4]

The share of the nation's older population made up of ethnic and racial minority group members has increased in recent years. In 1974, blacks, Hispanics, and other nonwhites accounted for only 11.3 percent of the population 55 and older; by 1987, that figure had risen to 14.5 percent.[5] The bulk of this increase occurred among Hispanics and Asians.

The formal educational attainment of the nation's older population improved markedly over the past two decades, reflecting primarily the greater number of years of schooling completed by the newer cohorts of older Americans. In 1968, nearly two-thirds of all persons 55 and over lacked a high school diploma; by 1987, only 41 percent of the older population had completed fewer than twelve years of formal schooling[6] (see figure 3.2). The proportion of older persons completing twelve or more years of schooling rose from 34 to 58 percent, the share with one or more years of college increased from 14 to 24 percent, and the share of college graduates from 7 to 12 percent.

The anticipated impact of these shifts in the demographic makeup of the older population on their labor force behavior and employment situation is somewhat mixed. The increased share of the population

4. Between 1986 and 2000, the male share of the civilian noninstitutional population of persons 55 and over is projected to rise from 43.8 to 44.6 percent (Fullerton 1987).

5. Data on the Hispanic origin of respondents were not included on the CPS public-use tapes until the early 1970s. The March 1968 tape thus cannot be used to identify Hispanics. Only a white/nonwhite race classification is possible for that year.

6. The CPS public-use tapes do not indicate whether a person actually possesses a high school diploma. It tells only the number of years of schooling attended and completed. We have assumed that persons reporting twelve years of schooling completed were high school graduates.

TABLE 3.1. Number and Percentage Distribution of Persons 55 and Older, by Age, Sex, Educational Attainment, and Race and Ethnic Group, 1968–1987

Category	Number (in 1000s)				Percentage of Total			
	1968	1974	1980	1987	1968	1974	1980	1987
Age subgroup								
55–59	9,538	10,157	11,243	11,106	26.6	25.5	25.3	22.3
60–62	5,037	5,552	5,993	6,633	14.1	13.9	13.5	13.3
63–65	4,414	5,194	5,498	6,389	12.3	13.0	12.4	12.8
66–70	6,217	7,145	8,138	9,160	17.3	17.9	18.3	18.4
71+	10,642	11,798	13,647	16,570	29.7	29.6	30.7	33.2
Total	35,848	39,846	44,519	49,858	100.0	100.0	100.0	100.0
Sex								
Male	16,249	17,607	19,595	21,856	45.3	44.2	44.0	43.8
Female	19,598	22,238	24,923	28,004	54.7	55.8	56.0	56.2
Total	35,847	39,845	44,518	49,860	100.0	100.0	100.0	100.0

TABLE 3.1. (cont.)

	Number (in 1000s)				Percentage of Total			
Category	1968	1974	1980	1987	1968	1974	1980	1987
Educational attainment								
High school dropouts	23,721	23,402	22,280	20,716	66.2	58.7	50.0	41.5
High school graduates	6,994	10,064	13,528	17,310	19.5	25.3	30.4	34.7
Some college	2,603	3,234	4,360	5,799	7.3	8.1	9.8	11.6
College graduates	2,530	3,145	4,351	6,034	7.1	7.9	9.8	12.1
Total	35,848	39,845	44,519	49,859	100.0	100.0	100.0	100.0
Race/ethnic group[a]								
White non-Hispanic		35,309	39,003	42,601		88.6	87.6	85.4
Black non-Hispanic		3,314	3,798	4,339		8.3	8.5	8.7
Hispanic		884	1,187	1,948		2.2	2.7	3.9
Other		339	530	970		0.8	1.2	1.9
Total		39,846	44,518	49,858		100.0	100.0	100.0

[a]Comparable data not available for 1968.

TABLE 3.2.   Trends in the Relative Size of the Civilian Noninstitutional
Population of Persons 55 and Older, 1967–1986 (annual averages)

Population Measure	1967	1973	1979	1986
Population 55+ as percentage of total population	18.0	19.2	20.1	20.8
Population 55+ as percentage of working-age population (16+)	27.2	27.0	27.3	27.4

FIGURE 3.1.   Distribution of Persons 55 Years and Older, by Age
Subgroup, 1968 and 1987

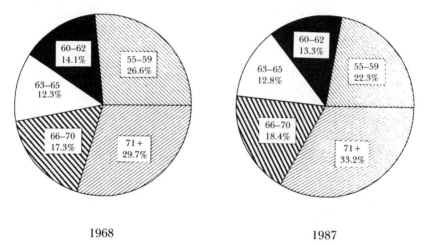

1968   1987

represented by those over 65, women, and minority males would tend
to depress aggregate civilian labor force participation rates and
employment-population ratios of the older population. At the same
time, both civilian labor force participation rates and employment-
population ratios of older persons typically rise with increasing years
of formal schooling. Further, research has shown that the educational
attainment of older workers has a substantial influence on their hourly
and annual earnings. The opportunity costs of withdrawing from the
labor force are clearly higher for better-educated workers (Parnes
1983; Parsons 1981). Thus the rising average levels of formal schooling among the older population should have boosted the participation
rates of the elderly and improved their employment prospects.

FIGURE 3.2. Distribution of Persons 55 and Older, by Educational Attainment, March 1968 and March 1974

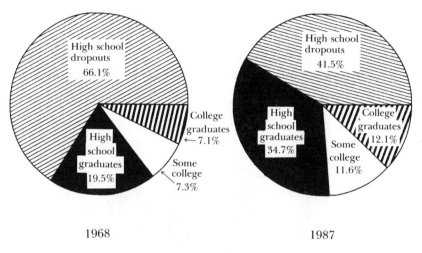

1968   1987

Projected Increases in Population

The Census Bureau has projected that the size of the total population of older persons in the United States will increase at an above-average rate between 1986 and the end of the century[7] (U.S. Department of Labor 1984a; Fullerton 1987) so that by the year 2000, the total population in this group will be 59.0 million, a gain of 7.6 million, or nearly 15 percent. Although this increase will occur among each major subgroup, the absolute and relative size of these increases will vary sharply by age (see figure 3.3).

The cohort born during the Depression decade (1930–40) was far smaller than would have been expected based on birth rates in the immediately preceding period.[8] As a result, the absolute number of persons aged 55 to 64 will decline by 870,000 between 1986 and 1993 but then will grow by 3 million until the end of the century (U.S.

---

7. In 1986, the estimated size of this group living in institutions was approximately 1.9 million or 3.7 percent of the total population of persons 55 and older. The ratio of the institutional population to this total population is projected by the Census Bureau to remain unchanged between 1986 and 2000 at 3.7 percent. According to our calculations, the absolute size of the institutional population 55 and older will rise from 1.9 million to nearly 2.2 million but will still account for the same 3.7 percent of the total population of older persons.

8. During the 1930s, the aggregate birth rate fell below the replacement level for the first time in American history. It has been estimated that 3 million fewer births took place during the decade than would have been expected (Mintz and Kellogg 1988).

FIGURE 3.3.   Actual and Projected Number of Persons 55 and Older,
by Age Subgroup, 1986 and 2000 (in millions)

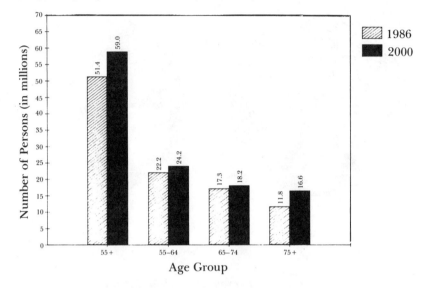

Department of Labor 1988a; Spencer 1989). Since smaller population
cohorts tend to experience more favorable employment and earnings
opportunities, the upcoming cohort of 55- to 64-year-olds may find
itself in greater demand in the labor market, particularly as the supply
of young labor force entrants declines.

The "middle-growth path" labor force projections of the Bureau
of Labor Statistics for the period 1986–95 suggested a continuing
decline in the labor force participation rates of 55- to 64-year-old
males and only a slight rise in the rates of women of the same age
(U.S. Department of Labor 1984a). Other analysts, including Malcolm
Morrison, have argued that the substantial increase in the number of
35- to 54-year-old workers over this time period will probably limit
any substantive expansion in employment opportunities for older persons, especially in higher-paying positions (Morrison 1983).

The 55- to 64-year-old cohort also will experience important
changes in its racial and ethnic composition between 1986 and 1995.
Although the total civilian population of this group was projected to
decline by nearly 855,000 during this period, all of the reduction was
projected to occur among white non-Hispanics (U.S. Department of
Labor 1988a). The number of ethnic minorities (Asians, blacks, Hispanics, and others) was projected to rise by nearly 800,000, increasing

their share of the entire 55- to 64-year-old population from 16 percent in 1986 to nearly 21 percent in 1995. The economic fortunes of older workers will thus be increasingly dependent on the labor market experiences of the nation's older minority population.

The projected population growth rates of the older population between 1986 and 2000 range from a low of 5.3 percent for those 65 to 74 to a high of 40.5 percent for those 75 and older. As a consequence, the population 55 and over will shift toward the older age groups at an accelerated pace. The shares of the older population represented by those 55 to 64 and 65 to 74 will decline between 1986 and 2000, while those 75 to 84 and those 85 and over will rise. By the year 2000, those persons over 75 will account for more than 28 percent of the population of older persons. This figure is well above their 23 percent share in 1986 and 20 percent in 1972.

The projected rapid growth of the oldest members of the nation's elderly population will have important consequences for their future aggregate labor force participation rates and for their poverty status. The labor force participation rates of those over 70 have plummeted sharply over the past two decades and are not projected to reverse course over the remainder of the century. As a result, an even lower share of the aggregate population aged 55 and over will be active in the civilian labor force. The growth in the pool of elderly individuals, especially women living alone, may result in increased poverty in this group (Commonwealth Fund Commission on Elderly People Living Alone 1987).

Labor Force Participation

Whether measured from a flows perspective throughout an entire calendar year or at a given time, the labor force participation rates of older persons decline consistently with age, particularly after ages 59, 62, 65, and 70[9] (see tables 3.3 and 3.4 and figure 3.4). During calendar year 1986, for example, 35 percent of all persons 55 and over either worked or looked for work at some time. The likelihood of active participation in the labor force, however, varied by age group. Nearly sixty-nine of every one hundred persons 55 to 59 years

---

9. The work experience supplement to the March CPS allows us to analyze the labor force attachment and employment experiences of older persons throughout an entire calendar year. Such data can be used to estimate the total number of persons who participated in the civilian labor force at some point during the year and their mean weeks of participation and employment. For examples of analysis of the work experience data, see U.S. Department of Labor 1987b; Sum 1977.

TABLE 3.3   Older Persons in the Labor Force at Any Time during the
Calendar Year, by Age, Sex, and Educational Attainment, 1967–1987
(in percent)

Category	1967	1973	1979	1986
Age subgroup				
55–59	73.7	72.5	69.1	69.3
60–62	67.8	65.8	58.5	57.8
63–65	55.7	50.1	44.1	39.5
66–70	36.1	29.8	25.3	22.4
71+	15.6	13.4	10.2	8.5
Total	46.9	43.5	38.5	35.1
Sex				
Male	64.5	60.3	52.4	46.9
Female	32.3	30.1	27.6	25.9
Total	46.9	43.5	38.5	35.1
Educational attainment				
High school dropouts	41.9	36.6	28.3	24.5
High school graduates	53.7	51.5	46.3	38.8
Some college	55.8	51.5	48.9	43.3
College graduates	66.0	60.7	56.2	53.2
Total	46.9	43.5	38.5	35.1

old participated in the civilian labor force at some point during 1986
versus 40 percent of those 63 to 65, 22 percent of those 66 to 70, and
only 8 percent of those 71 or older. Similar differences prevailed in
March 1987 (see table 3.4). Sixty-four percent of those persons 55 to
59 years of age were actively participating in the civilian labor force
in March 1987 versus only 17 percent of those 66 to 70 and 6 percent
of those over 70.

The fraction of older persons participating in the labor force at any
time during the year has declined over the past two decades[10] (National Commission for Employment Policy 1985; Parnes 1981, 1983).
During 1967, for example, nearly 47 percent of all persons 55 and
older either worked or looked for work at some point during the year.
This rate fell to 44 percent by 1973, to slightly below 39 percent in
1979, and to 35 percent in 1986 (see table 3.4). This trend represents

10. The civilian labor force participation rates of persons 55 and over have been
declining since the late 1940s; however, this decline accelerated after the late 1960s.
Between 1948 and 1968, the annual average civilian labor force participation rate of
this group fell from 43 to 39 percent.

TABLE 3.4. Civilian Labor Force Participation Rates of Older Persons, by Age, Sex, Educational Attainment, and Race and Ethnic Group, March 1968, March 1974, March 1980, and March 1987 (in percent)

Category	1968	1974	1980	1987
Age subgroup				
55–59	68.0	66.7	64.2	64.1
60–62	60.6	56.0	51.5	49.5
63–65	44.7	38.3	35.3	30.5
66–70	24.9	20.5	18.5	16.7
71+	9.2	7.9	7.0	6.1
Total	39.1	35.8	33.0	29.9
Sex				
Male	55.9	51.2	45.8	40.5
Female	25.3	23.6	23.0	21.5
Educational attainment				
High school dropouts	33.8	29.0	23.1	20.0
High school graduates	46.8	43.8	40.8	33.3
Some college	48.5	44.5	43.1	37.2
College graduates	58.3	52.2	49.8	47.1
Race/ethnic group				
White non-Hispanic		35.8	33.2	29.8
Black non-Hispanic		35.4	30.8	29.1
Hispanic		34.8	34.1	31.3

a decline of nearly 12 percentage points, or 25 percent, between 1967 and 1986. Declines in participation rates have occurred for every major age, sex, and educational attainment subgroup of older persons. The relative size of these declines, however, was highest for the older subgroups, for men, and for those with fewer years of schooling.

The sharp declines in participation rates among both men and women well before age 62 suggest that forces are at work other than the availability of Social Security retirement benefits. In 1988, annual average labor force participation rates of both men and women peaked in the 45-to-49 age group at 93 and 73 percent, respectively. The end of active (in some cases temporary) labor force participation well before ages 62 and 65 suggests that many men and women end their career jobs well before "normal" retirement age.

The gap between the aggregate participation rates of older men and women still remains large (47 percent versus 26 percent for cal-

FIGURE 3.4. Older Persons in the Labor Force at Any Time in the Year, by Age Subgroup, 1973 and 1986

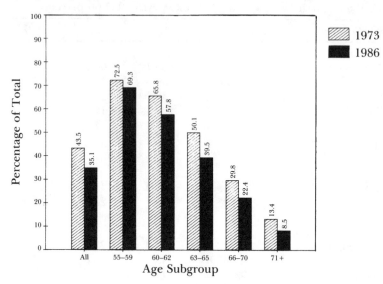

endar year 1986). The absolute and relative sizes of the gap have narrowed, however, particularly among those 55 to 59, and further reductions are projected for the remainder of the century as women 55 to 59 become more firmly attached to the labor market. The participation rates of older persons also vary considerably by years of schooling: only 25 percent of high school dropouts participated in the civilian labor force at some point in 1986 versus 39 percent of high school graduates and 53 percent of college graduates. Some of the difference between the participation rates of the less and most well educated is attributable to the greater representation of non-high-school graduates among the older subgroups; however, in each age subgroup, including those over 65, college graduates are much more likely to be active in the civilian labor force.

Participation in the labor force may well increase among older persons because of changes in national labor supply and demand. The reduced numbers of young entrants, particularly those in the 18-to-24 age group, should stimulate demand for older workers, and a number of national survey findings have suggested that older workers want part-time employment after retirement from career jobs (Parnes 1983). No basic shift in the labor force behavior of older persons is expected, however (Eisdorfer and Cohen 1983; Morrison 1983).

TABLE 3.5. Average Annual Civilian Labor Force Participation Rates of Older Persons, 1982 and 1987 (in percent)

Sex/Age Subgroup	1982	1987
Males	43.8	40.4
55–59	81.9	79.7
60–64	57.2	54.9
65–69	26.9	25.8
70+	12.2	10.5
Females	22.8	22.0
55–59	49.6	52.2
60–64	33.4	33.2
65–69	14.9	14.3
70+	4.5	4.1

Sources: U.S. Department of Labor, Bureau of Labor Statistics, *Employment and Earnings,* January 1983, Table 3, p. 142; U.S. Department of Labor, Bureau of Labor Statistics, *Employment and Earnings,* January 1988, Table 3, p. 160.

Between 1982 and 1987, the U.S. economy generated job opportunities for an additional 12.9 million persons, and the aggregate unemployment rate fell from 9.7 to 6.2 percent (Ulmer and Howe 1988). Yet the aggregate civilian labor force participation rate of older persons fell during this period from 31.9 to 30.2 percent. This was true for both older men and women and for each age and sex subgroup, except women in the 55-to-59 age group (see table 3.5).[11] Recent projections by the Bureau of Labor Statistics of the civilian labor force for the year 2000 indicate that the participation rates of older men and women will continue to decline throughout the remainder of the century (Fullerton 1987; U.S. Department of Labor 1989). Again, women in the 55-to-64 age group are the sole exception; their participation rate is projected to rise from 42.3 percent in 1986 to 45.8 percent in 2000.

Trends in Employment Patterns of Older Workers: Industry Attachment

The job market for older workers has undergone fundamental transformations during the past two decades. The continued and somewhat accelerated shift in national employment patterns toward service-

11. In 1988, the annual average participation rate of all older persons fell to 30.0 percent; however, a higher fraction of women in each age subgroup actively participated in the civilian labor force.

TABLE 3.6.　Distribution of Employed Older Persons by Major Industry Group, March 1968, 1974, 1980, and 1987 (in percent)

Industry Group	1968	1974	1980	1987
Agriculture, forestry, fishing, mining	9.1	8.0	6.0	5.5
Construction	5.1	5.0	4.9	5.7
Nondurable manufacturing	9.9	9.1	8.7	7.8
Durable manufacturing	12.4	12.8	13.2	11.0
Transportation, communications, utilities	5.5	5.9	5.6	6.6
Wholesale trade	3.3	4.0	4.2	4.1
Retail trade	14.9	15.0	14.3	13.2
Finance, insurance, real estate	4.7	4.9	5.9	6.8
Services	29.8	29.6	31.3	34.1
Public administration	5.4	5.7	6.0	5.1

producing industries and away from goods-producing industries has affected older workers as well as those under 55. Between 1968 and 1987, the share of older persons employed in goods-producing industries (agriculture, forestry, fishing, mining, construction, and manufacturing) fell from 36.5 to 30.0 percent[12] (see table 3.6). These shifts were sharply lower for older male workers than for younger workers, especially those under 30. The share of older workers employed in construction industries held fairly firm throughout this period; thus nearly all the decline in the goods-producing share of employment resulted from relative and absolute losses in manufacturing and farming, forestry, and fishing. Some of these losses resulted in the dislocation of older workers from career jobs in the goods-producing sector. Older persons who were displaced during the 1980s tended to experience more severe reemployment adjustment problems, including above-average earnings losses, lengthier periods of joblessness, and above-average rates of withdrawal from the labor force (U.S. Department of Labor 1984b, 1986, 1988d; Abt Associates 1985; Flaim and Sehgal 1985; Horvath 1987; Parnes, Gagen, and King 1981). Finding bridge jobs for more of these older dislocated workers would seem to be a desirable employment and training policy goal.

The service-related industries absorbing the greatest numbers of older persons over this period were the finance, insurance, real estate, and service industries, in which the combined share of employment

12. The "services" industries appearing in table 3.6 include both private sector firms and government agencies providing services to the public other than general administrative functions, such as police, tax collection, and the courts. An older worker employed as a public school teacher would be classified as an employee in the services industry.

of older workers expanded from slightly over 33 percent in 1968 to 41 percent in 1987. During March 1987, the broad sectoral distribution of employed older workers between goods and services was nearly identical to that of persons 18 to 54 years old. Within the services sector, however, older workers were somewhat more likely to be found in service industries and in public administration, while workers under 55 were more concentrated in retail trade.

Although the shift out of goods-producing industries has affected both older men and women, men are still far more likely to be dependent on industries in the goods-producing sector. During March 1987, nearly four of every ten employed older males were working in the goods-producing sector versus only 17 percent of women. In that month, 48 percent of older women were employed by firms in service industries (business, health, legal, educational, and professional services), while only one of every four older males held jobs in these industries.

Opportunities for bridge jobs in the service industries are likely to increase. Between 1986 and 2000, nonfarm wage and salary employment is projected to rise by 20.1 million under the "moderate" growth scenario (Personick 1987). All of this change is projected to occur in the service-producing sector, with services and retail trade industries accounting for nearly three of every four net new jobs.

Trends in Occupational Employment Patterns

The occupational composition of the jobs held by older workers has also shifted over the past two decades, influenced both by changes in industrial employment opportunities and by changes in technology within industries which have altered the skill content of jobs (Cyert and Mowery 1987; Flynn 1987; Tschetter 1987). Thus the proportion of older employees holding white-collar jobs rose from 44 percent in 1968 to nearly 56 percent in 1987. These gains were most pronounced in the sales and clerical occupations.[13] In March 1987, the share of older workers holding clerical and sales positions (27.8 percent) was identical to that employed in professional, technical, and managerial jobs. Each of the other major oc-

---

13. Part of the gain in the sales-related occupations' share of employment between 1968 and 1987 is attributable to changes in the occupational classification system used in coding jobs in the 1980s. Sales manager positions would have been coded as management positions in the late 1960s but today are classified under the sales occupation category. Similarly, cashier positions were previously classified as clerical occupations but are now considered to be sales occupations.

FIGURE 3.5.   Distribution of Employed Older Males, by Major
Occupation, March 1968 and March 1987 (in percent)

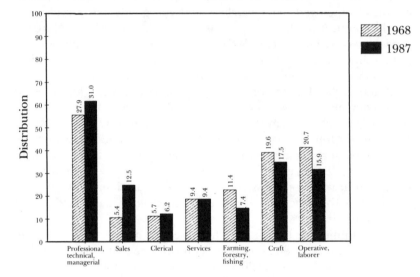

cupational groups has declined in relative importance over the past
two decades, with blue-collar operative and laborer and farming,
forestry, and fishing occupations experiencing the largest absolute
and relative declines. These developments reflect primarily the declining shares of older workers in the agricultural and manufacturing industries over the past two decades.

Both older men and women have experienced the shift from blue-
to white-collar employment (see figures 3.5 and 3.6), but men, who
are more concentrated in the goods-producing industries, remain far
more dependent than women on blue-collar jobs. In March 1987, for
example, the proportion of older men employed in blue-collar craft,
operative, and laborer positions was nearly three times that of women
(33.4 percent versus 11.7 percent).

Older workers in blue-collar positions are more likely to be affected
by economic dislocation and thus to depend on bridge jobs for employment before retirement at age 62 or 65. Of the 5.1 million dislocated workers age 20 and over identified by the January 1984
Bureau of Labor Statistics survey, 56 percent had been employed in
blue-collar occupations at the time of their displacement (U.S. Department of Labor 1984b; Flaim and Sehgal 1985). Dislocated workers
who held jobs as operators, fabricators, and laborers experienced

FIGURE 3.6.　Distribution of Employed Older Females, by Major
Occupation, March 1968 and March 1987 (in percent)

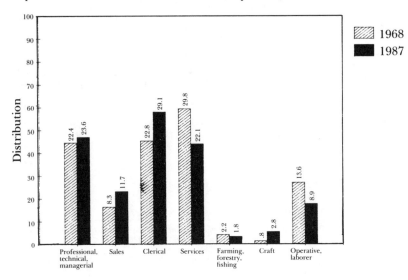

above-average unemployment rates and weekly earnings losses when
they became reemployed (Cyert and Mowery 1987; Podgursky and
Swaim 1987).

The share of older workers holding white-collar positions is likely
to increase over the remainder of the century for several reasons.
First, women are projected to account for a higher share of all employed older workers in 2000, and women are more likely to hold
white-collar jobs. Second, of the projected 21.4 million increase in
total employment between 1986 and 2000, white-collar occupations
are expected to account for an additional 14.1 million jobs or two-
thirds of the net gain (Silvestri and Lukasiewicz 1987). Better-
educated older workers with general skills should be able to transfer
to bridge jobs without incurring substantial periods of joblessness or
relative wage losses (Podgursky and Swaim 1987).

Size of Firm and Employment for Older Workers

Research has suggested that large firms tend to encourage the retirement, rather than the retention, of older workers. Attractive retirement benefits, the desire to make room for young workers, and
a host of seniority-based personnel practices are often cited as rea-

TABLE 3.7. Persons 65 and Older as a Percentage of Employment,
by Industrial Sector and Size of Firm, 1983 (in percent)

| | | Older Persons Employed in Firms with | | |
Industrial Sector	Older Persons Employed in All Firms	Under 100 Workers	100–499 Workers	500 or More Workers
All industries	2.1	3.1	1.9	1.0
Durable manufacturing	1.1	2.4	.2	.9
Nondurable manufacturing	1.1	2.1	2.2	.4
Wholesale trade	1.9	2.6	2.4	—
Retail trade	2.0	2.8	1.5	1.1
Finance, insurance, real estate	1.7	2.2	2.1	1.2
Miscellaneous services	3.5	4.6	2.7	1.9

Source: U.S. President, *The State of Small Business: Report of the President* (Washington, D.C.: U.S. Government Printing Office, 1986), Table C-21.

sons older workers, especially those 65 and over, are underrepresented in the nation's largest firms. In recent years, downsizing and plant closings in mature industries have contributed to this situation. In addition, larger manufacturing firms initiated new early retirement schemes in the face of pressures to reduce their labor costs and cut capacity (Mirkin 1987). Manufacturing industries with above-average levels of employment per firm accounted for 53 percent of dislocated workers between 1979 and 1984, although they represented only 22 percent of all wage and salary jobs in nonagricultural industries over the same period (Flaim and Sehgal 1985). In contrast, small and medium-sized firms are thought to be more flexible in their personnel practices and to provide fewer incentives to early retirement.

These hypotheses have not been examined systematically, but there is some evidence to support them. Recent national data show that workers 65 and older are three times more likely to be employed in firms with fewer than one hundred workers than in firms employing five hundred or more (see table 3.7). This association holds true for all major industry groups. Firms employing fewer than five hundred workers are providing a growing share of manufacturing employment. Because of their receptivity to employing older workers, these firms have the potential to become a significant source of bridge jobs (U.S. Small Business Administration 1988).

TABLE 3.8. Distribution of Employed Older Persons, by Class of Worker and Sex, March 1968, 1974, 1980, and 1987 (in percent)

Class of Worker	1968	1974	1980	1987
	All Workers			
Private	66.0	66.6	67.2	68.7
Government	14.9	16.3	17.0	16.8
Self-employed	17.5	15.8	14.8	13.8
Employed without pay	1.6	1.3	1.0	0.7
	Males			
Private	64.5	65.1	67.0	68.3
Government	12.8	14.4	14.5	14.1
Self-employed	22.4	20.3	18.2	17.5
Employed without pay	0.3	0.2	0.3	0.2
	Females			
Private	68.6	69.2	67.4	69.4
Government	18.7	19.6	20.8	20.7
Self-employed	8.7	8.2	9.6	8.4
Employed without pay	4.0	3.0	2.2	1.5

Self-Employment for Older Workers

Over the past two decades, as an increasing proportion of older persons held wage and salary positions in both the private and public sectors, self-employment and unpaid family work declined in relative importance, particularly among older males (see table 3.8). The share of self-employed women held fairly constant over this period at about 8.5 percent so that by March 1987, women accounted for nearly one of every four self-employed older workers, up from one of six in March 1968. The share of older workers employed without pay in family-owned businesses fell by half over this period, from 1.6 percent in 1968 to 0.7 percent in 1987.

The declining importance of self-employment and unpaid work in family enterprises was influenced by the sectoral shifts in employment. Large numbers of the older self-employed were previously found in agriculture, forestry, and fishing, a declining source of employment opportunities for older persons. In addition, agriculture has shifted away from self-employment and use of unpaid family workers toward employment of wage and salary workers as the family farm has diminished in importance.[14] The decline in these sources of employment has contributed to the reduced rate of labor force participation among older workers. This decline continues a trend that began in the late nineteenth and early twentieth centuries, when fewer self-employment opportunities were available for older men in the expanding urban-industrial economy (Haber 1985).

Although self-employment has become a less important source of jobs for all major age subgroups of the older working population during the past two decades, it accounts for a higher share of employment as age increases. In March 1987, only 11 percent of employed persons 55 to 59 years old were self-employed, as compared to 19 percent of those 66 to 70 and 25 percent of those over 70. Given the cross-sectional nature of the CPS survey data, we cannot determine whether this is because the self-employed are more likely to remain active in the labor market as they age or because a growing fraction of older persons shift into self-employment after retiring from career wage and salary jobs. National longitudinal studies of older men suggest that the self-employed, especially those in full-time jobs, are more likely to continue to work after age 62 (Parnes 1981, 1985).

Self-employment, which is projected to keep pace with overall job growth, has the potential to increase among older workers over the remainder of this century. Higher percentages of the new cohorts of older workers are better educated and hold white-collar jobs, the source for 60 percent of the occupations of the older self-employed in 1987. Unfortunately, public programs to prepare older dislocated workers or early retirees for self-employment are practically non-existent in the United States.

Part-Time Employment
for Older Workers

As is true for the entire work force, the proportion of employed older persons working part time (less than thirty-five hours per week) has increased over the past twenty years (Hedges and Gallogly 1977). In March 1968, slightly under 25 percent of all employed older persons were working part time. By March 1987, this figure had risen to nearly 30 percent. Part-time employment increased among older workers in all age subgroups, among both men and women, and

---

14. Between 1972 and 1986, the number of self-employed and unpaid family workers in agriculture fell by nearly 620,000 while wage and salary jobs in agricultural industries expanded by 353,000 (Personick 1987).

among all educational attainment subgroups (see table 3.9). The only group for whom part-time employment did not become relatively more important was that made up of black non-Hispanics,[15] although older blacks continue to remain more likely than whites to hold part-time jobs, often for economic (i.e., inability to obtain full-time jobs) rather than voluntary reasons.

The proportion of older employed persons working part time varies sharply by age subgroup and by sex. Only one of every five workers aged 55 to 59 worked part time during March 1987, a ratio only 2 percentage points higher than in 1968. Part-time employment as a share of total employment rises continuously with age. Slightly more than one-fourth of all employed 60- to 62-year-olds worked part time as did one-third of those in the 63-to-65 age group and nearly two-thirds of those over 70. Once past age 65, a clear majority of older persons shifts to part-time work. The increases in self-employment and part-time employment with rising age are mutually reinforcing in that the self-employed have more control over their working hours. Older women are nearly twice as likely as men to work part time. In March 1987, 40 percent of employed older women and 22 percent of employed older men were working part time.

Several researchers have argued that part-time employment among older workers would be expected to be even higher than it is given the possibility of workers gradually retiring from their jobs (Marcus, Jondrow, and Brechling 1987). Surveys show that older workers would like to work part time after leaving their career jobs (Kennedy 1980; Parnes 1983), but the perceived lower productivity of part-time workers and the existence of higher fixed costs per hour of work may discourage employers from offering it. The potential for using part-time jobs more widely in career firms as a bridge into and out of retirement should be examined by national and state employment policy makers and program administrators.

The industrial distribution of the jobs held by older part-time workers tends to differ somewhat from that of their full-time counterparts. Like all part-time workers, older part-timers tend to be relatively concentrated in retail trade, in finance, insurance, and real estate, and in the service industries. The extent of this concentration has increased over time (see table 3.10). During March 1987, for example, nearly seven of every ten older part-time workers were employed in

_____

15. Part of the explanation for this trend may lie in the different age distributions of older blacks and whites. Higher fractions of older white non-Hispanics are found in the 65 and over age groups for whom part-time employment becomes increasingly important as a source of job opportunities.

TABLE 3.9. Distribution of Older Employed Persons by Full-Time/Part-Time Status, by Age, Sex, Educational Attainment, and Race and Ethnic Group, March 1968, 1974, 1980, and 1987 (in percent)

Category	Employed Full Time				Employed Part Time			
	1968	1974	1980	1987	1968	1974	1980	1987
All	75.5	74.2	71.7	70.6	24.5	25.8	28.3	29.4
Age subgroup								
55–59	82.4	82.1	81.5	80.5	17.6	17.9	18.5	19.5
60–62	80.9	79.2	76.3	74.4	19.1	20.8	23.7	25.6
63–65	74.3	71.6	68.9	66.9	25.7	28.4	31.1	33.1
66–70	57.0	51.5	40.8	44.5	43.0	48.5	59.2	55.5
71+	43.2	39.5	36.0	34.9	56.8	60.5	64.0	65.1
Sex								
Male	80.7	80.5	78.3	77.7	19.3	19.5	21.7	22.3
Female	65.9	63.2	61.5	60.2	34.1	36.8	38.5	39.8
Educational attainment								
High school dropouts	72.0	69.1	64.9	66.9	28.0	30.9	35.1	33.1
High school graduates	79.1	78.1	73.7	69.0	20.9	21.9	26.3	31.0
Some college	77.8	77.8	75.8	71.4	22.2	22.2	24.2	28.6
College graduates	84.0	80.7	78.4	78.0	16.0	19.3	21.6	22.0
Race/ethnic group								
White non-Hispanic		75.1	72.1	70.4		24.9	27.9	29.6
Black non-Hispanic		64.0	65.0	67.3		36.0	35.0	32.7

TABLE 3.10. Distribution of Older Part-Time Workers, by Major Industry, March 1968, 1974, 1980, and 1987 (in percent)

Industry	1968	1974	1980	1987
Agriculture, forestry, mining	14.8	11.2	8.7	7.2
Construction	6.0	4.4	5.0	5.3
Nondurable manufacturing	5.2	5.6	4.7	4.0
Durable manufacturing	5.1	4.1	4.7	4.4
Transportation, communications, utilities	2.9	4.0	3.4	3.6
Wholesale trade	2.1	3.4	3.0	3.0
Retail trade	16.2	18.2	18.9	18.0
Finance, insurance, real estate	4.2	5.4	6.2	7.4
Services	39.7	39.7	41.2	43.5
Public administration	3.7	3.9	4.2	3.6

the retail trade, finance, insurance, real estate, and service industries, whereas only 54 percent of all older workers were engaged in these industries.

Between 1968 and 1987, the share of older workers employed part time in the retail trade, finance, insurance, and service industries increased from 60 to 69 percent. Nearly all of this shift occurred at the expense of the goods-producing industries, especially agriculture, forestry, fishing, and manufacturing. Manufacturing firms have not been major users of part-time workers of any age and do not seem to make efforts to retain their older career workers on a part-time basis after they retire. Persons leaving their career jobs in manufacturing typically must seek employment in other industrial sectors. These shifts are accompanied by a sharp drop in union-related positions among workers past the age of 65. During 1987, 25 percent of all employed persons 55 to 64 years old held jobs in which there was union representation, but only 11 percent of workers 65 and older were in this category (U.S. Department of Labor 1989).

These trends are likely to continue over the remainder of this century because new job growth is expected to predominate in the trade and service industries. The rise in the share of manufacturing jobs in smaller firms, however, may provide additional opportunities for part-time work because of their greater flexibility in staffing. The organization of production may require part-week, full-time work by older workers rather than the part-day hours found in the trade and services industries.

Older part-time workers have tended over time to move into white-collar occupations, especially professional, technical, sales, and clerical work. This trend is related to the growth of industries such as trade, finance, insurance, and services, which are relatively intensive users of white-collar workers.

In March 1968, only three of every eight older workers employed part time held jobs in white-collar occupations. By March 1987, a slight majority (52 percent) of all older part-time workers held jobs in such occupations, nearly one-third of them in sales and clerical positions. Not all of these sales jobs are in trade-related industries, the segment of the labor market most affected by the decline in the number of young entry-level workers. Older males are heavily represented in stock and real estate broker positions in finance industries and real estate. These sales jobs rather than retail clerk positions also tend to dominate the employment of full-time workers after they pass normal retirement age (Parnes et al. 1985).

Not all older workers choose their shorter hours voluntarily. Over the past fifteen years, a growing fraction of the employed throughout the nation have been working part time for economic reasons (because of slack work or material shortages in their current firms or because they were unable to find full-time work), and these trends have affected older workers as well (Ehrenberg, Rosenberg, and Li 1986; Blank 1987; Levitan and Conway 1988) (see figure 3.7).

During both March 1968 and 1974, only 3.2 percent of all employed older persons were working part time for economic reasons, but this ratio rose to 4.5 percent in March 1987, and approximately 36 percent of the increase in overall part-time employment occurred for economic reasons. The effect was most dramatic among blacks and older workers lacking a high school diploma. In March 1987, older black workers were 2.6 times more likely than white non-Hispanics to be employed part time for economic reasons (10.1 percent versus 3.9 percent). Older persons lacking a high school diploma were 80 percent more likely than high school graduates to work part time for economic reasons and five times more likely to do so than college graduates. Part of the difference between the involuntary part-time employment rates of poorly educated and more well-educated older workers is probably attributable to differences in job displacement rates and reemployment adjustment problems, with dropouts having more trouble securing full-time jobs once they have left their career jobs (Podgursky and Swaim 1987). Although older and more poorly educated dislocated workers appear to suffer the most severe adjustment problems, they tend to be heavily underrepresented in

FIGURE 3.7.   Older Persons Employed Part Time for Economic Reasons
and for Noneconomic Reasons, March 1968, 1974, 1980, and 1987

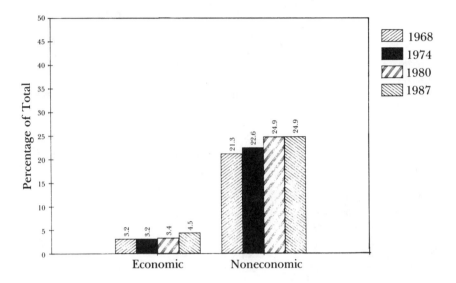

JTPA Title III dislocated worker programs (U.S. General Accounting Office 1986).

Part-Year Employment among Older Workers

During any given year, the total number of persons participating in
the labor force is greater than the average number in any given month.
Some individuals enter the labor force to earn a particular amount
of income and then withdraw once their goal has been achieved.
Others find employment in seasonal industries (construction, tourism,
real estate) that offer only part-year work. During calendar year 1986,
for example, the annual average number of civilian labor force participants was 117.8 million, but 128.1 million persons either worked
or looked for work at some point during the year (U.S. Department
of Labor 1987a and b).

Relative to their younger counterparts, especially those in the prime
age group (25 to 54), one would expect an above-average fraction of
older persons, especially those over 62, to work for only part of the
year. During 1986, the total number of older persons who either
worked or looked for work was approximately one-sixth larger than

TABLE 3.11. Older Persons Working Either No Weeks or 50 to 52
Weeks, by Age, Sex, and Educational Attainment, 1967, 1973, 1979, and
1986 (combined percentages)

Category	1967	1973	1979	1986
All	85.9	86.5	88.2	89.2
55–59	82.4	83.9	84.3	84.0
60–62	84.0	81.8	83.8	83.9
63–65	81.6	82.2	85.0	86.6
66–70	84.1	85.2	87.6	89.4
71+	93.1	93.7	95.0	96.0
Sex				
Male	83.5	83.8	86.1	87.0
Female	88.1	88.7	89.9	91.2
Educational attainment				
High school dropouts	85.9	86.8	89.4	91.1
High school graduates	86.6	86.6	87.0	88.4
Some college	85.6	85.3	87.5	87.8
College graduates	85.3	85.7	86.4	86.6

the average number actually working each month. This figure was
about twice that for all employed persons during that year. The rate
of part-year work during 1986 was nearly identical for older men and
women.

The desire among older persons for part-year work increases with
age. The ratio of the annual flow of labor force participants to the
average monthly stock among those 55 and older ranged from a low
of 1.08 for those aged 55 to 59, to 1.21 for those 60 to 64, and to
1.39 for those 70 and older. It should be remembered, however, that
the overall labor force participation rate of this last group is very low
so a higher turnover rate during the year does not raise the absolute
participation rate for such persons by more than a couple of percentage points.

Although part-year work is somewhat more common among workers over 65 than among their younger counterparts, older persons
are increasingly becoming all-or-nothing participants in the labor market (Ruhm and Sum 1989). Over the past two decades, the proportion
of older persons reporting either no employment or year-round employment has risen gradually from 85.9 percent in 1967 to 89.2 percent by 1986 (see figure 3.8 and table 3.11). During the latter year,
nine of every ten older persons in the United States worked either

FIGURE 3.8. Older Persons Who Reported Zero Weeks of Employment and 50 to 52 Weeks of Employment in the Previous Year, 1968, 1974, 1980, and 1987 (in percent)

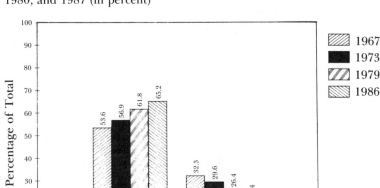

year-round or not at all. This trend has occurred for all age subgroups (with the exception of those aged 60 to 62), for both men and women, and for members of each educational attainment subgroup. As was true for our earlier findings on participation rates, these trends were most evident among the older subgroups (65 and over) and among those with the least formal schooling.

The high and rising fractions of older persons opting for year-round or no employment are somewhat surprising. One might have expected the shift toward part-time employment to have been accompanied by a movement toward more frequent part-year employment, particularly given the past earnings limits imposed by the Social Security system and by some private pension plans. Greater knowledge of the institutional and economic factors inhibiting part-year employment would be highly desirable in planning future human resource programs for older Americans. The increased availability of part-year employment opportunities may serve to reduce the withdrawal rates of older persons from their career jobs and attract retired older persons back into the labor force, thereby reversing the long-term trend of reduced attachment to the labor force. Successful efforts in this area may also help alleviate labor shortages in local economies.

TABLE 3.12.   Employed Persons 50 to 64 Who Moved into New Industrial Sectors, by Age, Sex, and Educational Attainment, 1974–1988 (1-digit SIC) (in percent)

Category	1974	1980	1987	1988
All 50–65	5.9	2.7	3.0	2.8
Age subgroup				
50–54	5.5	2.7	3.3	3.3
55–62	6.2	2.5	2.7	2.2
63–65	6.7	3.8	2.9	3.7
Sex				
Men	6.5	2.9	3.2	2.8
Women	5.0	2.4	2.6	2.8
Educational attainment				
Less than 12 years	6.0	3.3	3.0	2.8
12 years	5.9	2.4	2.6	2.6
13–15 years	6.2	2.8	3.5	3.4
16 or more years	5.5	2.4	3.1	2.6

Job Changing and Industrial Mobility among Older Workers

The CPS retrospective employment data provide information on the industry to which the respondent was attached for the longest time during a calendar year, while the March data indicate the industry of the respondent's current employer. By comparing these industries, mobility rates for older workers can be estimated. Estimates of industrial mobility rates for subgroups of older workers across major industrial sectors (one-digit Standard Industrial Classification codes) and more detailed industry groupings are presented in tables 3.12 and 3.13. Findings suggest a fairly high degree of year-to-year mobility, though the rates for the early 1970s clearly exceed those for the 1980s.

In March 1974, nearly 6 percent of all employed 50- to 65-year-olds held jobs in industrial sectors different from those in which they were employed in the previous calendar year. In the 1980s, this ratio has averaged a little under 3 percent, indicating that nearly one-third of these workers may shift into a new industrial sector by the time they reach 62. (These mobility rates are probably conservative because they consider only movement into different major industrial sectors,

TABLE 3.13. Employed Persons 50 to 64 Who Moved into New Industries (3-digit SIC) within a One-Year Period, by Age and Sex, 1974–1988 (in percent)

Category	March 1974	March 1988
All 50–65	7.5	3.9
Age subgroup		
50–54	6.9	4.4
55–62	7.8	3.3
63–65	8.9	4.7
Sex		
Men	7.7	3.5
Women	7.3	4.5

such as durable manufacturing, retail trade, and services, and ignore shifts into different industries within the same industrial sector.)

When the analysis is focused on more detailed industry groupings, mobility rates are even higher. In March 1988, for example, nearly 4.0 percent of all employed persons 50 to 64 were in jobs in an industry different from the one that provided their major source of employment in the previous calendar year. The corresponding rate for March 1974 was 7.5 percent. Whether viewed from a major industrial sector or a more detailed industry grouping, the mobility rates typically tended to be highest for those workers 63 to 65 years of age. This finding suggests a higher rate of interindustry mobility for workers who have reached the minimum age at which they are eligible for Social Security benefits. Retirement from career jobs is thus accompanied by shifts to jobs (including part-time jobs) in other industries.

Reentry into the Paid Work Force

Estimates of reentry rates into the paid work force among older persons with no employment experience in the previous calendar year are presented in table 3.14. During the 1980s, approximately 1 of every 125 persons in this group was employed by March of the following year. As expected, these rates vary uniformly by age group, with the likelihood of reentry falling with age. After the age of 70, only three of every one thousand became employed by March of the following year.

Table 3.14. Retired and Other Older Persons Reentering Employment, by Age, Sex, and Educational Attainment, March 1974, 1980, 1987, and 1988 (in percent)

Category	1974	1980	1987	1988
All 55+	1.4	.8	.8	.7
Age subgroup				
55–59	3.9	1.8	2.4	2.5
60–64	1.5	1.3	1.2	1.0
65–69	1.6	.9	.7	.7
70+	.7	.3	.3	.4
Sex				
Men	2.1	.8	1.2	.8
Women	1.1	.8	.5	.7
Educational attainment				
Less than 12 years	1.0	.6	.4	.5
12 years	.9	1.0	1.0	.8
13–15 years	1.2	1.2	.8	1.1
16 or more years	1.3	1.1	1.7	1.7

The reentry rates for men and women were nearly identical in two of the three years in the 1980s. A greater number of older women than men have no work experience during a given year, so women clearly represent an above-average fraction (60 percent in March 1988) of the pool of older reentrants. Reentry rates for older workers have also varied systematically in the 1980s by years of formal schooling completed. High school dropouts were the least likely to reenter, while college graduates were the most likely. The high demand for professional and managerial workers in the late 1980s probably exerted a strong influence on these differential rates.[16]

Combined with our previous findings on the high rates of withdrawal from the labor force by men and women before the age of 62 or 65, these latter findings suggest a substantial degree of flux in the labor markets for older workers. Many older workers appear to change employers in their fifties and early sixties, a high percentage

---

16. Between 1983 and 1987, the number of persons over age 16 employed in professional and managerial specialty occupations increased by nearly 18 percent versus an 11.5 percent growth rate for all occupations. During 1987, the annual average unemployment rate of professional and managerial workers was only 2.3 percent (U.S. Department of Labor 1988b).

withdraw from active participation before 62, and a number of those who withdraw, especially those under 65, eventually return to paid employment.[17]

Bridge jobs thus appear to play a fairly important role in the work lives of older workers. They serve as a substitute for continued employment in one's career job through retirement, as a source of immediate or near immediate employment following retirement from a career job, and as a safety valve for formerly retired workers who wish to return to the labor market to supplement family income or fill a social or economic void in their lives. As more regional and local labor markets reach full-employment conditions, bridge jobs may also serve to alleviate or prevent labor shortages and thereby facilitate sustained economic growth.

---

17. In her analysis of a 1979 survey of the retirement plans of female labor force participants ages 42 to 56, Lois Shaw discovered that 36 percent of the sample planned to retire from active labor market participation before age 62 (Shaw 1983).

LABOR MARKET AND POVERTY PROBLEMS OF OLDER WORKERS AND THEIR FAMILIES

Andrew M. Sum and W. Neal Fogg

T HE PREVIOUS CHAPTER DESCRIBED and assessed past and projected demographic developments with respect to the size and
composition of the nation's older population, trends in the labor force
behavior of older persons, the changing industrial and occupational
patterns of employment among older workers, and their job mobility
and labor force reentry behavior. This chapter examines the types
and severity of problems encountered by older workers in the labor
market and tracks trends in poverty among older persons and their
families. The potential role of bridge jobs and new institutional arrangements for facilitating access to them as partial solutions to several
of these problems will be described.

Unemployment Problems of
Older Workers

Most discussions and analyses of labor market pathologies emphasize
the problems of persons actively seeking paid employment and available for work but unable to obtain a job. Because of their greater
years of work experience and the frequent use of seniority in determining layoffs, older workers are more likely to be protected against
moderate downturns in business activity that necessitate reductions

FIGURE 4.1.   Unemployment Rates of Persons 55 and Older and of
Persons 25 to 54, 1948–1986

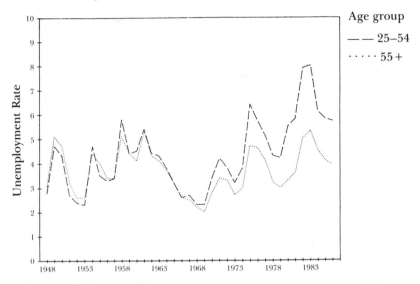

in a firm's work force. Their lower rates of entry and reentry into the
labor force should also reduce problems of frictional unemployment.
Nevertheless, the employment status of older persons is affected by
overall macroeconomic conditions and by plant closings, relocations,
and major reductions in force.

As has been true for the prime-age work force (25- to 54-year-olds),
the unemployment rates of older workers (here defined as those 55
and over) have drifted upward over the past two decades as national
labor market conditions became more slack (see figure 4.1). The average (mean) unemployment rate of older workers was only 2.7 percent from 1968 to 1973, rose to 3.5 percent in 1977 to 1979, and has
averaged 4.1 percent through 1987 (U.S. Department of Labor 1982b,
1988b). The aggregate unemployment rates of older workers, however, have remained below those of prime-age workers since the late
1960s (Rones 1983),[1] and in the last twenty years the unemployment
position of older workers has improved relative to that of prime-age
workers (Summers 1986). Thus, though the absolute unemployment

---

1. There is some variation by sex in the timing of these patterns. Older males typically
experienced unemployment rates above those of prime-age males in the 1968–70 period; but, after 1974, this situation reversed and has stayed that way since then (Rones
1983).

TABLE 4.1. Annual Average Unemployment Rates of All Persons 16 and Older and of Older Persons, by Sex, 1982, 1983, 1986, and 1987 (in percent)

Sex/Age Group	1982	1983	1986	1987
Both sexes				
All 16+	9.70	9.60	7.00	6.20
55+	5.00	5.30	3.90	3.30
55+/All	.52	.55	.56	.53
Males				
All 16+	9.90	9.90	6.90	6.20
55+	5.10	5.60	4.10	3.50
55+/All	.52	.57	.59	.56
Females				
All 16+	9.40	9.20	7.10	6.20
55+	4.80	4.70	3.60	3.00
55+/All	.51	.51	.51	.48

rates of older workers have risen since the late 1960s and early 1970s, their relative unemployment position has improved.

During the first five years of recovery from the 1982 national economic recession, the unemployment rates of older men and women have fallen as have those for all working-age individuals (defined here as all persons over 16) (U.S. Department of Labor 1988b) (see table 4.1). The aggregate unemployment rate for all older workers peaked in 1983 at 5.3 percent and fell to 3.3 percent in 1987. From 1982 to 1987, both older men and women experienced unemployment rates half those of their counterparts in the entire working-age population, and the unemployment rates of older women were about one-half percentage point below those of older men. One reason for this difference is that women were less adversely affected by the sharp economic downturn in 1982 (Klein 1983).

In recent years, the unemployment rates of workers over 65 have tended to be lower than for those under 65 (see table 4.2). In March 1987, the unemployment rate of those 55 to 62 years old was 4.0 percent, whereas for those 66 to 70 it was 2.9 percent, and for those over 70 it was only 2.0 percent. When we consider the low rates of labor force participation of the older age groups, the dimensions of the open unemployment problems among subgroups of older workers come into better perspective. In March 1987, approximately one of every forty individuals 55 to 59 years of age was unemployed. This

TABLE 4.2. Unemployment Rates and Unemployment/Population Ratios of Older Persons, by Age, Sex, and Educational Attainment, March 1968, 1974, 1980, and 1987 (in percent)

Category	Unemployment Rate				Unemployment/Population Ratio			
	1968	1974	1980	1987	1968	1974	1980	1987
Age subgroup								
55–59	2.7	3.0	3.0	4.0	1.8	2.0	1.9	2.6
60–62	1.9	2.5	3.8	4.1	1.1	1.4	2.0	2.0
63–65	3.2	3.7	3.8	4.6	1.4	1.4	1.3	1.4
66–70	3.5	3.2	2.8	2.9	0.9	0.7	0.5	0.5
71+	1.9	2.5	1.5	2.1	0.2	0.2	0.1	0.1
Total	2.6	2.9	3.2	3.9	1.0	1.1	1.0	1.2
Sex								
Male	2.6	2.7	3.3	4.2	1.5	1.4	1.5	1.7
Female	2.6	3.4	2.9	3.4	0.6	0.8	0.7	0.7
Total	2.6	2.9	3.2	3.9	1.0	1.1	1.0	1.2
Educational attainment								
High school dropouts	3.3	3.4	4.7	6.1	1.1	1.0	1.1	1.2
High school graduates	1.6	2.8	2.7	3.2	0.8	1.2	1.1	1.1
Some college	2.7	3.4	2.7	4.0	1.3	1.5	1.2	1.5
College graduates	0.7	1.2	1.1	2.0	0.4	0.6	0.5	0.9
Total	2.6	2.9	3.2	3.9	1.0	1.1	1.0	1.2

TABLE 4.3.   Estimate of the Number of Dislocated Workers as a
Percentage of the Adjusted Civilian Labor Force, by Age and Sex (based
on an average of the three BLS dislocated worker surveys, January 1984,
1986, and 1988)

Category	Dislocated Workers as Percentage of Civilian Labor Force
Age subgroup	
20+	4.6
20–24	1.6
25–54	4.9
55–64	6.2
65+	5.9
Males	
55–64	6.4
65+	4.6
Females	
55–64	5.8
65+	7.8

ratio was one of fifty for those 60 to 62 years old and only one per
one thousand for persons over 70. Strategies to reduce unemployment
among workers over 65 and especially among those over 70 would
therefore have a minimal influence on the overall economic well-being
of the older age group.

Job Loss and Unemployment
Problems of Older Workers

Although older persons are less likely to be unemployed than younger
ones, they are more likely to become unemployed as a result of job
loss and to experience greater difficulties in obtaining reemployment
when they lose their jobs. The late 1970s and early 1980s were characterized by economic turbulence, with major plant closings, corporate
restructuring, and downsizing efforts in key manufacturing industries
(Mirkin 1987). Concern for the plight of dislocated workers arose
during this period (Levitan and Gallo 1988; U.S. General Accounting
Office 1986; Flaim and Sehgal 1985).

Beginning with January 1984, the Bureau of Labor Statistics (BLS)
has conducted three surveys aimed at identifying the numbers and
characteristics of American workers who have been dislocated from

their jobs (U.S. Department of Labor 1984b, 1988d; Devens 1986; Flaim and Sehgal 1985; Horvath 1987). The BLS definition of a dislocated worker is a person aged 20 or over with job tenure of three or more years who lost or left a job in the previous five years as a result of a plant closing or relocation, slack work, or the elimination of a position or work shift.[2] To discover the degree to which older workers were affected during the 1980s, estimates have been made of the number of dislocated workers in each major age subgroup as a percentage of the adjusted civilian labor force in that same age subgroup at the time of the three BLS surveys of dislocated workers.[3] The mean percentages for the three surveys appear in table 4.3.

On average, 4.6 percent of the adjusted civilian labor force aged 20 and over had been dislocated from their jobs in the previous five years, although the overall rate of dislocation appears to have diminished somewhat in the mid- to late 1980s (U.S. Department of Labor 1988d). Dislocation rates rise with age, peaking at 6.2 percent in the 55-to-64 age group; thus, on average, nearly 1.3 percent of them had been dislocated each year during each previous five-year period. Males and females in the 55-to-64 age group experienced similar rates of dislocation, clearly indicating that the adverse effects of the economic turbulence of the 1980s were not confined to men, despite their greater concentration in key goods-producing sectors that bore the brunt of the dislocation. Once dislocated from their jobs, older workers are more likely than their younger counterparts to experience a spell of unemployment, and they incur longer periods of joblessness (Flaim and Sehgal 1985; Horvath 1987).

In January 1984, approximately one of every six unemployed adults had been displaced from a job in the previous five years[4] (see table

---

2. The total number of workers regardless of tenure who had lost a job in the previous five years was more than twice that of workers meeting the three-year tenure requirement (U.S. Department of Labor 1984b, 1988d; Flaim and Sehgal 1985). One would expect that the age distribution of the shorter-tenure dislocated workers would be more concentrated in the younger age groups.

3. The adjusted civilian labor force for any age and sex subgroup includes all persons in that subgroup who were in the civilian labor force at the time of each survey of dislocated workers (January 1984, January 1986, January 1988) plus those dislocated workers who were not participating in the civilian labor force at the time of the survey. Above-average fractions of older dislocated workers, especially those over 65, had withdrawn from the labor force by the time of each survey.

4. Values of these ratios were derived by dividing the estimated number of dislocated workers who were unemployed at the time of the January 1984 and January 1986 BLS surveys by the total number of unemployed workers in each age group in January 1984 and January 1986. Older dislocated workers were more likely than their younger counterparts to be unemployed at the time of both surveys. Similar findings also prevail for the January 1988 dislocated worker survey (U.S. Department of Labor 1988d).

TABLE 4.4. Age Distribution of All Unemployed Workers and Unemployed Dislocated Workers, January 1984 and January 1986 (in 1000s)

Age Group	1984			1986		
	(A) All Unemployed	(B) Dislocated Unemployed	(C) B/A (%)	(A) All Unemployed	(B) Dislocated Unemployed	(C) B/A (%)
20+	8,276	1,298	15.7	7,138	913	12.8
20–24	2,166	69	3.2	1,761	52	2.9
25–54	5,322	968	18.2	4,737	715	15.1
55+	786	261	33.2	639	146	22.8
55–64	682	238	34.9	545	139	25.5
65+	104	23	22.1	94	7	7.4

4.4). One-third of older unemployed persons had been displaced in the preceding five years, far more than every other age group, with workers aged 55 to 64 most likely to have been dislocated. The results of the January 1986 survey were similar, showing that unemployed workers aged 55 to 64 were twice as likely as all unemployed adult workers to have been displaced from a job over the preceding five-year period.

Once older workers become unemployed, they tend to face greater problems in securing reemployment and thus to experience lengthier spells of unemployment than younger workers (Doeringer and Sum 1984; Parnes, Gagen, and King 1981; Parnes 1982; Rones 1983). They are also more likely to withdraw from the labor force rather than obtain a job (Bould 1980; Parnes 1983). Recent evidence on the duration of unemployment among older workers is presented in table 4.5. In 1987, only one-fourth of all unemployed workers in a typical month had been unemployed for fifteen weeks or longer (the standard definition of long-term unemployment), and the mean duration of their unemployment was 14.5 weeks. Among unemployed 55- to 64-year-olds, however, 41 percent had been out of work for fifteen or more weeks, and their mean duration of unemployment was twenty-two weeks. Males aged 55 to 64 were the most likely to report long-term unemployment. Their mean duration of unemployment was nearly twenty-five weeks, or half a year. These figures imply that unemployment problems of older workers are concentrated among a relatively small group.

To study further the concentration of unemployment among older

TABLE 4.5.   Distribution of the Unemployed by Current Duration of Unemployment and Median and Mean Weeks of Unemployment, by Age and Sex, Annual Averages, 1987

Age/Sex Subgroup	Unemployed Less than 5 Weeks	Unemployed 15 or More Weeks	Median Weeks of Unemployment	Mean Weeks of Unemployment
All (16+)	43.7%	26.7%	6.5	14.5
55–64	31.6	40.9	10.9	22.0
Men	27.3	46.0	13.2	24.7
Women	38.8	32.4	7.9	17.6
65+ years	41.0	33.3	7.4	17.8

workers, we analyzed the work experience supplement to the March 1987 CPS survey, with emphasis on the unemployment experiences of older workers who were unemployed for one or more weeks during calendar year 1986[5] (see tables 4.6 and 4.7). We estimate that in 1986, 1.3 million older persons were unemployed for one or more weeks. This group represented nearly 8 percent of the total number of older persons who were active in the civilian labor force at some point during that year.[6] One-half of these persons were unemployed for fifteen or fewer weeks and one-fourth for more than six months. Periods of long unemployment were most prevalent among males.

We estimate that older workers experienced 26.0 million weeks of unemployment during 1986 (see table 4.7). Although half of this group were unemployed for fifteen or fewer weeks, they accounted for only 19 percent of all weeks of unemployment among older workers. The one-fourth of the group who were unemployed for more than six months accounted for 52 percent of the total weeks of unemployment, and males accounted for 54 percent of this total.

This evidence suggests that slightly less than 2 percent of the older labor force experienced more than half of all weeks of unemployment among the older work force in 1986. How many of these very long-term unemployed individuals were dislocated workers cannot be determined with the available data; however, it is quite likely that a

5. An individual may have been unemployed for two or more different spells during the year. Total weeks of unemployment for any individual thus do not necessarily reflect the length of a typical spell.

6. The actual figure of 7.7 percent is twice that of the annual average unemployment rate during 1986. The multiple of two is attributable to movement of older workers into and out of the ranks of the unemployed during the year.

TABLE 4.6. Distribution of Unemployed Older Workers by Total Weeks Unemployed during Calendar Year 1986, Total and Males

	All		Males	
Group	Number (in 1000s)	Percent	Number (in 1000s)	Percent
Persons with one or more weeks in civilian labor force	17,500	100.0	10,259	100.0
Persons unemployed at some point during 1986	1,343	7.7	852	8.3
Length of unemployment				
1–5 weeks	273	20.3	152	17.8
6–15 weeks	393	29.2	232	27.2
16–26 weeks	332	24.7	225	26.4
27+ weeks	347	25.8	243	28.5

TABLE 4.7. Total Weeks of Unemployment among Older Persons during 1986, All and Males Only, March 1987

	All		Males	
Length of Unemployment (weeks)	Weeks of Unemployment (in 1000s)	Percentage of Total Weeks	Weeks of Unemployment (in 1000s)	Percentage of Total Weeks
1–5	979	3.8	564	3.2
6–15	3,938	15.1	2,475	13.9
16–26	7,470	28.7	5,089	28.6
27+	13,646	52.4	9,657	54.3
Total	26,033	100.0	17,785	100.0

sizable fraction of them had been displaced from their career jobs. Building more effective bridges to new jobs would reduce the personal and social costs of dislocation among older workers.

Lost Earnings from Unemployment of Family Heads and Their Wives

The personal costs of unemployment include the lost earnings of the unemployed and a decline in their perceived sense of self-worth and social status. In addition, society loses because these people are not

TABLE 4.8.   Estimated Lost Earnings from Unemployment of Older
Heads of Families and Estimated Impact on Family Incomes, 1986
(number of family heads as of March 1987)

Category	Mean Lost Earnings	Mean Family Income	Lost Earnings as Percentage of Family Income
Age subgroup			
All 55+	$ 9,768	$26,899	36.3
55–64	10,405	26,733	39.1
65+	5,079	28,037	18.1
Race/ethnic group			
White not Hispanic	10,941	28,371	38.5
Black not Hispanic	4,029	20,080	20.1
Hispanic	6,741	19,055	35.4

producing goods and services.[7] To estimate the costs of unemployment in terms of lost earnings, we examined the unemployment experiences of older family heads and wives during 1986 and calculated
the gross earnings that they would have received if they had been
employed during those weeks[8] (see table 4.8).

During 1986, approximately 714,000 of the nation's 20.0 million
older heads of families experienced a spell of unemployment. The
estimated mean value of the lost earnings for this group, $9,768, was
equal to 36 percent of the mean income of their families during that
year. Although less than 4 percent of all older heads of families were
unemployed during that year, their lost earnings were nearly $7 bil-
lion. These losses were substantially larger for family heads in the 55-
to-64 age group than they were for those 65 and over, and they were
larger for whites than for blacks or Hispanics.

Wives in older families also incur unemployment and experience
their own earnings losses.[9] During 1986, 16.7 million married couple

---

7. For a review of the loss of status and authority among jobless older workers in
the United States throughout the nineteenth and early twentieth centuries see Haber
1985.

8. Our estimates of the earnings losses of unemployed heads of families were derived
by multiplying total weeks of unemployment during calendar year 1986 by their mean
weekly earnings during the time they were employed. If an unemployed older head
had no work experience during 1986, he or she was assigned a weekly earnings figure
equal to $134, or forty hours at the prevailing federal minimum wage of $3.35. This
last assumption was intended to be extremely conservative to avoid any upward bias
in our estimates.

9. The foregone earnings of wives were calculated in the same manner as described
in the preceding note.

TABLE 4.9.   Estimated Lost Earnings from Unemployment of Husband
and Wife in Older Married Couple Families and Estimated Impact on
Family Income, 1986

Category	Mean Lost Earnings	Mean Family Income	Lost Earnings as Percentage of Family Income
Age subgroup			
All 55 +	$8,635	$30,190	28.6
55–64	9,330	31,139	30.0
65 +	5,278	25,607	20.6
Race/ethnic group			
White not Hispanic	9,544	31,599	30.2
Black not Hispanic	3,333	22,454	14.8
Hispanic	6,564	24,007	27.3

families were headed by a person 55 or over. In these families, 621,000
heads were unemployed and an additional 419,000 spouses.[10] Unemployment of both the head and the spouse occurred in only 10
percent of the cases. The mean earnings loss of such families was
$8,635, equivalent to nearly 29 percent of their mean family incomes
during that year. Despite these earnings losses, the mean incomes of
these families ($30,190) remained well above the poverty line[11] (see
table 4.9). The mean earnings loss was nearly twice as large in families
headed by an individual 55 to 64 as in families in which the head was
65 and over. The aggregate economic loss resulting from unemployment of the heads and spouses in older married couple families was
$8.4 billion.

Job Desires of Older Nonparticipants
in the Labor Force

The official unemployment statistics may not fully capture the desire
of jobless older individuals to be employed. Some of those classified
as not in the labor force may wish to be employed even though they
are not actively looking for work at the time of the survey. Since the
late 1960s, the Bureau of Labor Statistics has attempted to estimate

---

10. The family householder can be either the husband or the wife. Among older
married couple families, the husband is classified as the householder in more than 95
percent of the cases.

11. This finding for older families is similar to that for all families with an unemployed husband or wife in earlier years (Hayghe 1979; Terry 1982).

the number of nonparticipants who desire employment and to identify their reasons for not actively seeking work (Flaim 1973; Finegan 1978a, b). Older persons expressing a desire for employment will be referred to as the "labor force overhang," a term developed by Eli Ginzberg (1977).[12] A subset of the individuals constituting this labor force overhang consists of "discouraged workers," that is, those who expressed a desire for employment at the time of the survey but were not actively seeking work because they had previously looked for work and could not find it, did not believe any jobs were available in their local economy, or believed they would not be hired for existing jobs because of their age, limited skills, or lack of experience. These two groups, though related, need to be treated separately because the labor force overhang is typically three to four times larger than the pool of discouraged older workers.

METHODOLOGICAL ISSUES

Estimates of the size of the pool of older nonparticipants who express a desire for employment tend to vary widely from one survey to another (Harris 1986; Parnes 1968, 1981a; Parnes et al. 1975, 1985). This variability is probably attributable to differences in the questions used to ascertain the job desires of nonparticipants and to the administration of the surveys. The wording of the CPS survey questions that are used to elicit responses from nonparticipants differs from that used by the NLS surveys of older workers and by the Louis Harris and Associates survey of elderly Americans (Harris 1986; Parnes 1981; Parnes et al. 1968, 1975; Sum 1988a).

The CPS survey obtains information on the current job desires of only a sample of those individuals who were not actively participating in the civilian labor force at the time of each monthly survey, whereas others such as the Louis Harris survey ask these questions of all older individuals who did not work in the preceding year. These latter surveys thus encompass many more individuals than does the CPS, including unemployed persons as well as all nonparticipants.

There are also differences in the methodologies used in the various surveys. The CPS survey asks these questions only of persons who have been surveyed repeatedly, and there is some evidence that nonparticipants are less likely to express an interest in a job when they have been interviewed repeatedly than when they are interviewed for the first time (Flaim 1973). The CPS survey asks respondents if they

---

12. For a discussion of the concepts of discouraged workers, hidden unemployment, and the labor force overhang, see Gastwirth 1973; Ginzberg 1977; and Mincer 1973.

want a regular job now. The desire for a job must be existent at the time of the survey, not for an unspecified period of time as is true for related questions in the NLS older worker surveys (Parnes et al. 1968, 1975).

Moreover, the CPS survey allows for proxy respondents, that is, any "responsible adult" member of the family may answer questions for any household member. Wives in older married couple families can thus answer questions regarding their husbands.

Finally, like most earlier survey work in this area, individuals expressing a desire for immediate employment are not asked to identify the type of job they would like to obtain or the terms and conditions under which they would accept an employment offer. Little substantial information is available on the hours of work, hourly wages, fringe benefits, locations of jobs, job duties, characteristics of co-workers, and other factors that would entice these older nonparticipants to accept a job if one were offered (Sum 1988a; Kennedy 1980).

Estimates of the Older
Labor Force Overhang

The Bureau of Labor Statistics publishes quarterly and annual estimates of the proportion of nonparticipants aged 60 and over who express a desire for current employment. Annual averages for the years 1972 to 1987 are shown in table 4.10. The share of older nonparticipants expressing a desire for employment averaged 2.1 percent and varied within a narrow range over this sixteen-year period from 1.8 percent to 2.4 percent. These estimates of the relative size of the labor force overhang are well below most of those given by Herbert S. Parnes (15 percent) and Harris Associates (12 percent), and they were only one-third to one-fifth as high as the CPS estimates for all nonparticipants aged 16 and over for the same time period.[13] During 1987, for example, 9.0 percent of all nonparticipants in the United States expressed a desire for employment (U.S. Department of Labor 1988b). The vast majority of nonparticipants aged 60 and over thus appear to prefer to remain outside the labor force.

---

13. The 1981 NLS survey of older workers was focused on 60- to 74-year-old men who were out of the labor force. Although 16 percent of the sample expressed a willingness to accept a hypothetical job offer, only 2 percent said they would do so unconditionally. The 1985 Harris survey was focused on persons 70 years of age and older, including an oversampling of persons 75 and over. Sample results have been weighted to reflect each respondent group's estimated share of the nation's civilian noninstitutional population of 70+-year-olds.

TABLE 4.10.   Job Desires of Persons 60 and Older Not in the Civilian
Labor Force, Annual Averages, 1972–1986

Year	Number Wanting Job (in 1000s)	Percentage of Those Out of Labor Force
1972	430	2.1
1973	421	2.0
1974	411	1.8
1975	511	2.2
1976	428	2.0
1977	505	2.3
1978	594	2.4
1979	544	2.2
1980	537	2.1
1981	556	2.0
1982	601	2.1
1983	556	1.9
1984	553	1.9
1985	605	2.0
1986	605	2.0
1987	616	2.0
1972–87 average	530	2.1

To obtain greater insight into the job desires of various subgroups
of older nonparticipants, including those 55 to 59 years of age, we
analyzed data on the March 1980 and March 1987 CPS public-use
tapes (see figure 4.2). At the time of the March 1987 CPS survey,
2.4 percent of the sample of older nonparticipants expressed a desire
for a job. The estimated total number of such individuals was 835,600,
a fairly large number, particularly when one considers that the estimated total number of unemployed persons 55 and over during that
same month was only 572,000. The size of the pool of older persons
making up the labor force overhang is thus important for employment
and training policy making.

The percentage of nonparticipants expressing a desire for a job at
the time of the March 1987 survey varied sharply by the age, sex, and
race and ethnic origin of respondents. More than 6.0 percent of the
nonparticipants in the youngest subgroup (those 55 to 59 years of
age) expressed a desire for a job, yet fewer than 1 of every 160
nonparticipants over the age of 70 wanted a job at that time. Males
were one and one-half times more likely than females to indicate a

FIGURE 4.2.   Percentage of Persons 55 and Older Who Are Out of the
Labor Force but Want a Job, by Age, March 1980 and March 1987

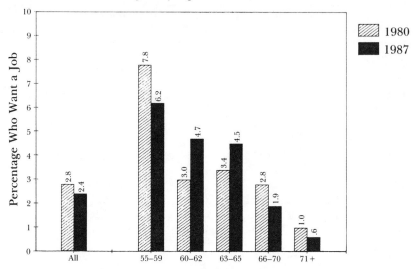

desire for employment, a finding consistent with those for earlier
years.

Both black and Hispanic nonparticipants were far more likely than
white non-Hispanics to express a desire for immediate employment.
Similar race and ethnic differences prevail for younger age groups
as well. Nearly 6.0 percent of all black older nonparticipants and 5.0
percent of Hispanics wanted a job in March 1987 versus only 2.0
percent of white non-Hispanics. Large differences between blacks and
whites on this issue have been evident throughout the decade, indicating involuntary withdrawals from the labor force by older black
persons. Given the high poverty rates experienced by older black
Americans in the 1980s, human resource policies designed to attract
black and Hispanic nonparticipants back into the labor force should
be given serious consideration by the nation's employment and training policy makers. A separate analysis of the job desires of older
nonparticipants living in poor and near poor households revealed an
above-average incidence of job desires on their part.[14] Nearly 3.5
percent of all such nonparticipants expressed a desire for current
employment, and this ratio increased to nearly 7.0 percent for poor
and near poor individuals 55 to 65 years of age.

14. The near poor are those individuals who live in households with incomes above
but less than 125 percent of the federal government's poverty line.

Apart from these expressions of interest in current employment, little is known about the types of jobs these older individuals would like. Future surveys of elderly Americans need to capture information on the characteristics of bridge jobs these potential labor force participants would be willing to accept and the terms and conditions of employment that would entice them into the labor force (Sum 1988a). Policies regarding bridge jobs should be tailored to meet the desires and needs of older workers and potential employers.

Reasons for Not Seeking Work

Older nonparticipants expressing a desire for an immediate job cite different reasons for not actively seeking work. Discouragement has accounted for about one-third of the responses of persons aged 60 and over surveyed from 1984 to 1987. Discouragement includes both economic reasons ("looked for work, but could not find it"; "does not believe any jobs are available") and personal reasons ("employers think I am too old" or "too poorly educated"). Health and disability factors were cited by 30 percent of the older nonparticipants who wished to work. Home responsibilities and transportation barriers account for the remainder of the responses. More specific knowledge of the job barriers faced by this potential pool of older workers would be highly desirable for the formulation of human resource programs to induce them back into the labor market.

Combined Incidence of Labor Market Problems among Older Persons

The problems of open unemployment, involuntary part-time employment, and "hidden unemployment" among older persons have been described and assessed separately. Because these three problems are mutually exclusive at any given time, they can be combined to provide an overall measure of their incidence among the older population[15] (see table 4.11). During March 1987, approximately 2.02

---

15. These three problems may be subject to some overlap during the year. For example, a person who was unemployed at the time of the March 1987 survey may have become employed part time for economic reasons later in the year. The number of individuals experiencing one or more of these problems during a year will be some multiple of the number doing so in any given month. For example, the estimated number of unemployed persons 55 and over in March 1987 was 575,000. Yet we earlier estimated that 1.34 million older persons were unemployed at some point during calendar year 1986, representing a pool of unemployed individuals that was 2.33 times larger than the number of older unemployed persons during March 1987.

THE LABOR MAKET

TABLE 4.11. Number of Persons 55 and Older Experiencing Open
Unemployment, Involuntary Part-Time Employment, or Hidden
Unemployment, by Sex, March 1987 (number in 1000s)

Category	All		Males		Females	
	Number	Percentage	Number	Percentage	Number	Percentage
Civilian population	49,850	100.0	21,850	100.0	28,004	100.0
Unemployment	575	1.2	369	1.7	205	.7
Involuntary part-time employment	611	1.2	326	1.5	285	1.0
Labor force overhang	836	1.7	393	1.8	443	1.6
All three problems combined	2,022	4.1	1,088	5.0	933	3.3

million older persons experienced one of these three problems. There
were 836,000 members of the labor force overhang in this group in
March 1987, accounting for 41 percent of the total number of older
persons with one of the three labor market problems. The remainder
were fairly evenly divided between the unemployed and those older
persons working part time for economic reasons.

The proportion of older persons affected by one of these three
problems was approximately the same in March 1987 as it was in
March 1980 (4.1 percent versus 3.9 percent); however, the incidence
of such problems appears to have increased for those under 65, males,
and blacks and Hispanics (see figures 4.3 and 4.4).

At the time of the March 1987 survey, older males were nearly 50
percent more likely than females to incur one of these three problems,
with open unemployment and involuntary part-time employment occurring more frequently among males. The incidence of these problems also varied sharply by age subgroup. Approximately 7 percent
of those 55 to 62 years old experienced one of these problems during
March 1987. In contrast, only 3 percent of those in the 66-to-70 age
group and less than 1 percent of those over 70 did so. The relative
incidence of these combined problems is thus nearly eight times higher
among those 55 to 62 than among those over 70. Older blacks and
Hispanics were more than twice as likely as white non-Hispanics to
be affected by one of these three labor market problems (see figure
4.4). Eight percent of older blacks and Hispanics but only 3.4 percent
of white non-Hispanics were unemployed, employed part-time in-

FIGURE 4.3.   Proportion of Persons 55 and Older with Some Labor
Market Problem, by Age, March 1980 and March 1987

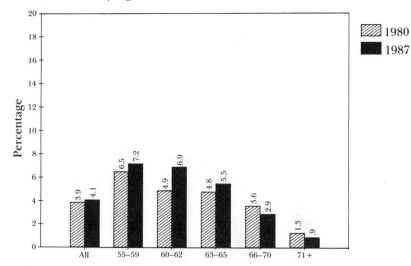

voluntarily, or members of the nation's labor force overhang during
that month. Because an increasing share of the older work force will
be composed of racial and ethnic minorities over the remainder of
the century, the labor market problems of older blacks and Hispanics
should be given greater attention by the nation's employment and
training policy makers.

Poverty and the Older Worker

TRENDS AMONG OLDER PERSONS
AND OLDER FAMILIES

To determine how well older individuals and their families have fared
in avoiding severe problems of income inadequacy over the past two
decades, estimates of the poverty rates for all older persons, older
families, and several important subgroups of the older population
have been made. The income thresholds used by the federal government to identify persons and families as being poor take into consideration the age of the householder as well as the number of persons
in a family. For example, the 1986 weighted average poverty threshold
for all unrelated individuals was $5,572[16] (U.S. Bureau of the Census

---

16. The poverty measures are based on the cash income received by individuals and

FIGURE 4.4.   Proportion of Persons 55 and Older with Some Labor
Market Problem, by Race and Ethnic Group, March 1980 and March 1987

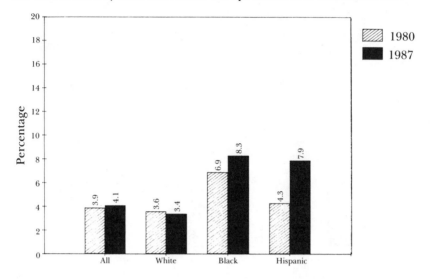

1987a). If the person was 15 to 64 years old, the poverty threshold
was $5,701; however, for unrelated individuals 65 years and over, it
was only $5,255, or about 8 percent less. For a two-person family with
a householder 15 to 64 years of age, the poverty threshold was $7,372;
however, if the same two-person family was headed by a person 65
or over, the poverty threshold was only $6,630, or 10 percent less.

   The poverty rates of all older persons have declined in both an
absolute and a relative sense over the past two decades (Moynihan
1986b; Preston 1984) (see table 4.12). During 1967, the poverty rate
among all older persons was 21.4 percent. It fell to 13.7 percent by
1973, 12.5 percent in 1979, and 11.6 percent in 1986, a near halving
over two decades. Poverty rates of older persons have also fallen
sharply relative to those of younger persons during the last twenty
years. In 1967, the poverty rate of older persons was 1.5 times that
of all persons in the nation. The relative rate of poverty among older
Americans fell to 1.07 in 1979 and to .85 during 1986.

   The poverty position of families with a householder 55 or over also

---

their families, including pensions, Social Security retirement income, public assistance
income, and property income. In-kind benefits such as food stamps, Medicare, and
Medicaid are excluded from the totals.

TABLE 4.12. Poverty Rates of All Persons and of Persons 55 and Older, by Age, 1967, 1973, 1979, and 1986 (in percent)

Population Group	1967	1973	1979	1986
All	14.2	11.1	11.7	13.6
Age 55+	21.4	13.7	12.5	11.6
55–59	11.8	8.1	8.3	10.2
60–62	15.7	11.5	10.2	10.7
63–65	17.6	13.4	11.5	10.1
66–70	23.5	14.0	12.4	9.6
71+	33.2	19.4	17.4	14.5
Sex 55+				
Men	16.8	10.5	9.3	8.6
Women	25.3	16.1	15.0	13.9
55+/All	1.51	1.23	1.07	.85

improved both absolutely and relatively over the past twenty years (see table 4.13). During 1967, the poverty rate of families with a householder 55 and over was 14.2 percent, which was 25 percent higher than the poverty rate among all families (11.4 percent) throughout the nation that year. By 1973, the poverty rate of families headed by a person 55 or over had fallen to 8.6 percent and was slightly below that of all families. By 1986, 7.4 percent of older families were in poverty, only two-thirds as high as the rate for all families in the nation.

The expansion in Social Security benefit coverage over time, the above-average increases in the minimum benefit payments during the early 1970s, and the annual indexing of benefits to the rate of inflation were critical in reducing poverty among elderly families during this period (Moynihan 1986a, b). In 1983, the share of households headed by an individual over 65 that would have been poor in the absence of transfer income was twice as high as the actual posttransfer share (43 percent versus 21 percent) (Danziger, Haveman, and Plotnick 1986). Poverty rates among this elderly group were twice as high in 1967 as in 1983. In sharp contrast to the trend among the nation's elderly families, the poverty rate among young families, especially those with children in the home, rose sharply in the 1980s (Edelman 1986; Moynihan 1986a, b; Preston 1984; Sum, Fogg, and Parekh 1988).

Although there has been less poverty among every major subgroup

TABLE 4.13. Trends in Poverty Rates of All Families and of Families
Headed by Persons 55 and Older, 1967, 1973, 1979, and 1986 (in percent)

Family Group	1967	1973	1979	1986
All families	11.4	8.8	9.2	10.9
Families with a householder 55+	14.2	8.6	7.5	7.4
Families 55+/all families	1.25	.98	.81	.68

TABLE 4.14. Poverty Rates of Families with a Householder 55 and Older
and of Unrelated Individuals 55 and Older, by Race and Ethnic Group,
1986 (as of March 1987)

Race/Ethnic Group	Families	Unrelated Individuals
All	7.4	25.5
White not Hispanic	5.4	21.5
Black not Hispanic	21.3	49.5
Hispanic	17.7	49.5
Other not Hispanic	12.1	27.7

of older persons over the past two decades, there are substantial differences among key subgroups of this population. The poverty rates
of persons over 70, of women, of blacks and Hispanics, and of individuals living alone remain well above those of each of their respective
counterparts (see tables 4.13 and 4.14). For example, during 1986,
the poverty rate among persons 71 and over was 14.5 percent, a rate
40 to 50 percent higher than that of each of the other age subgroups
of the older population. In 1986 the poverty rate among older black
families was four times as high as that of white non-Hispanic families,
and older families with a Hispanic householder experienced a poverty
rate more than three times higher than that of white non-Hispanic
families. Older women, especially those who live alone, have continued
to live in poverty about 60 percent more frequently than men. Older
women living in families (as householder, spouse, or other family
member) have encountered poverty problems only one-third as high
as those of older women living on their own during the 1980s (Commonwealth Fund Commission of Elderly People Living Alone n.d.).
The changing demography of the nation's older population, including
the rising share of persons over 70 and the growing numbers of racial
and ethnic minorities, will complicate the task of combating future
poverty problems among the elderly.

FIGURE 4.5. Labor Force Participation Rates of Poor Persons 55 and Older, by Sex and Age, March 1987

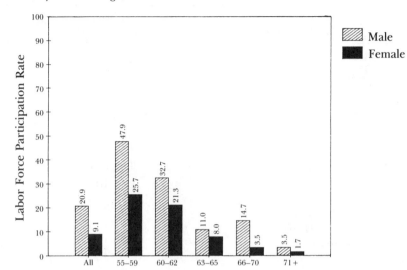

Labor Force Behavior and Employment Experiences of the Older Poor

The role of labor market strategies for combating older Americans' problems of inadequate income is dependent on the degree of their participation in the labor market, the nature of the employment problems faced by the working poor, and the potential for new or expanded programs to attract elderly nonparticipants back into the civilian labor force. Strategies for assisting the working poor are likely to be different than those designed to attract the dependent poor into the labor force.

During March 1987, only 13 percent of all older poor persons were actively participating in the civilian labor force (see figure 4.5). As expected, participation rates varied widely by age subgroup, ranging from 34 percent for those 55 to 59, to 26 percent for those 60 to 62, to a low of 2 percent for those over 70. In the aggregate, poor older men were more than twice as likely as poor women to be working or looking for work in March 1987, although the relative size of these differences varied by age group. Participation rates for poor women over 65 are very low, never rising above 4 percent.

These estimates of the labor force attachment of the elderly poor are in close accord with findings of an analysis of the employment

Table 4.15. Older Poor Who Worked at Some Point during 1986
(N = 5.763 million)

Demographic Subgroup	Percentage with Employment Experience
All 55+	14.6
55–59	36.5
60–62	27.1
63–65	13.0
66–70	8.9
71+	3.1
Sex	
Male	23.0
Female	10.5
Race/ethnic group	
White not Hispanic	14.1
Black not Hispanic	16.2
Hispanic	15.2
Educational attainment	
Less than 12 years	11.4
12 years	21.0
13–15 years	21.3
16 or more years	23.7

experiences of the elderly poor throughout calendar year 1986. Slightly more than 85 percent of all poor persons 55 and over reported no employment whatsoever during 1986. As expected, the proportion of the elderly poor with no employment during 1986 also varied sharply by age subgroup. Among those 55 to 59 years old, only 63 percent reported no employment. This ratio rose to 73 percent for those 60 to 62, to 87 percent for those 63 to 65, and to 97 percent for those over 70. Again, poor males were more than twice as likely as women to have worked at some point during 1986 (see table 4.15). The likelihood of employment during 1986 varied only slightly among poor whites, blacks, and Hispanics. The elderly poor without a high school diploma were the least likely to have worked during 1986.

A more refined analysis of the employment experiences of the working elderly poor revealed substantial attachment to the labor market. Of the estimated 840,000 older working poor, approximately one-third worked year-round, full time during 1986, and another 18 percent worked year-round, part time (see table 4.16). Males were about

Table 4.16. Full-Time and Year-Round Employment Rates of the Older Working Poor during 1986, by Sex, Age, and Race and Ethnic Group (number of persons as of March 1987)

Demographic Subgroup	Worked Year-Round, Full Time	Worked Year-Round, Part Time	Worked Full Time, Part Year	Worked Part Time, Part Year
All	31.2	17.9	19.3	31.7
Sex				
Male	39.9	10.1	22.8	27.1
Female	22.0	26.1	15.5	36.5
Age				
55–59	35.2	17.1	24.7	23.0
60–65	26.5	16.1	19.1	38.3
66+	28.9	23.2	4.8	43.1
Race/ethnic group				
White not Hispanic	36.5	16.5	20.1	26.9
Black not Hispanic	21.1	20.8	10.6	47.5
Hispanic	23.0	16.6	32.5	27.9

twice as likely as poor women to work year-round, full time; however, about half of both groups worked year-round (50 to 52 weeks) during 1986. Poor women were more likely to have worked year-round on a part-time basis.

The elderly working poor were employed on average for 35.4 weeks during 1986 and worked nearly 32 hours per week when employed. Mean weeks of employment among those working did not vary widely by age or sex, although the younger subgroups and males tended to work more hours per week. Mean weekly hours of work ranged from a high of 35 for those 55 to 59 to a low of 21 for those over 70. Many members of the older working poor clearly do "earn their poverty"; that is, despite over 1,100 hours of work, they and their families do not obtain a total income above the poverty line.

Wives in Poverty

Because of the high rates of poverty among elderly women living alone, efforts to strengthen the labor force attachment and earnings

TABLE 4.17.　Current Labor Force Status and Recent Employment
Experiences of Wives in Older Poor Families, by Age, March 1987

Category	All Wives 55+	Wives 55–65	Wives 66+
Number of poor wives (in 1000s)	749	455	294
Percentage of all wives	5.6	5.7	5.4
Current labor force status			
Percentage in labor force	11.4	18.8	.0
Percentage employed	10.5	17.3	.0
Full-time/part-time status of employed			
Percentage full time	35.4	35.5	—
Percentage part time	64.6	64.5	—
Weeks worked in 1986			
Zero weeks	86.6	78.6	98.9
50–52 weeks	7.0	11.1	.6

potential of older women likely to become poor widows may have the
potential for reducing future poverty among this group. The labor
force behavior and recent employment experiences of wives in poor
older families were examined separately because they are at greatest
risk of becoming poor widows upon the deaths of their husbands
(Mott and Haurin 1981). In March 1987, there were approximately
750,000 older wives in poor families across the nation. They represented 5.6 percent of all older wives (see table 4.17). Only one of nine
of these women was actively participating in the civilian labor force,
and only one of ten was employed. Of those who were working, slightly
more than one-third were working full time (thirty-five or more hours
per week). Thus fewer than four of every one hundred poor wives
held a full-time job. All of these women were 55 to 65 years of age.
None of those 66 and over were in the civilian labor force at the time
of the survey.

　　The limited attachment to the labor force among these poor women,
including those 65 and under, places them at particularly great risk
of remaining poor after the deaths of their husbands. The low earnings of their husbands will limit the size of the Social Security survivors'
benefit that they will receive, and their lack of recent work experience
combined with their frequently limited formal schooling will place
them at a severe competitive disadvantage in future labor markets.

Preventive strategies for combating future poverty among these older Americans deserve a higher priority than they have received to date.[17]

Most existing employment and training programs for poor American adults, such as JTPA Title IIA programs, have provided only limited services to the elderly poor. Of the nearly 450,000 adults aged 22 and over who terminated from JTPA programs during program year 1987, only 16,200, or less than 4 percent, were 55 or older. The limited participation of older disadvantaged adults in JTPA programs does not seem to be attributable to their lack of interest in employment and training programs. The Senior Community Service Employment Program funded under the Older Americans Act has been able to attract relatively large numbers of poor and near poor older Americans into its part-time subsidized employment programs. During the program year ending June 30, 1988, the SCSEP program provided job opportunities for 100,000 older Americans, and over half of those remaining enrolled at the end of the program year were 65 years of age or older (Senior Community Service Employment Program 1987).

Summary and Conclusions

In many respects, older persons and their families have fared relatively well in avoiding severe labor market and poverty problems in the 1980s. Older workers are less likely than their younger counterparts to be unemployed, to be part of the pool of the hidden unemployed, and to be poor. These relative advantages, however, have not affected all major subgroups of older persons equally, and some of them could benefit from an expansion and strengthening of the network of bridge jobs and of support systems to facilitate movement into bridge jobs. With minor exceptions, older workers in need of job placement assistance are less likely than younger persons to use formal placement services, including the public labor exchange and most federally funded employment and training programs (Pursell and Torrence 1979; U.S. General Accounting Office 1986).

There are at least four key subgroups of older persons who could benefit from expanded and more diverse bridge job opportunities. First, older displaced workers who have experienced relatively high rates of dislocation from career jobs in the 1980s, especially those with limited formal schooling and firm-specific skills, could benefit from

---

17. For a recent review of the magnitude, characteristics, and labor market problems of all of the nation's working poor, see Levitan and Shapiro 1987a and b.

bridges into new jobs that could more effectively use their existing skills, reduce the likelihood of large relative earnings losses, and prevent premature withdrawal from active participation in the labor force. Greater national and state leadership in this area is needed. Existing programmatic responses to the problems of displaced workers, such as JTPA Title III dislocated worker programs, have performed poorly in attracting older and less well-educated dislocated workers.[18]

The second group of older persons that could benefit from an expansion of bridges back into the labor force consists of those who desire current employment but are not actively seeking work (i.e., the labor force overhang). Although estimates of the size of this group vary considerably, even the most conservative estimates (those based on the CPS) suggest that a fairly substantial pool of such older individuals does exist, including above-average fractions of persons aged 55 to 62, blacks and Hispanics, and the poor and near poor under 65. The development of a more comprehensive set of bridge jobs for such individuals could help alleviate general labor shortages in local economies experiencing full employment, expand real output, and contribute to an improvement in the real income position of older persons and their families.

Although older workers are less likely than their younger counterparts to be poor, employment by itself does not guarantee an escape from poverty. The older working poor are in need of bridges out of poverty. Such bridges would have to include retraining and upgrading opportunities that would enable them to acquire the literacy and vocational skills necessary to boost their productivity and real wages and gain access to more full-time, year-round jobs. The nation's federally funded employment and training system has placed little or no emphasis on retraining and upgrading for the currently employed poor, and the older working poor are seldom targeted for further training by their employers. New institutional arrangements for upgrading the skills of low-wage workers of all ages, especially the elderly, would fill a major void in the nation's existing employment and training system.

Finally, there is a clear need to address the labor market problems of older poor wives, who are at great risk of remaining poor for the

---

18. At the time of the January 1988 dislocated worker survey, older displaced persons accounted for 17 percent of the unemployed and 35 percent of the combined pool of displaced workers who were either unemployed or withdrawn from the labor force. Yet during program year 1987, which ended on June 30, 1988, older persons accounted for less than 8 percent of all JTPA Title III program terminees.

remainder of their lives. Few of the wives in poor older families are attached to the labor market, and many appear to lack the skills and work experience needed to secure future employment that would raise them out of poverty. This group needs bridges into the labor market, and many will likely require home-based services for the care of husbands or other family members to enable them to devote more time to the labor market. An expansion of unsubsidized jobs for these older women in the private sector and of subsidized jobs in the public and nonprofit sectors, such as those provided under the Senior Community Service Employment Program, could assist in the attainment of important economic and social goals. Among these would be an expansion of real economic output, provision of additional public and social services to the community at large, and an amelioration of problems of poverty and social isolation among the nation's elderly.

5

CAREER JOBS, BRIDGE EMPLOYMENT, AND RETIREMENT

Christopher J. Ruhm

THE SPECTACULAR DECLINE IN labor force participation rates of elderly Americans, combined with their increasing population share, has provoked an explosion of interest in the labor force behavior of older persons. Nonetheless, the process by which individuals move from stable career employment to retirement remains poorly understood, and the gaps in our knowledge lead to inadequately focused analysis, poorly constructed theories, and questionable policy recommendations.

This chapter briefly outlines the results of a statistical analysis of the Social Security Administration's Retirement History Longitudinal Survey (RHLS). The RHLS was designed to investigate changes in the economic and social characteristics of men and women as they approach and enter retirement.

The evidence presented here suggests that most individuals enter stable career jobs during their late twenties or thirties. The age at which these jobs end, however, is variable and often occurs well before retirement. In such cases, career positions are followed by a fairly lengthy period of postcareer or bridge employment. The groups that are slowest to enter career jobs (females, nonwhites, and less-educated workers) also leave them the soonest.

The combination of early ending of career employment, relatively less stable postcareer bridge jobs, and frequent partial retirement (almost outside in the career job) yields the surprising finding that most workers retire from jobs of relatively brief duration. It thus becomes questionable whether adverse pension incentives and employers' desires to reduce the work commitments of their most senior employees are major factors causing premature retirement.

Data and Sample

This chapter uses data on heads of households from all six waves of the RHLS. The RHLS contains information on a representative sample of men and unmarried women aged 58 through 63 in 1969 (the initial survey year). Respondents were reinterviewed at two-year intervals through 1979. Fairly detailed data on labor force histories during the survey period are available, as is less specific information on work in the presurvey years. Questions are included about the job held for the longest time before 1969 (if different from 1969 employment), which allows the construction of data on career jobs.

After excluding persons with no work experience between 1949 and 1969 and nonhousehold heads, the sample contains 10,150 respondents—7,884 males and 2,266 females.[1] When the analysis focuses on changes occurring during the survey period, the sample is limited to the 6,630 persons who responded in all six waves of the survey.[2]

The majority of workers moved from full participation in the labor force to retirement during the years covered by the survey. Fewer than one-quarter of respondents considered themselves retired or partially retired in 1969, but over 90 percent did so ten years later (see table 5.1).[3] The probability of retirement increases with age and, at any given age, males, whites, and educated workers are less likely to be retired than their counterparts. Partial retirement also appears to be fairly common among workers in their middle to late sixties. As will be demonstrated, data on the mobility of younger age groups would be helpful when considering the transition out of career employment.

Nature of Career Employment

The notion of a career job implies attachment to a *single* employer for a substantial portion of an individual's working life.[4] With this in

---

1. Nonhousehold heads are excluded because information on them is limited in the RHLS.
2. Approximately 30 percent of the attrition in the sample is attributable to death of the respondent; the remainder is because they refused to answer or could not be located.
3. Retirement status is self-reported.
4. Frequent turnover need not be inconsistent with job advancement, but long-term

TABLE 5.1. Retirement Status in 1969 and 1979 (in percent)

Category	1969			1979			N
	Not Retired	Partially Retired	Retired	Not Retired	Partially Retired	Retired	
All workers	78.0	8.4	13.6	9.0	16.6	74.4	6,633
Age in 1969							
58–59	87.1	5.1	7.8	11.1	18.7	70.2	2,391
60–61	79.3	7.8	12.9	8.1	16.5	75.4	2,194
62–63	65.9	13.0	21.1	7.4	14.3	78.3	2,048
Sex							
Male	80.6	7.8	11.6	9.3	17.6	73.1	5,179
Female	68.7	10.7	20.7	7.6	13.3	79.2	1,454
Race							
White	78.8	8.0	13.2	8.9	16.8	74.3	5,931
Nonwhite	71.8	11.5	16.7	9.4	15.2	75.4	702
Educational attainment							
Less than 9 years[a]	73.9	9.9	16.3	8.2	16.7	75.2	3,373
9–12 years	81.9	7.2	10.9	8.3	16.0	75.7	2,275
More than 12 years	83.0	6.3	10.7	13.1	18.0	68.9	985

Source: Retirement History Longitudinal Survey. Includes heads of households remaining in sample through 1979.
[a]Includes persons not reporting the number of years of education received.

TABLE 5.2.   Duration of Career Jobs (in percent)

Duration (years)	All Workers	Sex		Race		Education		
		Male	Female	White	Nonwhite	<9[a]	9–12	>12
0–10	22.3	16.9	41.8	21.3	31.0	25.1	20.8	16.3
11–15	14.9	14.7	15.9	14.8	15.8	14.8	14.7	15.5
16–20	15.6	15.9	14.6	15.9	13.0	15.6	15.7	15.5
21–30	27.0	29.2	19.3	27.0	27.5	26.6	26.9	29.1
More than 30	20.2	23.5	8.4	21.0	12.8	17.9	22.0	23.6
Job in progress in 1979	2.5	2.8	1.7	2.5	2.9	1.9	2.4	4.9

Source: Retirement History Longitudinal Survey. The table shows completed durations except for jobs in progress in 1979.

[a]Includes persons not reporting number of years of education received.

mind, I define an individual's career job as the longest spell of employment with a single firm up to and including the job held in 1969 (the beginning of the RHLS survey). Completed rather than interrupted job durations are used in arriving at this measure, thus length of the job in progress in 1969 is calculated by tracking forward in time until the position terminates.[5]

Most workers are employed in at least one lengthy job during their prime working years, and a substantial minority are employed at a single job for the majority of their working life. Almost two-thirds of the sample held a career job lasting more than fifteen years, for approximately half it exceeded twenty years, and a fifth were employed by the same firm for more than thirty years (see table 5.2).

Near lifetime employment was especially prevalent for males and whites. Two of five females failed to work at any job for more than ten years, and only one in twelve was with a single employer for more than thirty years. Conversely, almost a quarter of the males held career jobs lasting at least three decades, and only one in six worked less than ten years on any one job. Whites were 1.6 times as likely as

---

employment relationships, which generate worker-firm attachments, appear to be an important feature of U.S. labor markets.

5. The duration is truncated at 1979 for the 2.5 percent of career jobs that continued through this date. Because so few career jobs lasted through the end of the survey, the measurement of duration of career employment is insensitive to the treatment of these in-progress jobs.

TABLE 5.3.   Age Career Job Ends (in percent)

Career Job Ends before Age	All Workers	Sex		Race		Education		
		Male	Female	White	Nonwhite	<9[a]	9–12	>12
45	14.7	13.8	18.0	14.4	17.8	15.9	14.0	12.4
50	23.8	22.8	27.3	23.4	27.6	25.7	22.6	20.1
55	35.5	34.1	40.3	34.9	40.3	38.0	33.3	32.0
60	53.7	52.1	59.8	52.6	63.9	56.6	51.6	49.3
64	78.3	77.5	81.5	77.9	82.4	80.7	77.9	71.4
67	93.7	93.6	94.0	93.7	93.5	95.1	93.7	88.9
70[b]	96.9	96.7	97.5	96.9	96.6	97.8	97.1	93.9

Source: Retirement History Longitudinal Survey.
[a] Includes persons not reporting number of years of education received.
[b] Includes 68- and 69-year-olds with career jobs in progress in 1979.

nonwhites to hold a job for thirty years, and nonwhites were almost 50 percent more likely to work less than ten years for any one employer.[6]

There were also differences based on level of education. For example, 52.7 percent of the college-educated workers held career jobs for more than twenty years, and only 16.3 percent had completed durations of less than ten years. Corresponding percentages for persons with less than nine years of education were 44.5 and 25.1 percent.[7]

Although most individuals are employed in a lengthy job at some point in their working lives, there is striking evidence that, for a large proportion of workers, career jobs terminate long before retirement. By age 60, more than half of all persons had left their career jobs, but only one in nine had retired (see tables 5.3 and 5.4). Only one 67-year-old in fifteen remained in career employment, even though four in ten continued to participate in the labor force.

What is surprising is not that retirement occurred so late—more

6. Akerlof and Main (1981) and Hall (1982) also find that females have shorter job durations than males, but Hall does not uncover significant race disparities. The difference between his results and mine could be a result of the specific job analyzed. I consider only the longest employment held during the lifetime; he considers all jobs (career and noncareer) held at a given time.

7. The group with less than nine years of education also includes persons not reporting educational attainment. This group was initially considered as a separate category, but because their experiences were very similar to those of the least educated group, the tables merge the two categories.

TABLE 5.4. Age at Retirement (in percent)

Retired Before Age	All Workers	Sex		Race		Education		
		Male	*Female*	*White*	*Nonwhite*	*<9[a]*	*9–12*	*>12*
45	0.3	0.2	0.9	0.3	0.9	0.4	0.2	0.2
50	1.3	1.0	2.5	1.2	2.1	1.6	1.0	1.0
55	4.1	3.1	7.6	3.8	6.8	5.3	3.2	2.2
60	11.1	9.7	16.2	10.4	17.4	13.7	9.0	7.8
64	35.5	33.2	43.4	34.7	42.2	39.6	33.7	26.0
67	61.8	60.4	66.7	61.1	67.9	66.1	60.4	51.0
70[b]	70.1	68.5	75.3	69.2	77.6	73.4	69.2	60.2

Source: Retirement History Longitudinal Survey.
[a] Includes persons not reporting number of years of education received.
[b] Includes persons aged 68 and 69 in 1979 and not retired in that year.

than two-thirds of the sample retired before age 70 and most of the remainder were partially retired—but rather that career jobs ended so early. Although career employment sometimes continued to the time of retirement, the data indicate that this is the exception rather than the rule. Over a third of the workers left career employment before age 55 and half before age 60.

Termination of the career job and full retirement occurred even earlier for women, nonwhites, and the less educated. For example, 33.2 percent of males and 34.7 percent of whites retired before age 64, as compared to 43.4 percent of females and 42.2 percent of nonwhites. Differences among educational subgroups were even larger—almost two-fifths of the least-educated group retired before age 64 versus only a quarter of the college-educated workers. The 40 percent of college-educated persons remaining at work past age 70 far exceeded that of any other category. Similarly, career jobs ended later for whites, males, and educated workers than for the other groups.

Early departures from career jobs and short durations of career employment generally go together because minorities, females, and less-educated workers both end career employment at relatively young ages and start career positions relatively late. Approximately half of whites and males but less than a third of females and approximately 40 percent of nonwhites were employed in career jobs by age 35.[8]

---

8. See Ruhm 1988a for a further discussion of the entry into career employment.

TABLE 5.5. Characteristics of Last Job Held before Retirement (in percent)

Probability of	All Workers	Sex		Race		Education		
		Male	Female	White	Nonwhite	<9[a]	9–12	>12
Retiring from career job	44.4	44.8	43.1	45.1	37.7	42.6	45.3	47.9
Starting bridge job before 1969[b]	59.2	59.2	58.9	59.3	58.2	58.7	60.0	58.6
Moving from career to bridge job after 1969[c]	33.8	33.5	35.2	33.1	40.9	35.7	32.6	31.0
Final preretirement job lasting less than								
5 years	28.0	27.0	32.3	27.3	34.5	30.8	26.5	23.0
10 years	45.8	44.2	53.0	45.2	52.0	48.2	43.9	41.2
20 years	66.9	64.7	76.7	66.5	70.4	68.9	65.8	63.3
30 years	84.7	82.7	93.3	84.1	90.8	86.4	83.7	82.0

Source: Retirement History Longitudinal Survey.
[a] Includes persons not reporting number of years of education received.
[b] Conditional on holding a bridge job at some point in work life.
[c] Conditional on working in career job in 1969.

Postcareer Bridge Jobs

The early end to career employment implies that most workers retire from positions that bridge the period between the end of the longest job and retirement. Because these bridge jobs start relatively late in life and tend to be less stable than career employment, people typically retire from positions of relatively short duration. Nevertheless, a significant minority of bridge jobs last for a considerable period of time, suggesting that in some cases bridge employment represents a second career.

Only four of every nine workers retired from their career jobs, and the percentage was smaller still among the groups whose career jobs ended the soonest (table 5.5).[9] Approximately three-fifths of respon-

9. Career jobs lasting through 1979 are assumed to end in retirement. Since some

TABLE 5.6.   Relative Duration of Career and Bridge Jobs Ending in
Retirement (in percent)

Probability that Job Lasts Less than	*Career Job*	*Bridge Job*
5 years	1.7	49.0
10 years	6.0	77.7
20 years	30.6	95.9
30 years	66.9	98.9

Source: Retirement History Longitudinal Survey.

dents holding postcareer jobs at some point in their working lives first
did so before 1969, and around one-third of persons still in career
employment in 1969 took a bridge job at some point during the next
decade (table 5.5).

Table 5.5 also shows the duration of jobs held immediately before retirement. Fewer than a third of the final jobs lasted for
more than twenty years and less than one in five for more than
thirty years. More than a quarter, however, were of less than five
years' duration, and almost half failed to reach ten years. Even
among whites and males, the groups with the most stable career
employment, only about a third of the terminal jobs lasted twenty
years, and more than a quarter fell short of five years. Nonwhites
and women almost never retired from thirty-year jobs but did so
from jobs lasting less than five years approximately a third of the
time.

Not surprisingly, career jobs that terminated in retirement were
almost always of fairly long duration—two-thirds exceeded twenty
years and one-third surpassed three decades—whereas bridge jobs
ending in retirement were generally quite short (see table 5.6).
Nonetheless, not all bridge jobs were unstable. For example, almost
a quarter of final postcareer jobs lasted more than ten years; in
many cases, these may have constituted a second career.

Virtually nothing is known about the characteristics of bridge jobs.
This ignorance makes it difficult to determine how workers might
respond to changes in pension and Social Security incentives, part-
time employment initiatives, or programs aimed at increasing the
labor force retention rates of older workers. The response to each
initiative depends on the type of employment held before retirement
and on the reasons for holding it.

The RHLS does provide some information on the transition from
career to bridge employment. Although 41.3 percent of employed

workers leaving career jobs after this year would continue to work, the calculation
slightly overestimates the probability of retiring from career employment.

sample members remained on their career jobs in 1969 (table 5.7, column 1), there is substantial variation by age, sex, race, education, and retirement status.[10] For example, males, whites, and 58- to 59-year-olds were about one-third more likely to continue in their career jobs than were females, minorities, and 62- to 63-year-olds, while the college educated were about one-quarter more likely to do so than persons who did not attend high school. Most interestingly, persons describing themselves as partially retired were only one-third as likely to remain on career jobs as those who were not retired.[11] This finding suggests that partial retirement on the career job is an option available to relatively few workers.

The transition from career to bridge employment almost always involves a change of either industry, occupation, or both. Almost three-quarters of the sample switched industry *or* occupation when moving to a bridge job (table 5.7, column 2), and almost half changed both industry *and* occupation (column 3). Partially retired persons were more than twice as likely to have changed both industry and occupation as their fully employed counterparts, which probably explains why such changes increase with age of the cohort. Sectoral change was also more common for less-educated workers and minorities than for others.

Somewhat surprisingly, women were slightly more likely than men to remain in the same industry when moving from career to bridge employment and much more likely to remain attached to their career occupation. There is no indication whether this occurs because men more frequently undertake second careers, because discrimination limits the occupations available to women, or for other reasons.

Persons leaving their career job before age 55 were much more likely to change employment sectors than those who departed later. This result is consistent with the possibility that a minority of individuals pursue second careers following early termination of their career jobs but could also indicate the involuntary destruction of occupation- or industry-specific skills. It also suggests that persons leaving career employment at later ages prefer not to change sectors.

---

10. One-seventh of the sample retired before 1969. The percentage of workers retiring from career jobs is therefore slightly higher than the proportion remaining in such employment by 1969.

11. Gustman and Steinmeier (1984) present a similar finding, and Honig and Hanoch (1985) point out that partial retirement is frequently associated with a change in jobs.

TABLE 5.7.   Characteristics of 1969 Job by Individual and Career Job
Characteristics (in percent)

Group or Individual Characteristic	Job Characteristic[a]				
	(1)	*(2)*	*(3)*	*(4)*	*(5)*
All workers	41.3	26.7	43.4	42.8	40.6
Employment status (1969)					
Not retired	54.1	28.6	41.0	45.2	42.6
Partially retired	18.3	14.8	57.6	28.5	28.8
Age (1969)					
58–59	46.6	28.8	40.9	45.8	42.1
60–61	41.8	26.6	43.0	42.0	41.8
62–63	35.1	24.2	47.0	39.9	37.3
Sex					
Male	43.5	25.3	45.0	40.3	40.1
Female	33.3	32.8	36.1	53.8	42.9
Race					
White	42.4	26.9	42.6	43.1	41.2
Nonwhite	32.1	24.6	49.8	39.6	35.2
Educational attainment					
Less than 9 years[b]	37.6	25.0	47.4	39.2	38.4
9–12 years	44.1	26.6	41.4	43.9	41.4
More than 12 years	47.2	32.5	35.0	51.7	45.9
Age career job ended					
Under 55	—	24.0	45.7	40.0	38.3
55 or over	—	33.0	38.0	49.1	45.9

Source: Retirement History Longitudinal Survey.
[a]Definitions of 1969 job characteristics:
    (1) employed in career job
    (2) same industry and occupation as career job
    (3) different industry and occupation from career job
    (4) same occupation as career job
    (5) same industry as career job
    (2) to (5) apply only to persons who left their career jobs before 1969.
[b]Includes persons not reporting the number of years of education received.

Partial Retirement

Many individuals express a desire to reduce the extent of their involvement in the labor force or "partially retire" at the end of their
working lives. Despite research by Gustman and Steinmeier (1984)
and Honig and Hanoch (1985) highlighting the importance of partial
retirement, the general belief is that this form of reduced labor force

participation occurs relatively infrequently and that, when it does occur, it lasts for only a short period of time.[12]

Partial retirement is both more prevalent and longer lasting than is commonly believed. At least half of all workers partially retire at some point in their lifetimes, and the average period between the onset of partial retirement and complete withdrawal from the labor force exceeds five years.

Partial retirement is uncommon before age 58 but becomes much more probable from ages 60 to 67, after which it gradually declines. At ages 66 and 67, more than one-fifth of all individuals are partially retired and at least one-seventh of 64- to 73-year-olds will be partially retired at any given time (table 5.8). Although only 15 percent of the RHLS sample was partially retired in any single survey wave, more than 45 percent partially retired in at least one of the six waves. Some spells of partial retirement are of considerable duration, with almost 60 percent of the persons partially retiring at some point in the ten-year period maintaining the status for at least two survey waves and almost 30 percent for three or more. Nonwhites and less-educated workers were more likely than their counterparts to retire partially, but women did so less often than men.

Table 5.8 understates the prevalence of partial retirement because spells occurring before 1969 or after 1979 are not counted. Approximately half (49.2 percent) of the persons retiring after 1969 partially retired at some point between 1969 and 1979, and using reasonable assumptions about out-of-sample behavior and the duration of in-progress spells, I estimate that at least 50 percent and probably closer to 55 percent of respondents partially retired at some point during their working lives.[13]

The typical partial retirement spell was fairly short—more than 40 percent of spells ended within two years—but a significant proportion lasted for a considerable period of time.[14] For example,

---

12. For example, Burtless (1986:785), in his careful study on the labor supply effects of unanticipated Social Security benefit changes, writes, "The average duration of partial retirement is only about three years. By implication partial retirement accounts for only a very small proportion of lifetime labor supply...and will be treated as indistinguishable from full retirement."

13. For example, if 40 percent of partial retirements observed in any period originated in the previous two years (see table 5.9), partial retirement probabilities are 1.0, 3.0, 11.5, 8.5, and 5.0 percent for persons aged 54 to 55, 56 to 57, 74 to 75, 76 to 77, and 78 to 79, respectively (with no partial retirement among workers younger than 54 or older than 79), and if actual partial retirement probabilities are used for 58- to 73-year-olds, then 52.9 percent of the sample partially retired at some point during their lives.

14. Partial retirements beginning before 1969 are excluded from the table to eliminate initial condition problems, which occur if probabilities for the continuation of

TABLE 5.8. Probability of Experiencing Partial Retirement (in percent)

			Probability if survey year age is				
58–59	60–61	62–63	64–65	66–67	68–69	70–71	72–73
5.0	7.8	13.0	18.1	20.3	18.7	16.5	14.4

	Probability in		
	a given wave	> 1 wave	> 2 waves	> 3 waves
---	---	---	---	---
All workers	15.4	45.2	25.6	13.2
Age (1969)				
58–59	10.5	44.1	23.4	9.6
60–61	15.9	45.5	26.0	14.7
62–63	16.9	46.1	27.7	15.7
Sex				
Male	13.1	45.7	26.0	13.3
Female	14.4	43.3	23.9	12.5
Race				
White	15.3	44.8	25.4	13.1
Nonwhite	15.9	48.4	27.2	13.5
Educational attainment				
Less than 9 years[a]	16.2	46.6	26.7	14.4
9–12 years	14.7	44.7	24.5	12.1
More than 12 years	14.3	41.2	24.1	11.3

Source: Retirement History Longitudinal Survey.
[a]Includes persons not reporting years of education received.

almost 30 percent of partial retirements exceeded six years, and more than one-fifth exceeded eight years (see table 5.9).[15] I estimate that the expected completed duration of all partial retirement experiences is 5.2 years.[16]

---

existing spells differ from those of new spells. The duration of partial retirement is defined as the number of years from the first occurrence of partial retirement until full retirement. Thus transitions from partial retirement to "not retired" are included in the measure.

15. The extended right tail of the distribution results because hazard rates (exit probabilities) decline with the duration in partial retirement. The full sample two-year hazard rates are 0.413, 0.325, 0.288, and 0.256 for moving from zero to eight years duration. If exit probabilities remained constant at 41.3 percent (the initial level), only 11.9 percent of partial retirees would remain in the state at the end of eight years; conversely, at 25.6 percent (the final hazard rate), 30.6 percent of spells would last eight years or more.

16. This estimate assumes that partial retirement spells that terminate before a survey

TABLE 5.9. Number of Years from Time Partial Retirement Was Begun until Complete Retirement (in percent)

	Number of Years					Expected Completed Duration[a]
	0–2	> 2	> 4	> 6	> 8	
All workers	41.3	58.7	39.6	28.2	20.9	5.2 years
Sex						
Male	40.3	59.7	40.0	27.9	21.9	5.6
Female	45.2	54.8	37.7	29.1	17.8	4.6
Race						
White	41.4	58.6	39.6	28.5	21.1	5.2
Nonwhite	40.1	59.9	39.0	25.7	19.8	5.2
Educational attainment						
Less than 9 years[b]	40.9	59.1	39.3	27.8	19.9	4.9
9–12 years	43.4	56.6	40.1	26.8	20.2	5.1
More than 12 years	37.2	62.8	39.4	33.8	28.8	7.6
Age[c]						
60–61	39.6	60.4	38.8	30.2	21.6	5.1
62–63	41.9	58.1	39.8	27.5	22.3	5.9
64–65	43.1	56.9	39.9	26.9	19.5	4.9
66–67	38.6	61.4	40.3	32.1	–[d]	6.2

Source: Retirement History Longitudinal Survey. Data are for respondents who partially retired between 1971 and 1977 (N = 2,172).
[a]Expected completed duration is calculated as discussed in text.
[b]Includes persons not reporting the number of years of education received.
[c]Age at beginning of partial retirement.
[d]Spells of this duration do not occur in sample period.

The expected duration of partial retirement (shown in table 5.9) is around five years for most demographic categories with slightly longer durations for men than women and no observable differences between ethnic groups. There is striking dispersion across groups by education. Although college-educated workers partially retired less frequently than their less-schooled peers, when they did so they stayed in that condition for approximately 50 percent longer. One possible explanation is that educated persons have more opportunity to retire par-

end at the midpoint between that wave and the previous one. In addition, hazard rates are assumed to remain at the final observed level after the end of the sample period.

TABLE 5.10.   Probability of Reversing Retirement (in percent)

Category	(1)	(2)
All workers	23.4	5.0
Sex		
Male	24.3	5.2
Female	20.0	4.3
Race		
White	23.0	4.8
Nonwhite	26.3	7.3
Educational attainment		
Less than 9 years[a]	23.8	5.5
9–12 years	23.0	4.4
More than 12 yeas	22.5	5.0
Age at retirement		
60–61	31.4	9.5
62–63	24.5	5.6
64–65	21.2	4.4
66–67	23.0	3.9

Source: Retirement History Longitudinal Survey. Data are for persons retiring in 1971 or 1973 (N = 2,419).

Column definitions: (1) Probability of reentering the labor force after retiring; (2) probability of reentering the labor force more than four years after retiring.

[a]Includes persons not reporting years of education received.

tially on their career jobs and that continued employment in such jobs delays retirement.

Reverse Retirement

A significant number of persons reversed their retirement decision. Roughly a quarter of sample members retiring between 1969 and 1973 reentered the labor force before 1979, the vast majority within four years after first withdrawing (see table 5.10).[17]

Males and nonwhites were somewhat more likely to reverse retirement than females and whites, but the differences were not very large.

17. These figures are two to three times as high as the reentry probabilities cited by Diamond and Hausman (1984). The difference is attributable to the longer time period over which I follow individuals. For example, the one- and two-year reentry rates for men aged 60 to 64 are 13.4 and 9.6 percent in Diamond and Hausman (p. 100). The two-year reentry rate for men aged 60 to 67 in this sample is 13.1 percent.

Young retirees (60- and 61-year-olds), however, reentered the labor force 30 to 50 percent more frequently than those retiring after age 63, and they were more than twice as likely to reenter after an extended period of retirement.

Conclusion and Implications

The final stages of the working lives of many individuals are characterized by a job-stopping process in which career jobs terminate well before retirement. The end of such employment is likely to be followed by various combinations of full-time work in bridge jobs, partial retirement, temporary retirement, and reverse retirement before permanent departure from the labor force.

This new information about the labor market behavior of older persons suggests many questions for future research. Is an early end to career employment generally voluntary or involuntary? What are the consequences of such premature terminations? To what extent are bridge positions less stable than career employment, and does such instability occur more because of attributes of individuals or of jobs? Why do workers so rarely stay on their career jobs when they partially retire? To what extent does the necessity of moving from career to bridge employment speed ultimate retirement?

Even without answers to these questions, the evidence presented in this chapter has important implications for research on older workers. First, existing theoretical models need to be enriched to explain the early termination of career jobs and the forms of reduced labor force participation exhibited by the elderly. Second, theoretical and empirical work should not assume that factors associated with early transitions out of career positions necessarily cause premature retirement. Recent research on pensions (i.e., Mitchell and Fields 1984; Kotlikoff and Wise 1989), for example, stresses that discounted lifetime pension benefits typically decline for workers who remain on career jobs past their early sixties and infers that these pension profiles lead to early departure from the labor force. As shown above, however, workers generally retire from jobs of fairly short duration. In such positions, pension benefits are relatively unimportant, making it less clear how adverse pension incentives influence the labor supply decisions of older individuals.[18]

---

18. This does not deny that the pension structure could have an impact. For example, if pensions encourage movement into bridge jobs and retirement occurs sooner out of bridge than career jobs, the pension incentives could indirectly cause earlier retirement.

Finally, the findings reported in this chapter have important policy implications. That a large proportion of career jobs end well before retirement indicates that even relatively stable employment attachments are not synonymous with lifetime employment.[19] Increasing the portability of pensions and other employee benefits would therefore aid older workers. Workers need to be prepared for the possibility that they will change jobs one or more times fairly late in their working lives. To the extent that individuals retire more quickly from bridge than career employment, increasing their ability to retire partially on career jobs might also increase the labor force participation of mature adults. Finally, the relatively early retirement of women and nonwhites is almost certainly related to the greater difficulties they face in obtaining and retaining career employment. Therefore, policies that increase their ability to do so may pay dividends in the form of increased labor force participation and delayed retirement.

---

19. To the extent that structural change is now greater than it was in earlier decades, job changes will be even more common today than in the period studied here.

PART II

*Flexible Employment and
Bridges to Retirement*

FLEXIBLE EMPLOYMENT: THE EMPLOYER'S POINT OF VIEW

Richard S. Belous

INCREASED COMPETITIVE PRESSURES CAUSED vast changes in employment and pay practices at many American corporations in the 1980s. In many cases practices that were unthinkable only a few years ago are now standard operating procedures.

These changes have created benefits and costs for workers, with some workers being "winners" and others being serious "losers." Employers and academic analysts often see older workers as potential gainers under more flexible corporate human resource systems because increased flexibility could provide bridge jobs for older workers in the transition from full-time employment to full-time retirement.

In theory, this new flexibility may be beneficial to older workers, but there seem to be significant obstacles to their actually gaining such flexible bridge jobs. This chapter addresses the following questions: (1) What are employers doing to enhance employment flexibility? (2) Why are they making these changes? (3) How do older workers fit into this new strategy?

Various published and unpublished data from both private and public sector sources, along with insights obtained from more than fifty case studies of leading U.S. employers that I conducted during

Richard S. Belous is vice-president, international affairs, and a senior economist for the National Planning Association. This chapter presents his personal opinions and does not necessarily represent the opinions of the National Planning Association.

the past year, will be used in an attempt to answer these questions (Belous 1989).

What Are Employers Doing?

In the 1980s many American employers adopted new methods to increase the flexibility of their human resource systems, with the result that labor markets are less rigid than they were in the 1970s. Labor markets are now behaving more like commodity and capital markets than at any time in the postwar era (see, e.g., Kochan et al. 1986; Belous 1987; OECD 1986; Freedman 1985).

There are many different ways to define flexibility. Webster's dictionary defines it using such terms as *adaptable, elastic, supple, resilient,* and *pliable.* In the context of corporate human resource systems and labor markets in general, flexibility means that compensation, employment relationships, work assignments, work rules, and career paths are highly responsive to economic variables and business strategies.

There are many different ways employer-employee relations can be made more flexible. In the 1980s, however, three basic methods have predominated:

1. Employers have altered compensation systems to tie wages and benefits more closely to corporate economic realities and less to customs and traditions.

2. Employers have made the employment relationship more flexible and contingent upon corporate economic factors. Temporary workers, for example, may have no long-term contract with an employer and may be let go at the first signs of a business slump. A growing percentage of workers do not have a long-term relationship with one employer.

3. When employers have retained long-term relationships with employees, they have tried to make these relationships more flexible and based on corporate economic conditions. Included in these shifts are changes in job ladders and more redeployment of workers (e.g., geographic and/or occupational arrangements).

The application of these three methods has altered the job mix of the large enterprise sector. Although the pay and employment security of the work force in this sector have been affected, more flexible work arrangements have also made it easier for employers to accommodate the job preferences of their older workers. Thus the experience with flexible employment in large corporations can shed considerable light on the prospects for bridge employment for workers who are nearing retirement.

Why Are Employers Doing It?

A few years ago it would have seemed pretentious to talk about strategic choices and labor costs in the same breath. Strategic choices that influenced the entire direction of a company were made in such areas as finance and marketing. The personnel department was not viewed as a bastion of strategic thinking. Human resource staffs had to create and design forms and help in recruitment, hiring, development, and separation of employees. They also had to help form compensation policies and plans to comply with government regulations. Although all this was very important to the life of a corporation, it often brought to mind such words as *administration* and *bureaucracy* (Kochan et al. 1986).

But in a world of stronger competitive pressures, top corporate managers have increasingly discovered that human resource decisions provide a vital and effective strategic lever and in some cases may be the most important short-run control mechanism available to management.

Although the experiences of each corporation are unique, several common threads run through the labor-related choices that all companies face. The recent shifts in the human resource landscape become clearer when one examines these common threads.

One of these threads involves the concept of affiliation, or the degree to which workers are associated with a specific employer. The model of lifetime employment represents one end of the affiliation spectrum (see table 6.1). This lifetime model has often been compared to a marriage in which both partners make a deep commitment to each other and have significant responsibilities in the course of the relationship.

The other end of the affiliation spectrum is represented by the day-laborer model. In this system, neither the worker nor the employer makes any enduring commitments. Workers under a lifetime employment system tend to have a very strong identity with their company, whereas workers under the day-laborer model tend to identify with their occupation rather than with their employer.

The lifetime model, of course, represents very strong affiliation, and the day-laborer model represents very weak affiliation. Both sides of the spectrum have benefits and costs for an employer. The primary benefit for employers of a weak affiliation system is that their future options in the realm of human resources and labor costs are wide open. An employer may place a high value on the flexibility generated by a weak affiliation system. The primary cost to workers of a weak

TABLE 6.1.　The Employer-Employee Affiliation Spectrum

Very Strong Affiliation	*Very Weak Affiliation*
The Lifetime Employment Model	*The Day-Laborer Model*
• Workers spend their entire career with one company.	• Workers and employers make agreements that cover only a very short period of time.
• Workers and employers make a deep commitment to one another and have long-term responsibilities to one another.	• Since neither employers nor workers have a deep commitment to one another, both sides retain a very high degree of flexibility and freedom in the long run.
• Employees link their future to the fate of a company, and they have a strong identity with the company.	• Since workers do not link their future to the fate of any specific employer, workers build up a strong identity with their occupation (and not their employer).
• Employer has a strong incentive to make significant human capital investments (i.e., skill development, training, and education) in a worker.	• Employer does not have a strong incentive to make significant human capital investments in specific workers. Employers may have an incentive to support some system that provides worker human capital investments as a public good.
• Employer-employee relationships at many Japanese companies are often cited as a prime example of the lifetime model.	• Employer-employee relationships in some agricultural markets are often cited as a prime example of the day-laborer model.

affiliation system is the lack of a strong common identification with an employer or with a firm's long-term goals.

Most employer-employee relationships fall between these two poles on the affiliation spectrum. Nevertheless, the evidence presented in this chapter—and in other reports—documents that in recent years many employers and employees have chosen (or been forced) to make a significant strategic move on this spectrum away from stronger affiliation and toward weaker affiliation (Belous 1987).

A second common thread all companies face in the area of human resources involves the concept of *stakeholding*—the legal, moral, political, and economic claims various groups can make on a corporation. All employers function within a specific legal and cultural framework. But within these boundaries employers often have great discretion in establishing the stake employees have in their jobs. Many employers are shifting these stakes.

These two common threads—affiliation and stakeholding—combine to fashion the human resource system used by a company. Two very general categories of workers may be defined: core workers and contingent workers. Core workers are those who have a strong affiliation with an employer and are treated as though they have a significant stake in a company. They show long-term attachment to a company and have a good measure of job stability. To use the language of economists, core workers have an *implicit contract* with their employers that if they follow certain rules and norms and meet certain standards, they will receive a long-term home and some measure of advancement (Rosen 1985).

In contrast, contingent workers have a weak affiliation with a specific employer and do *not* have a significant stake in a company. Contingent workers are *not* part of the corporate family. They do not show long-term attachment to a company, and they often do *not* have much job stability. Employers usually do *not* make implicit contracts with contingent workers.

In forming a human resource system, a corporation can use various proportions of core and contingent workers. The data presented in this chapter show that many employers in recent years have altered their basic human resource systems to reduce their core work force and to use an increasing number of contingent workers. The major reasons for this shift have been to increase flexibility, to reduce labor costs, and to improve corporate competitiveness.

Work Flexibility

A Conference Board survey of leading American employers has examined the relative importance of the factors used in setting corporate wage objectives (Freedman 1985). These data show major shifts in compensation practices between the 1970s and 1980s.

As indicated in table 6.2, in 1978 American employers placed "industry patterns" at the top of the list and ranked "productivity or labor cost trends in this company" only fourth in relative importance. In 1983, however, these same employers placed "productivity or labor

TABLE 6.2.   Relative Importance of Factors Used in Setting American
Corporate Wage Objectives[a]

1978	1983
1. Industry patterns	1. Productivity or labor cost trends in this company
2. Local labor market conditions and wage rates	2. Expected profits of this company
3. Expected profits of this company	3. Local labor market conditions and wage rates
4. Productivity or labor cost trends in this company	4. Industry patterns
5. Consumer price index increases	5. Consumer price index increases
6. Influence of this settlement on other wage settlements and/or nonunion wage levels	6. Internal (company) wage patterns (historical)
7. Potential losses from a strike	7. Influence of this settlement on other wage settlements and/or nonunion wage levels
8. Internal (company) wage patterns (historical)	8. Internal (company) benefit patterns (historical)
9. Internal (company) benefit patterns (historical)	9. Potential losses from a strike
10. Major union settlements in other industries	10. National labor market conditions and wage rates
11. National labor market conditions and wage rates	11. Major union settlements in other industries

Source: Audrey Freedman, *The New Look in Wage Policy and Employee Relations* (New
York: Conference Board, 1985), p. 8.

[a]The sample includes 197 major U.S. corporations which in both 1978 and 1983
ranked the relative importance of factors used in setting company wage objectives at
their company, on a scale with 1 as the most important factor and 11 as the least
important factor.

cost trends in this company" at the top of the list, and "industry
patterns" fell to fourth place. Conference Board survey data of employers indicate that "corporations have switched their wage-setting
policies from imitation of other companies' wage increases toward
internal criteria. Under growing competitive pressures, companies
now base wage changes on labor costs per unit of output, and on
expected profits (Freedman 1985:iv).

Other evidence supports the Conference Board survey data on
employers' shifting attitudes. Area wage survey data collected by the
Bureau of Labor Statistics indicate a growing deviation in wage patterns. In the 1970s, for example, the standard deviation of the wage
levels paid in Detroit for tool-and-die workers was very small, whereas
in the 1980s this standard deviation has been quite large. In many

local labor markets, wage patterns that were once quite tight have become very wide (Belous 1984:31–34).

Why have employers become more interested in increased compensation flexibility? As Conference Board labor economist Audrey Freedman has noted:

> Wage rigidity and wage sensitivity to industry conditions is fading fast with the fragmentation of pattern bargaining....The cause of this custom-tailoring is competition. Companies that previously had sufficient market power (or position) to pass on labor cost increases could accept the national formalization of wages. Now, however, these companies and industries are being pressed on costs by domestic nonunion competition and by international competition....There will be no going back to the "model" of the 1970s (Freedman 1982:7).

CONTINGENT WORK

Beyond compensation flexibility, many American employers have recently slashed the size of their core work forces and vastly increased their use of contingent workers. Between 1979 and 1983, roughly seven hundred thousand managers and professionals who had been employed at a firm for three years or more lost their jobs; and in the period 1985 to 1986, another six hundred thousand middle- and upper-level executives lost their jobs, according to private industry estimates, despite improved business conditions (Sanderson and Schein 1986).

The result of these changes has been a dramatic reduction in the percentage of the American labor force that is employed by the leading and largest U.S. corporations. In 1970, for example, the Fortune 500 corporations represented 18.9 percent of American civilian employment, but by 1986 that figure had shrunk to 12.2 percent (data from *Fortune*'s statistical department).

Although measuring the size of the contingent work force is difficult at best, there is evidence that this group has experienced significant increases. There has been a growth in the forms of contingent work, including part-timers, temporary workers, employment subcontractors, consultants, "life-of-project" workers, and leased employees. Although there is no official government measure of these different types of contingent workers, the National Planning Association has used various data sources to construct an estimate.

As indicated in table 6.3, between 1980 and 1986 most parts of the contingent work force increased at a faster rate than the entire labor force (Belous 1989). Part-time employment, for example, climbed by

TABLE 6.3.   Growth of the Contingent Work Force (millions of workers)

Category	1980	1986	Percent Change
Temporary workers	.4	.7	75
Part-time workers	16.3	19.5	20
Business services	3.3	4.8	45
Self-employed	8.5	9.3	9
Upper bound on the size of the contingent work force[a]	28.5	34.3	20
Lower bound on the size of the contingent work force[a]	25.0	28.3	13
Total civilian labor force	106.9	117.8	10

Source: Author's estimates based on data from the U.S. Bureau of Labor Statistics.
[a]See text for definitions.

20 percent, while the total civilian labor force increased by roughly 10 percent. In measuring the size of the contingent work force, however, one runs into two serious problems: double-counting and undercounting.

An upper-bound estimate on the size of the contingent work force can be obtained if one adds all of the various segments of contingent workers together, which yields 34.3 million contingents in the United States in 1986. If a person were both a part-time and a temporary worker, however, adding the various totals would double-count this worker.

A lower-bound estimate can be formed if one makes conservative estimates about potential double-counting. It appears, for example, that about 40 percent of temporary workers are part-timers. Thus, instead of counting 700,000 temporary workers as contingents, a conservative estimate would count only 420,000. Similarly, a very conservative estimate might assume that all business service workers are already counted in the contingent total (i.e., these workers are assumed to be either temporary, part-time, or self-employed). If this is done, then a conservative estimate would indicate that 28.3 million workers were contingents in 1986.

Undercounting is also a serious problem. For example, temporary workers are often measured by looking at employment totals for the temporary help industry. But National Planning Association case studies of major American employers indicate that many corporations are starting their own internal pools of temporary workers to avoid using temporary help agencies. These internal pools are not captured in the data presented in table 6.3. Also, leased employees appear to be a growing category in the U.S. labor market. One estimate placed the number of leased employees at 120,000 in 1986 (Day 1987). Nevertheless, since there is no sound data source on leased employees, these contingent workers are often not counted in the totals.

Despite these uncertainties, we do appear to be on safe ground in making the following general observations:

1. The contingent work force appears to be growing at a faster pace than the entire labor force.

2. The contingent work force appears to make up one-fourth, or more, of the American labor force.

3. A significant fraction of the jobs generated by the U.S. economy in the 1980s have involved contingent employment.

How Do Older Workers Fit into Employers' Strategies?

How do older workers stand in this new environment of increased corporate human resource flexibility? Contingent work could provide bridge jobs, for example. In compiling its case studies on human resource flexibility, the National Planning Association asked employers their views on the above question. Numerous senior human resource executives working for companies in many different industries and parts of the country expressed strong agreement on several key points:

1. Employers believe that the employment opportunities for older workers will show significant increases because of increased human resource flexibility.

2. Stronger interest in wage flexibility and contingent workers means that employers will turn to older workers to meet a greater part of their human resource needs.

3. Employers believe that older workers—more often than many other categories of workers—will want to be part-timers, temporary workers, and so forth.

4. Employers believe that older workers, on average, have the key characteristics employers are looking for in contingent workers. They believe, for example, that older workers often have a strong work ethic and other cultural values that make them good employees. Also, older workers often have demonstrated a very strong track record in the world of work. As one senior human resource executive put it: "Older workers represent a gold mine to us. They are just what we want."

5. Employers believe that they can provide a service to older Amer-

icans beyond a source of earned income because an active and productive work life can be a strong emotional boost for older Americans.

The bottom line is that flexible employment practices in large corporations would seem to be creating new bridges to retirement for
older workers. The range of flexible job opportunities available to
incumbent employees is being extended, and the options for entry
jobs are being enlarged in ways that should favor the employment of
older workers. Moreover, these changes are paired with the expec-
tation among employers that older workers will be the labor pool of
choice to fill these flexible jobs.

REALITY OF FLEXIBLE EMPLOYMENT
FOR OLDER WORKERS

Despite these changes in work options and the preference of employers for placing older workers in flexible jobs, the question remains
whether older workers are benefiting from this employment potential.
Preliminary evidence suggests that the reality may be very different
from this picture of expanding opportunities for bridge employment.

One way of measuring the movement of older workers into flexible
employment is to look at their share of part-time employment. Bureau
of Labor Statistics data show that people 55 years and older represent
a smaller portion of the part-time than of the full-time labor force.
People in this age group represent 7.0 percent of all part-timers and
8.1 percent of full-timers. Also, though people 55 years and older
represent 9.7 percent of the temporary work force, they represent
12.5 percent of the combined temporary and permanent work force
(Plewes 1988). Thus the estimates above indicate that people who are
55 years and older may represent a *smaller* portion of various segments
of the contingent work force than of the more traditional work force.
In the long run the employers' views expressed above could result in
a vast expansion of employment opportunities for older workers, but
in the recent past older workers have actually been underrepresented
in key areas of flexible employment.

Data by Sum and Fogg (chapter 3) do show an increasing trend in
both part-time and part-year employment among older workers during the 1980s. These data show, however, that much of this increase
is involuntary and that part-time and part-year work among older
persons is concentrated in the service sector and in smaller firms, not
among the parts of the large enterprise sector that have been experiencing much of the growth in flexible employment. If new bridges

to retirement are emerging, the large enterprise sector does not appear to be a major source of such jobs.

A set of detailed case studies of flexible workplace practices will illustrate why this might be. All of the corporations that were examined were large, mostly ranking among the Fortune 500. Many had experienced recent major economic and cultural shocks. The case studies are of employers who wanted to use more older workers in their newer flexible systems but who encountered various problems in implementing that goal.

TECHNOLOGICAL FEARS

Company E is a bank that has experienced a world of change in recent years (Belous 1989). "Deregulation has made us change," a human resource executive at the bank explains. In the past the bank had a fairly stable market for its services, and it also enjoyed a fairly stable market for its key input—money. Deregulation altered this business environment. Other types of financial institutions sought the business of many of the bank's customers. At the same time, the cost of obtaining financial resources increased.

Under these competitive conditions, the bank had to work extra hard to control expenses. A key area of cost control turned out to be labor costs. Meanwhile, the bank had to be willing to service customers when and where they wanted to be serviced. Customer patterns showed a wide range of differences not only on a daily, seasonal, and cyclical basis, but in the bank's various branches. Thus the bank had to expand customer service at the same time that the competitive market dictated that it trim its labor costs. "We felt like we were being pulled at both ends," one bank executive commented.

The bank started an active part-time program for tellers and customer service representatives and vigorously recruited for these positions. On any given day, from 17 to 25 percent of the bank's tellers and customer service representatives are part-timers. The bank has given these part-timers some centralized training, but most training is done on the job in the branches. Branch managers have had to be retrained to teach and manage part-timers. Bank executives assert that they have obtained a good number of "quality workers with low turnover" through this program. The use of part-timers has helped this bank meet erratic customer demand and control labor costs.

When the bank started this part-timer program, its human resource executives expected that a large percentage of the part-time tellers and customer service representatives would be older workers. But very few older workers are in this program. The vast majority of the part-time tellers and customer service representatives are young and middle-aged women with family responsibilities.

"We had wanted to hire many older workers," an executive with the bank noted. "We felt that many older workers had the skills and background we needed. But very few older workers showed up." The bank has not tried to redesign the part-time program to interest more older workers. Since there is a good supply of female workers in their younger and middle years, the bank has not felt any need to alter the part-time program.

Why have few older workers been interested in this bank's part-time program? Although the bank has not conducted a formal study of this question, bank executives have formed some views on the subject. Part-time tellers and customer service representatives must work with computers and other microelectronic equipment. Several of the bank executives believe that many older workers have strong fears concerning working with advanced technological equipment, which have prevented them from applying for these positions.

This example, of course, does not prove that many older workers have technological fears that are blocking an active work life, but it does indicate that management may see older workers' lack of interest in this light. This example also indicates that if employers are able to meet their demands for contingent labor from other sources, they may have no incentive to alter their programs to interest more older workers.

RECRUITMENT PROBLEMS

Besides potential technological fears, employers may face general recruitment problems in their efforts to hire more older workers. Company J, for example, a major regional retailer, has lived with tight labor markets for the last several years and has had to expand its use of part-time and temporary help. In one of its stores located in the business district of a major American city, the company has recently been able to keep managerial workers for an average of only sixty days.

This company has had to start "seeing each store as having its own culture," an executive with the retailer asserted. The various stores employ part-timers with quite different demographic characteristics. Some stores use a large number of students, others employ a large number of women, and still others use a large number of Third World part-timers. The company has wanted to hire older workers, but it has run into serious recruitment problems in efforts to hire them. "Nothing we do seems to work with older workers. We do want them," an executive at the firm explained.

The company has tried various recruitment methods directed at older workers, including magazine and newspaper ads, notices in the store, and recruitment suggestions to current workers. The company has even tried to hold special "parties" for older individuals, which include a social period, refreshments, and a presentation of the company by senior executives and older workers at the company. So far, these parties have not proven to be a success.

This company's recruitment experiences do not seem to be unique. The Bureau of National Affairs recently reported:

> "Older workers can help the food services industry solve its labor shortage problems, but recruiting them requires innovative techniques," say participants at a Washington, D.C., conference sponsored by Kentucky Fried Chicken and coordinated by the National Restaurant Association and the American Association of Retired Persons. . . . Companies that have hired older workers give them top ratings in such areas as dependability, job performance, and rapport with customers, according to a survey of 140 full-service and fast-food restaurant executives attending the conference. . . . The respondents cited recruitment difficulties as the biggest obstacle to hiring workers age 55 and older. . . . A majority of the respondents said Social Security limitations were an impediment to hiring older workers.
>
> Traditional recruitment techniques, including newspaper advertising, ads placed on radio and television, and window signs, have had only limited success in attracting older workers, conference participants agree. (Bureau of National Affairs 1987:258, 263)

Some firms in the food service industry have tried recruitment methods such as "team interviewing" using one recruiter who is middle-aged and a second recruiter who is elderly. An employer may have to show a potential older worker that the company already does employ elderly people. Other companies in the industry have emphasized pleasant working conditions. These firms believe that it is important to convince older individuals that the company's restaurants are "fun, vibrant places to work" (Bureau of National Affairs 1987:258, 263).

The parties for senior citizens cited by this retail company could be a third example of new recruitment methods. The company hopes to revise and redesign the party formula to recruit more older people for the firm. In this company's case labor markets have been so

tight—and unemployment so low—that it has not been able to ignore the lack of older people in its work force. Older people may
be viewed as good potential workers, but they are very difficult to
recruit.

If labor shortages are large enough to cause employers concern,
they may be willing to make major efforts to redesign their recruitment programs to gain more senior workers. But if labor shortages
are not serious, many employers may not be willing to make the added
effort to make special adjustments in their recruitment programs. If
recruitment programs are not directed toward the special needs and
concerns of older workers, their employment may not increase at
many firms despite employers' interest in hiring them.

Labor cost and labor shortage considerations appear to have motivated this retailer to make special efforts to attract older workers,
but these considerations were not strong enough to motivate the bank
in the previous case study to make such a special effort.

"JUST-IN-TIME" WORK FORCES

In an effort to reduce costs, many corporations have introduced so-
called just-in-time inventory systems. Instead of carrying more parts
and raw materials than are needed, business executives have tried to
reduce the size and costs of inventories based on production flows.
Contingent workers can be viewed as just-in-time work forces that are
designed to minimize labor costs and total corporate employment.

Many corporate employers have discovered that the temporary help
industry is a very good source of just-in-time workers in tight labor
markets. Company K is a publisher located outside a major city. In
the past, the company met its human resource needs easily. But "management knows that many workers would tell us good-bye if we told
them that they had to be permanent full-time employees," a human
resource executive at the publishing company noted. The use of contingent workers has helped this publishing company reduce the
growth of labor costs. "In the past people lined up outside the door
to work permanent full-time. Our compensation levels and benefits
are well above the local market rates," this company executive noted.

The publisher has increasingly turned to temporary help agencies
to supply workers. These agencies have even brought city workers
out to the company's suburban facility by bus. "They [temporary help
agencies] seem to be much better than we are at shaking the trees
and discovering new sources of labor supply," the company executive
noted.

When the publishing company first became interested in the just-in-time work force concept, company executives believed that a good number of these workers would be older individuals who lived in the company's suburban labor market. Instead, the just-in-time workers often live outside the suburban community, and very few of them are older individuals.

Since temporary help agencies have found enough workers to meet the publishing firm's labor demands, this firm has not had any strong incentive to redirect its program so that more just-in-time workers are older individuals.

More Older Flexible Workers

The case studies did show some examples in which a corporation's drive to increase employment flexibility resulted in older workers being hired as contingents. These older workers, however, often tended to be former employees of the company.

Several insurance, drug, chemical, and manufacturing firms have rehired former older core workers as contingents to serve as consultants for various projects. Some firms have viewed these former employees as "coaches" or "mentors" for their younger workers. As one human resource executive at a drug company put it: "With downsizing we need older workers with an institutional memory. These older workers act as coaches and help younger sales staff in the field."

Most employers who mentioned such coach, mentor, or consultant programs said that many older former employees like being able to work part time or on a temporary schedule. A few employers mention, however, that some former older core workers feel resentment at becoming contingent workers.

Employee Benefits

The food service industry conference cited above also indicated that fringe benefits can be a key tool in the recruitment of older workers. It was reported that "benefits are almost as important to older workers as wages. Recruiters should emphasize the employer's total compensation package, rather than the job's hourly wage" (Bureau of National Affairs 1987:263).

Our knowledge of employee benefits for contingent workers is limited. Two George Washington University economists, Sar A. Levitan and Elizabeth Conway, have provided some basic estimates in this area. As indicated in table 6.4, employers of part-time workers often do not have to pay for such employee benefits as health insurance.

TABLE 6.4. Sources of Health Insurance Coverage for Full-Time and Part-Time Workers, 1985 (in percent)

Category	Own Employer	Someone Else's Employer	Other Nonemployer Plan	No Coverage
Full-time, full-year workers	78.6	7.0	6.3	8.1
Part time for noneconomic reasons	26.2	34.3	21.4	18.1
Part time for economic reasons	34.8	17.3	17.4	30.6

Source: Sar A. Levitan and Elizabeth Conway, "Part-Time Employment: Living on Half-Rations" (Washington, D.C.: Center for Social Policy Studies, George Washington University, 1988), pp. 11–12. Estimates based on Current Population Survey data from its March 1985 supplement.

More than three-quarters of individuals who worked full time, full year in 1985 received health insurance coverage from their employers, but roughly one-third or fewer part-time workers received this benefit. As indicated in table 6.5, part-timers are usually excluded from pension plans.

Interviews with employers did indicate that some firms have provided systems of prorated benefits for many of their contingent workers, but these systems remain the exception rather than the norm at a majority of companies. One of the major reasons employers expressed interest in expanding the use of contingent workers was that they could give contingents fewer benefits than core workers.

As was true for the recruitment examples cited above, if labor shortages are serious enough, more employers may provide more employee benefits for contingents. But without the pressure of labor shortages, it may be unrealistic to expect that many employers will introduce systems of prorated benefits. If employee benefit packages are as important to older workers as wages are, many of these workers could view employers' attitudes in this area as an obstacle to employment.

SHORT RUN VERSUS LONG RUN

The basic conclusions of the evidence presented in this chapter are as follows:

1. Many employers are in the process of making their human resource systems more flexible.

TABLE 6.5.   Full-Time and Part-Time Workers Covered by Their Employers' Pension Plan, 1985 (in percent)

Category	No Plan	Plan Exists, Not Included	Plan Exists, Included
Men			
Full time, full year	35.8	4.6	59.7
Part time for economic reasons	73.0	7.7	19.6
Part time for noneconomic reasons	72.2	10.5	17.3
Women			
Full time, full year	34.4	7.7	57.9
Part time for economic reasons	69.6	12.5	17.9
Part time for noneconomic reasons	71.3	13.2	15.5

Source: Sar A. Levitan and Elizabeth Conway, "Part-Time Employment: Living on Half-Rations" (Washington, D.C.: Center for Social Policy Studies, George Washington University, 1988), pp. 12–13. Estimates based on Current Population Survey Data from its March 1985 supplement.

2. Employers seem to have very positive views toward hiring older workers.

3. In the long run, the shift toward more flexible human resource systems could expand the employment opportunities of older workers, and older workers may be among the winners in this new labor-management environment.

4. There seem to be numerous obstacles in the short run to the employment of older workers, particularly technological fears and recruitment problems.

5. Employers seem to be driven by cost-benefit analysis. If they can meet their labor demands by hiring nonelderly workers, they will not make the effort to redesign their employment programs to attract more older people. But if employers cannot meet their labor demands by hiring nonelderly workers, they will have an incentive to redesign their programs to favor older workers.

In light of these conclusions, what role can older workers expect to play in a more flexible work force? The key variable appears to be labor supply. If employers can meet their human resource demands without using older workers, they will not make the added effort and pay the added expenses to hire older workers in the expanded contingent work forces. But if labor supplies become very tight, market forces will force employers to go out of their way to include more older workers in these newer contingent systems.

In 1989 the national unemployment rate fell under 5.3 percent, and in various parts of the country (including New England and the

Mid-Atlantic states) employers seem to be making an active effort to redesign their hiring programs with older workers in mind. Of course, tax and other public programs could be created that would in effect lower the price employers have to pay to hire older workers. These public programs could also increase the economic rewards older people gain from working. This would increase the potential labor supply for employers. Most employers, however, have not taken an active position in this area.

A majority of employers have shown much more concern about educational issues than about older workers (Morrison, McGuire, and Clarke 1988:1–6). They hope that an improved educational system will provide more better-educated young workers to fill positions (Morrison, McGuire, and Clarke 1988:vii).

The bottom line is that despite employers' beliefs that older individuals are very good workers, market forces so far have *not* been strong enough to move most employers to deal with the specific concerns of older workers. Changes in the large enterprise sector are creating more bridge jobs, but older workers do not seem to be obtaining their proportional share of such jobs. The main exceptions appear to be firms that are creating special programs for their own older employees.

Appendix to Chapter 6

The data used in this study come from many different sources. Since the U.S. government has no official measure of contingent work forces, data from the Bureau of Labor Statistics, the Census Bureau, and various private sector surveys have been used. Many different international data sources were also used, including Statistics Canada, the OECD, and the International Labour Organization.

The case studies, though not randomly selected, are drawn from a diverse group of industries and represent considerable regional diversity. Of the fifty case studies, the companies represented the following sectors of the economy:

Natural resources and agriculture	3
Manufacturing	19
Services	16
Private nonprofit	8
Government	2
Unions	2

The geographic distribution (by location of company headquarters or principal offices) of the case studies was as follows:

Mid-Atlantic	15
New England	7
Southeast	6
Midwest	10
Southwest	5
Pacific	7

Interviews were also conducted with many business, labor, and government executives from foreign countries. The case studies used in this report were based on U.S. organizations. The interviews with foreign executives were used only as background in this study.

---------------------------------- 7 ----------------------------------

FLEXIBLE EMPLOYMENT: UNION PERSPECTIVES

Eileen Appelbaum and Judith Gregory

Flexible Employment Relations

Conventional wisdom in economics suggests that the increase during the 1980s in part-time work, temporary employment, home-based work, subcontracting, and other contingent work arrangements is the serendipitous outcome of changing labor demand and labor supply conditions. It is argued that increased requirements for flexibility in scheduling work by firms occurred just as the proportion of the work force that desires more flexible hours was rising. According to this interpretation, the increase in the number of part-time jobs from 18 million in 1979 to 20 million in 1987 as well as the temporary nature of up to 80 percent of the 10 million full-time jobs added since the end of the 1982 recession (Uchitelle 1988; U.S. Department of Labor 1985) are benign, even welcome, developments.

On the demand side, traditional peak-load problems in retail sales, restaurants, and personal services are exacerbated by the needs of a still-rising number of two-earner families for longer shopping hours. Part-time work in the United States has grown along with the expansion of these industries, and fluctuations in demand in this sector of the economy are met by varying the hours of part-time employees.

In addition, primary labor market firms, facing increased competition for markets at home and abroad, want a buffer of workers who are easily dismissed when demand conditions change. Some primary labor market firms that employ expensive but soon-to-be-obsolete hardware want to keep the equipment in use for longer than the standard eight-hour day so as to spread their high fixed costs over a larger volume of output and recoup their investments. The result is the emergence of alternative employment arrangements—ranging from part-time data-processing work after regular hours to electronic home work, temporary jobs, and subcontract employment for clerical and professional workers—in firms that traditionally offered full-time, permanent employment.

On the supply side of the labor market, mothers struggling to earn an income while meeting family responsibilities, teenagers trying to reconcile the demands of school and work, and older workers no longer up to the rigors of full-time employment and seeking bridge jobs before retirement have been choosing part-time work, temporary jobs, and other alternative work arrangements.

In this conventional economic view, the lower compensation (wages plus benefits) paid by firms to workers in contingent jobs reflects employers' perceptions of differences in productivity or absenteeism and turnover between permanent and contingent workers. Acceptance of lower compensation is viewed as a price willingly paid by workers who place a premium on convenience in scheduling work.

An Alternative View

Although it is true that many workers in jobs that either are not full time or lack permanent status have chosen these jobs, this free-market view of alternative work arrangements is overly sanguine and is challenged by the few data that are available. The evidence suggests that increased flexibility in employer-employee relations and the increase in contingent employment have occurred largely at the discretion of management. Neither the increase in part-time employment nor the explosive growth of temporary jobs can be explained by changes in the characteristics of the labor force.

The proportion of workers employed part time voluntarily, for example, peaked in 1979 and has edged down since then for women as well as men (Appelbaum 1987). The number of people who usually work part time increased by 2.4 million between 1979 and 1985, but only six hundred thousand of these workers sought part-time employment voluntarily (Nardone 1986:15). The rest wanted full-time jobs but were unable to obtain them. Involuntary part-time employment increased from 1.6 million in 1967 to 3.2 million in 1977 and 5.5 million in 1987, edging down slightly in the current tight labor market. Thus, though most part-time employment remains voluntary, the proportion in this category is shrinking, not rising. Almost all of the recent growth in part-time employment has been involuntary.

Similarly, a recent study of the temporary help services (THS) industry found no support for the view that women with family responsibilities are choosing employment in the temporary help industry for the flexibility in scheduling it affords (Lapidus 1988). On the contrary, the study found that nearly 73 percent of THS employees worked full time in 1985, and half of those working part time did so involuntarily.

Although employers have taken various steps to make the employment relationship more flexible and contingent on the firm's perception of its economic situation, the traditional pool of workers seeking contingent work arrangements is shrinking. In addition to the changed aspirations of women, changing demographics also contribute to this situation. The number of younger workers—an important source of low-wage, part-time, or temporary workers—is declining. The Bureau of Labor Statistics projects a total of 7.4 million workers between the ages of 16 and 19 in the labor force in 1992, compared with 9.4 million in 1980 (Collins 1987). Thus firms are finding it increasingly difficult to fill contingent jobs.

OLDER WORKERS: AN ALTERNATIVE LABOR POOL

The search for alternative labor pools is already under way in industries that rely on a low-wage labor force, such as retail trade, restaurants, motels, day care and early childhood education, and nursing homes. Older people, especially those who retired early, whose retirement income is inadequate, and who are willing to accept bridge jobs in preference to full retirement, are an important candidate population for these and other part-time or contingent jobs. Not only is this group growing in numbers but, as management points out, many in its ranks are experienced workers.

An increasing number of older people may, in fact, be available for such jobs. Surprisingly, this is not because increased longevity has increased the proportion of older Americans. The number of people in the United States, including those older than 55, has increased steadily, but the proportion of the population aged 55 to 64 has remained virtually unchanged since 1950, and only a small increase has been registered in the proportion aged 65 to 74. Not until 2010, when the baby boom cohort begins to pass the 55-year mark, will the proportion of older Americans rise sharply (9 to 5 1987).

Instead, it is the decline in labor force participation rates of older men and the leveling off of participation rates of older women since 1970, resulting in a rapid increase in the proportion of people over the age of 55 outside the labor force, that marks this age group for recruitment to contingent work. One reason older workers have left the labor force is that they have been laid off and are discouraged about finding another job. Among all workers who lost their jobs because of plant closings or employment cutbacks between January 1981 and January 1988, approximately 14 percent left the labor force; among workers over 55 years of age, however, more than 33 percent left (Horvath 1987). Early retirement is the other reason for declining labor force participation in the over-55 age group. Since 1974, many of the private pension plans at large companies have reduced the normal retirement age. Nearly all allow early retirement, and many have reduced the penalties associated with retiring at age 55 (Bell and Marclay 1987). The percentage of the population aged 60 to 64 electing early retirement under Social Security pension provisions also increased, from 14.1 percent in 1970 to 23.2 percent in 1984 (Mirkin 1987).

The result is that by 1984, 50 percent of the women aged 55 to 59 and 20 percent of the men were outside the labor force; among those 60 to 64, 87 percent of the women and 44 percent of the men were outside the labor force (Mirkin 1987). Combined with the expressed desire of a large majority of older workers for partial, as opposed to complete, retirement, the sharp decline in median household income after age 55 (Kahne 1985:65–66, 87), and the failure of most firms to allow older workers to reduce their hours (Kahne 1985:36, 133; Gustman and Steinmeier 1983), the over-55 age group is potentially a significant source of new recruits for part-time and contingent work schedules.

Reports in the popular press indicate that some firms in low-wage industries have already begun actively seeking new employees among older people. In the child care industry, one small Arizona company that pays $3.35 to start, with an increase to $3.85 after a year, has an intern program, funded by the state, to train and employ workers over the age of 55 whose income is less than $5,700. The program has been cited as "a model for efforts to bring older Americans into day care" (Collins 1987:191). At the largest U.S. national chain of child care centers, which has 1,100 facilities in forty states, wages for child care workers vary from minimum wage ($3.35) to $5 an hour in most states, with a high of $6 an hour in a few areas with a high cost of living. Here, too, older workers are sought for employment, and the firm reports an increase in the number of its elderly workers (Collins 1987).

Fast food is another industry that is turning to older people as it seeks to expand hiring. Labor shortages are projected for 1995 in the food service and lodging industries, where many jobs are part time and low paying. McDonald's efforts to cope by hiring older workers, exemplified by the McMasters Program that trains and hires older workers and the New Kid commercials, are probably best known; but other firms are expected to follow suit (Kingson 1988).

UNION RETIREES AND BRIDGE JOBS

A recent national survey of 6,543 retired union workers provides important insights into the attitude of these retirees toward postcareer bridge jobs, including part-time, part-year, and temporary jobs (all data in this section are from Charner et al. 1988). There are two important differences between union retirees and older Americans generally. First, union retirees have higher average total incomes. Only 23 percent had incomes of less that $10,000 in 1985, compared with almost two-thirds of all retired workers. Second, in comparison with the general population of older Americans, union retirees are more likely to be male. This finding reflects the composition of the work force and the unions when these retirees were employed. Nevertheless, one-quarter of the sample of union retirees is female. The survey found very few differences among male and female retirees with respect to paid employment.

The survey results provide support for the proposition that a significant proportion of older workers retired from their career job desire bridge employment and many prefer part-time or temporary jobs. The survey found that 2 percent of all union retirees work full time, 5 percent work part time, and 6 percent held temporary jobs. Among workers 64 years of age or younger, the percentages of workers in each category are much higher: 6 percent work full time, 8 percent work part time, and 10 percent work in temporary jobs. An additional 15 percent of the retirees in this age group would like to work. Thus nearly 40 percent of the retirees below the age of 65 hold or desire bridge jobs. Only 13 percent of the retirees who work or would like to work prefer a full-time work schedule; 61 percent prefer to work less than eight hours a day, 76 percent prefer to work less than five days a week, and 38 percent prefer to work less than twelve months a year.

Retirees report a variety of reasons for working or wanting to work. The need for money for necessary expenses is important for those with annual incomes under $10,000—77 percent give this as a reason compared with 68 percent of those with incomes of $10,000 to $14,999 and 51 percent of those with incomes of $15,000 or more. Female retirees report a desire to increase Social Security benefits as an important economic reason for working, with 48 percent of women versus 37 percent of men giving this as a reason. Nonfinancial motives for working are also important to union retirees. More than three-quarters of retirees report that they work or want to work in order to make a contribution or feel useful and as a way to spend time and keep busy; nearly 70 percent want the enjoyment of being with others and the stimulation or pleasure of the work.

But retirees who would like to work find that they face many obstacles. More than half seeking a paid job report that low pay is an obstacle, and a similar percentage report a lack of suitable opportunities. One-third report unsuitable hours, and one-third report lack of suitable skills as obstacles; 20 percent report unsuitable working conditions. These findings suggest that older workers and teenage workers may not be fungible. Like teens, older workers prefer flexible work-time arrangements, but they are seeking jobs with wages, working conditions, and skill content consonant with their lifetime work experiences. Jobs traditionally held by younger workers may not be suitable for older workers. In addition, 40 percent of older workers report facing age discrimination.

"NEW CONCEPT" VERSUS "OLD CONCEPT"
FLEXIBLE SCHEDULES

Increased employment opportunities for groups disadvantaged by circumstances, including advanced age, are much to be applauded. Many workers—among them, students, women with young children, and older workers seeking bridge jobs before full retirement—have expressed a strong desire for alternative work schedules.

The economic marginalization of these workers through consignment to low-wage jobs, however, is another problem. The union concern is twofold: to prevent the economic exploitation of easily stigmatized groups that lack economic clout, and to keep the growth of part-time and contingent work arrangements from undermining the wages and working conditions of full-time workers. It would be unfortunate, for example, if employers were to discount the need of older workers for job security and income and hire them as casual workers and worse yet if they were able to count on them to accept low wages, few benefits or even none, and intermittent employment.

Hilda Kahne, in *Reconceiving Part-Time Work* (1985:33), distinguishes between what she calls "old concept part-time work" and "regular, new concept part-time work," which may include job sharing and phased retirement as well as permanent part-time employment. Old concept part-time work refers to the proliferation of short-hour jobs in the United States in which firms have at best a weak commitment to workers. Without such a commitment, firms have little incentive to provide job stability and to offer wage and benefits packages that link workers more tightly to the firm. In contrast, in new concept part-time work, the job is permanent rather than temporary and intermittent in its nature, and fringe benefits are generally included in the earnings package. Unfortunately, new concept reduced-hour work scheduling is not widespread (Kahne 1985:41).

Legitimate requirements by firms for part-time or other alternative work arrangements, to meet scheduling problems, for example, do not depend on the payment of low wages or the absence of a long-term commitment to employees. And workers who prefer flexible schedules should not have to sacrifice pay and job stability by accepting them. New concept flexible scheduling does not rely on the ability of firms to offer part-time workers reduced compensation, nor does it undermine the pay and working conditions of those who work full time. Moreover, new concept flexible scheduling reduces the incentives employers now have to eliminate full-time positions and replace them with part-time jobs simply to evade the responsibilities most firms have toward permanent full-time employees.

Where will the impetus for change to new concept flexible scheduling come from? How will the struggle for decent compensation and working conditions be waged? The legislative process—through which minimum wages can be raised, minimum benefit standards mandated, and the standard workweek reduced—is one arena of struggle; the office, store, or shop floor is the other. Unions have an important role to play in each.

Changing Union Responses

Unions were slow to recognize the legitimate needs of workers and firms for flexibility in scheduling work. In the past, most U.S. unions were staunchly opposed to part-time work. The change in the hours and terms of employment of so many U.S. workers, however, has forced the trade union movement to rethink previously held attitudes toward contingent work arrangements and the workers who hold these jobs.

Until recently, most traditional unions have explicitly or tacitly opposed the creation of jobs with part-time hours or other alternative work schedules. Unions have done little to extend contract protections to part-time, temporary, or other contingent workers, who have often been outside the bargaining unit. Unions with high proportions of women members, however, and those based in public or private service sector industries—the United Food and Commercial Workers Union (UFCW), the Service Employees International Union (SEIU) and District 9–5/SEIU, District 65/UAW of the United Auto Workers, and the American Federation of State, County and Municipal Employees (AFSCME) are prominent examples—have pioneered in developing job-sharing programs, providing equitable and permanent part-time positions, organizing part-time and long-term temporary employees, and arranging for the transition of temporary positions into permanent ones. They have sometimes been successful in requiring some say for the union regarding the use of contingent workers, including when they may be hired, the conditions under which they work, and the effects of contingent employment on the mainstream work force.

With some justification, unions have traditionally viewed the extension of part-time work as a management strategy for replacing full-time jobs, intensifying work, reducing wages, denying fringe benefits, and excluding workers from promotion and access to training and skills within the company (see, for example, AFL-CIO 1985). In addition to opposing the introduction of part-time or contingent work, unions have consigned part-time workers (typically defined as those working less than twenty hours per week) and other contingent workers to a "no-man's land" outside the bargaining unit. Not only are such workers left without union protections or pay scales, but this arrangement can be used by an aggressive management as a loophole to hire more contingent workers while simultaneously diluting union strength. Management has sometimes used home worker programs or part-time employment to undermine the job security of full-time workers and to reduce the ratio of bargaining unit members in relation to the total work force, thus undermining the union's strength in the next round of bargaining and in future relations with the company (for examples, see Gregory 1983; Costello 1984).

The accumulation of such experiences has taught unions that it is folly to leave part-time and contingent workers outside the bargaining unit. Unions have begun to develop a more active and sympathetic approach to the organizing of contingent workers in response to two distinct concerns: the need for parity in pay and working conditions and a less precarious employment relationship for workers who require flexible schedules and the protection of the economic status of incumbent, permanent, full-time workers. Unions continue to oppose the marginalization of workers and the growth of involuntary part-time employment. But they have begun to see their role as assuring that such workers earn wages and benefits comparable to those of full-time workers and have access to grievance procedures and other job protection and due process mechanisms.

As a result, unions have increased their organizing efforts in the long-neglected service sector, in which a substantial minority of employees work part time, many of them voluntarily, and the number of part-time and other contingent workers continues to increase. Furthermore, they have begun to develop general principles for assuring that the choice of alternative work schedules is voluntary and that workers who make such choices achieve parity with full-time workers.

TRADE UNION PRINCIPLES AND CONCERNS

The thrust of trade union initiatives has been to halt the marginalization of jobs and of the workers who hold these casual jobs and to assure that flexible, temporary, or reduced-time schedules are voluntary. 9 to 5, which has been deeply involved in efforts to organize such workers, has defined the needs: adherence to the principle of a livable wage, with decent pay and employer-provided benefits for part-time, temporary, and home-based workers; family policies such as child care, parental leave, and flexible work schedules in permanent jobs so that parents are not forced to choose marginal jobs in order to care for their families; union organization of contingent workers to give them a voice in pay and working conditions; government recognition of the importance of these social goals and of its responsibility to set social policy; and business planning for long-term economic growth in a world context (Nussbaum and Meyer 1987).

Union concern over part-time and contingent employment is not limited to women workers. Unions are sometimes seen as barriers to part-time or part-year employment for all older workers (Paul 1988). Recently, however, the trade union movement has endorsed union bargaining over phased retirement programs, which allow workers to continue working for their current employer on a part-time or part-year basis, and has encouraged unions to aid retired members in finding bridge jobs. Recommendations adopted by the AFL-CIO in August 1988 call on unions to "work with employers to develop flexible schedules for retirees who wish to continue working in workplaces where flexible schedules are appropriate" and also suggest that unions should "maintain job banks for members interested in post-retirement work" (AFL-CIO 1988:8).

To redress the worst inequities associated with part-time work, the 1985 AFL-CIO "Draft Resolution on Part-Time Work," which spells out the trade union movement's position on this issue, demands that part-time workers "(1) be protected from the social point of view through an overall inclusion into social security schemes; (2) be guaranteed all benefits accruing from company policy and collective bargaining agreements; (3) be covered by the provisions laid down in the collective bargaining agreements also when they work on a capacity-oriented working time basis; and (4) be eligible for promotion, further training and retraining in the same way as full-time workers" (page 3).

The "Draft Resolution" characterizes individual flextime as unsuitable and objects to job sharing. Unions have been wary of job sharing and flextime programs for a number of reasons: concern that the hours of the day may be extended; that programs are not truly voluntary, either because of management or peer pressure; that opportunities for overtime or premium pay may be lost; and that the number of full-time jobs may be reduced. Despite these objections, however, union locals confronting particularly difficult situations have shown a willingness to bargain realistically and creatively over new forms of working arrangements. Opposition in principle to particular work arrangements does not mean refusal of union locals to compromise; and a collective bargaining agreement covering particular forms of contingent work does not necessarily signify union endorsement in principle of the work arrangement.

Unions stress that pilot programs must be carefully evaluated by both union and management. Locals interested in alternative work schedule programs are advised to create a labor-management committee to analyze employees' needs and interests, ensure that participation by employees is voluntary, develop and evaluate a pilot project, and allow either management or the union to initiate termination of the program. Unions emphasize the importance of a needs assessment conducted by the union to provide information for devising contract provisions that can be used to design solutions to stresses and strains in workers' lives (New York City Coalition of Labor Union Women

1985). Such an assessment would be especially valuable to workers and firms considering phased retirement and to organizations developing experimental programs for reemploying older workers.

COLLECTIVE BARGAINING OVER
ALTERNATIVE WORK ARRANGEMENTS

Although the national labor movement has announced its support for extending collective bargaining coverage to workers on part-time schedules, for organizing service industries in which contingent workers are most numerous, and for directing organizing efforts specifically toward part-time and other contingent workers, it is at the local level that such policies must be implemented. Unions have found it especially difficult to organize these workers because of their lack of attachment to a particular employer. Workers who view these jobs as a temporary expedient while still in school or while home responsibilities are particularly burdensome may not feel the need to join a union. Young workers, in particular, may not appreciate the importance of health and pension benefits, may view their interests as different from those of permanent full-time employees, and may have negative opinions of unions. At the same time, the precarious position of contingent workers, who can easily be fired by employers, may make them reluctant to join a union organizing drive.

The result is an extremely low level of unionization among part-time workers. Only 1.27 million part-time workers belonged to unions in 1985, about 7.3 percent of the labor force, and only 8.8 percent were covered by union contracts. This is about one-third the rate of unionization of full-time workers, 20.4 percent of whom belong to unions and 23.1 percent of whom have union representation. Only about one in fourteen union members works part time (Monthly Labor Review 1986:45). Unionization among temporary workers and contract employees is virtually nonexistent.

Despite the difficulties encountered in organizing contingent workers, there are notable examples of union locals that have organized and bargained for these workers, negotiating contract provisions that provide equitable working conditions for workers on alternative schedules. Such new concept work arrangements respect the needs of firms and workers for flexibility in scheduling work, but they do not have the impermanence or low pay characteristic of old concept contingent employment relations.

The context in which negotiations over flexible scheduling take place has a very strong effect on union attitudes. Three broad contexts for bargaining on this issue can be identified: bargaining for voluntary reductions in work time desired by workers; bargaining under conditions of legitimate crisis, such as a budget crisis in the public sector or industrial restructuring in the private sector, when the union faces the threat of layoffs; and bargaining when management is engaged in cost-cutting measures that undermine the job security or working conditions of the incumbent work force, often involving simultaneous layoffs of permanent workers and expanded use of contingent workers.

The development of contract provisions to address the needs of workers who require flexibility and efforts to achieve a shorter work-week or options for more leisure time through voluntary reduced time/income trade-offs are seen by unions in the most positive light. Older workers who would prefer reduced hours to full retirement and those who wish to reenter the labor force and are seeking bridge jobs are among those who would benefit from the more widespread availability of such options.

Unions would like to broaden the occupational range of part-time jobs and assure that workers in these jobs are classified as permanent employees and included in the bargaining unit. Such changes would make these jobs more attractive to older workers as well as to women with family demands. Unions have mainly addressed child care responsibilities, yet the home care of frail spouses or other dependent relatives is a concern of many older workers seeking employment. In particular, wives may need to work to support older husbands who need home care and may want less than full-time hours while still requiring decent wages and benefits.

Voluntary reduced-time options have been successfully negotiated by some locals (McCarthy, Rosenberg, and Lefkowitz 1981; Olmstead 1983). Reductions in hours in these cases have usually been temporary, allowing some employees transient time off to pursue other endeavors with guarantees that they can return to full-time status at the end of the agreed-upon period. Voluntary reduced-time options may be a welcome alternative for older workers before retirement. The illness of a spouse or a preference for greater leisure or partial retirement may motivate the voluntary transition to shorter hours, though older workers may prefer a more permanent arrangement than envisioned in current voluntary reduced-hour programs. In bargaining over alternative work schedules, unions need to develop a greater recognition of the opportunities such new arrangements provide for older workers, particularly older women.

Unions are most favorably disposed toward bargaining over flexibility in scheduling work when it is to meet workers' preferences. Bargaining during a financial crisis or when management's goals are strictly to reduce compensation is much more difficult. Unions have been innovative in negotiating alternative work arrangements as a job-saving strategy when bargaining with employers who face a legitimate crisis. They have helped devise programs that saved money for the employer during a period of distress while retaining more of the newer employees and keeping the union work force more intact than would have been possible otherwise. Some of the programs developed in response to a crisis were subsequently built into ongoing contract provisions under normal business conditions.

Not all reductions in work time negotiated as an alternative to outright layoffs work out so well. In cases involving reductions in force, there are underlying strains and pressures, and it is often questionable whether participation is really voluntary, though part-time work may be accepted as the lesser of two evils.

The least favorable context for negotiating over flexible work arrangements occurs when firms have implemented these arrangements primarily to realize budgetary savings and not in deference to the preferences of workers or the requirements of the production process. In this context, unions are concerned with creating permanent and, when appropriate, full-time positions based on the identification of situations in which temporary or part-time work is actually continuous or virtually full time. They are mainly interested in negotiating a transition from casual to permanent status for workers and in prohibiting the simultaneous layoff of full-time workers and the expansion of part-time, temporary, or contract jobs. Failing this, unions put forward demands for wage parity for contingent workers, increased hours, rest breaks, vacations, seniority rights, and health and pension benefits to reduce the disparities between permanent and marginal employment.

In general, unions have pressed for contract provisions that would make part-time work an option for many individuals at some point during their working lives, rather than as a permanent status for some workers. Voluntary job sharing, phased retirement, or other reduced-time options to enable workers to pursue education, training, parental responsibilities, care of an elderly spouse or parents, or increased leisure are examples of such provisions.

Unions have been concerned in the past that policies to aid working parents may lead to de facto discrimination against workers with children unless antidiscrimination rights are guaranteed explicitly. Similar problems are likely to emerge as unions negotiate contracts that provide alternative work options for older workers. Provisions barring discrimination on the basis of age will have to be included if these contracts are not to reduce rather than expand opportunities for these workers.

Conclusion

Unions have accumulated important experience in bargaining for part-time and temporary employees. Collective policies have been developed that facilitate individually tailored solutions to workplace stresses on workers while ensuring that the employers' work requirements are met. Contractual agreements help build an equitable, across-the-board "floor" for benefits. They also define transitions for temporary and part-time workers to permanent or full-time status and outline procedures for the creation of full-time positions when ongoing contingent work indicates that there is sufficient work to warrant this change. Mechanisms for guaranteed minimum hours, paid rest breaks, access to training, accumulation of hours for step increases in pay for part-time and temporary workers, as well as regular evaluations and accumulation of hours toward promotion to more experienced job classes, are all means of addressing affirmative action concerns for otherwise marginal or peripheral workers. In addition, unions have bargained to restrict the use of contingent workers to preserve the job security and working conditions of the full-time work force.

Such provisions protect the wages and working conditions of full-time as well as part-time or temporary workers. At the same time, they restrict the ability of employers to use flexible work schedules to drive down wages and benefits or to develop two-tier arrangements that marginalize large numbers of workers. They do not, however, discourage the use of these arrangements to meet such legitimate needs for flexibility as those associated with peak-load scheduling problems of firms or further formal education for workers.

IMPLICATIONS FOR OLDER WORKERS

Although union contract provisions that improve the quality of contingent jobs and eliminate the contingent aspect of new work options also increase the choices available to older workers, few unions have bargained for contract language that specifically addresses the needs of this group. In part, this is because of the relatively small number of older workers currently found in contingent jobs, which are held predominantly by young people and women. Unions negotiating for workers in such jobs have been most sensitive to the needs of incumbents. If changing demographics lead to the substitution of older workers for younger or to the aging of women now in these jobs, unions can be expected to increase the emphasis on contract provisions that specifically meet the requirements of older employees.

Another reason that new work schedules for older workers have not received more attention from unions is that older male workers, who have achieved the higher pay and benefits that accompany seniority in full-time unionized jobs, are the group most threatened by, and resistant to, these alternatives. They fear the spread of contingent work arrangements into the industries and plants where they are employed and are distrustful that short-hour options, once they are sanctioned by union contracts, will be strictly voluntary. Phased retirement or other flexible retirement provisions for older workers, if they are not strictly voluntary, may prove to be little more than a management strategy for circumventing seniority rights. Quite reasonably in this era of two-tier contracts and union give-backs, unions tread cautiously before embracing new work options that, without appropriate guarantees, could be punitive to older workers.

There is some evidence, however, that unions are becoming more receptive to the opportunities, as well as the challenges, presented by increased employment of older workers in contingent jobs. At a recent conference on contingent work in New York City, jointly organized by Cornell University's School of Industrial and Labor Relations and District Council 37 of AFSCME, the two presenters at the session on part-time and temporary workers were an organizer for 9 to 5, the National Association of Working Women, and the director of the Senior Employment Division of New York City's Department for the Aging. This, in itself, is a significant development.

Two important issues emerged at that session, neither of which was lost on the union members present. The first is that the increasing awareness of the plight of households headed by females has shifted the public perception that women work for pin money to the realization that they work because they need an income. As low wages for women become harder to justify, low-wage employers have begun to turn to older workers to fill these jobs, arguing that older people work only to escape from boredom and do not really need the money. This is not true of most older job seekers, of course, any more than it is of most women workers. Many older people seeking employment are experienced workers who are used to being compensated fairly for a day's work and to being treated with dignity on the job; they do not wish to work in marginal jobs or to be viewed as disposable employees. Only those whose need for income is most acute accept these low-paying jobs. The parallels with the position of most women in contingent jobs are obvious, as are the common interests of women and older workers in winning decent pay and working conditions. It would be a mistake for unions to counterpose the needs of these two groups of workers rather than bargaining on behalf of both.

The second point to emerge is that although employers value the stability that older experienced workers bring to contingent jobs, their previous work experience may make them an easier employee population for unions to organize. Older workers view poverty wages as exploitive and arbitrary behavior by managers as an insult, and they are old enough to remember the difference a union can make. Their attitudes toward unions appear to be more positive than those of young workers or women, who may never have belonged to a union or worked in a union shop. Increased employment of older workers in jobs may provide unions with new opportunities for reaching contingent workers.

Unions remain generally reluctant to endorse the creation of still more short-hour positions, including those suitable for older workers. Their concern is that such jobs will simply add to the rapidly growing number of contingent jobs characterized by low pay, few employee benefits, and precarious rather than permanent employment. At the same time, the contractual safeguards unions have won for workers on less than full-time hours have gone far toward making contingent employment relationships more committed and responsible. These changes benefit older workers, among others, seeking employment in today's job market.

Unions are engaged in a quest to restructure contingent jobs so that they pay decent wages and provide employees with a range of benefits and protections while meeting the needs of workers who prefer flexible schedules. Consideration of the special needs of older workers should be added to other union concerns. Trade unions have a stake in the evolution of alternative job opportunities for older workers and would do well to take an active role in protecting the interests of these workers.

--------- 8 ---------

BUSINESS NECESSITY, BRIDGE JOBS, AND THE NONBUREAUCRATIC FIRM

Peter B. Doeringer and David G. Terkla

T HE LABOR MARKET FOR older workers has traditionally been
studied from the perspective of labor supply. The literature has
dealt mainly with retirement processes and the effect of retirement
incentives on individual decisions (chapter 2 above; Lazear 1986;
Fields and Mitchell 1984; Burkhauser 1979; Boskin 1977; Boskin and
Hurd 1984; Pellechio 1979; Rosen 1980; Barzel 1973).

This emphasis on the supply side of the labor market for older
workers is also reflected in the designs of programs to increase their
employability. Such programs have tended to concentrate on job
search, short-term "brush-up" training (usually for older female workers to renew clerical skills), and counseling and work orientation services. Few programs have been directed at restructuring employment
opportunities.

The main exceptions to this focus on supply have been a limited
number of experimental, private sector initiatives directed at flexible
retirement and work sharing (ICF 1988; American Association of
Retired Persons 1986). These programs, however, appear to be confined to a few large companies. Even though these companies report
business advantages resulting from their programs, discussions with
program executives suggest that concern with the well-being of their
older employees, rather than a compelling business need, was often
the initial stimulus for the programs.

A broader survey of large firms, however, indicates an emerging
trend toward job flexibility that is driven by business necessity (chapter

6 above). Yet preliminary evidence suggests that this new flexibility does not seem to be resulting in substantial increases in opportunities for stable bridge jobs among older workers.

The study discussed in this chapter supports these findings with respect to the limited potential for improving employment opportunities for older workers through job restructuring in large companies. We also find, however, that there are significant opportunities for expanding bridge jobs in small and medium-sized nonbureaucratic firms.

This study focuses on the structure of demand for older workers and on identifying those sectors of the labor market in which business necessity is likely to motivate the expansion of employment opportunities for older workers. It then examines the extent to which such business necessity results in changing employment practices that might enlarge the number of bridge jobs available to such workers.

Our major finding is that although business necessity is an important motivator for firms considering changes in their employment practices, small firms often find it easier than large firms to make their jobs more flexible. Small firms are less burdened by rigid job structures and are thus more quickly able to modify job opportunities to accommodate older workers seeking bridge jobs. Public sector initiatives have largely overlooked the substantial potential for hiring older workers in smaller firms and need to focus more on this neglected sector.

Retirement Bulge and Youth Squeeze Industries

There is some controversy over how the aging of the U.S. population will affect the work force. Some projections have indicated that the number of working persons in the 62-to-64 age class will increase by almost 8 percent by the year 2000 and by 48 percent between 2000 and 2010 (Cooper and Torrington 1981). Others argue that the trend toward early retirement will continue, thus holding constant the proportion of older persons in the work force and somewhat reducing the overall number of workers (Kahne 1985).

Even if the trend toward early retirement is reversed, particular industries will still feel the effects of the aging population on their labor pools because older workers are not evenly spread throughout all industries. Even though older workers (age 55 and above) constitute less than 14 percent of the nonagricultural work force (U.S.

Bureau of the Census 1987a), the proportion in different industries ranges from less than 9 percent in toy and sporting goods manufacturing to almost 27 percent in the household services industry. Similarly, the proportion of young workers ranges from less than 6 percent in the petroleum and primary metals industries to almost 40 percent in some retail trades, with a nationwide average of 20 percent.

Sectors that are most likely to come under increased labor market pressures to expand their employment of older workers are those with a "retirement bulge"—a large fraction of their current work forces reaching the customary retirement age during the next decade—and those facing a "youth squeeze" because they depend heavily on a contracting supply of younger workers.

Firms with a retirement bulge may be encouraged to adopt more flexible retirement practices and to redesign some jobs so that their experienced workers can be retained rather than retired. Similarly, firms experiencing a youth squeeze as the size of the pool of young labor entrants begins to shrink may seek older workers as a source of replacement labor.

Table 8.1 lists industries likely to be feeling pressures from retirement bulge, youth squeeze, or both. In the industries classified as facing retirement bulge, more than 15 percent of the work force (10 percent or more above the national average) consists of older workers. Likewise, workers aged 16 to 24 make up at least 22 percent of the work force of the youth squeeze industries. In general, youth squeeze industries are concentrated in the service sector of the economy, and retirement bulge industries are more heavily represented in older manufacturing industries.

Identifying those industries that are likely to experience substantial needs for replacement labor in the near future does not indicate anything, however, about the staffing practices of employers or the extent to which these practices are changing to create bridge jobs that would accommodate older workers as replacement labor. To explore how business staffing practices affect the employment opportunities for older workers, we conducted a case study of firms in retirement bulge and youth squeeze industries.

The Case Study

Our sample of employers is drawn from the Montachusett region of central Massachusetts, a relatively self-contained area about fifty miles northwest of Boston with a population of almost 190,000 and a labor

TABLE 8.1.   Retirement Bulge and Youth Squeeze Industries in the
United States

Industry	Percent of Work Force 55 and Older
Retirement bulge	
Fabricated metals	16.1
Nonelectrical machinery	16.2
Primary metals	16.5
Aircraft manufacturing	19.2
Transportation equipment (except motor vehicle and aircraft)	15.4
Apparel	15.1
Petroleum	22.7
Leather	23.0
Utilities and sanitation	15.7
Insurance and real estate	16.5
Household services	26.8
Personal services (barbers, shoe repair, etc.)	15.2
Social services	16.1
Public administration	15.8
National average	13.8
Youth squeeze	
Entertainment and recreation	38.8
Repair services	22.2
Household services	35.3
Retail	38.5
Furniture and fixtures	22.0
National average	20.0

Source: Current Population Survey, Public Use Sample, March 1987.

force of about 75,000. Montachusett was selected as a research site because the characteristics of its population and labor force roughly parallel those of the United States in age, education, labor force participation, and income (see table 8.2). It also has a large concentration of manufacturing industries facing retirement bulge pressures and a growing service sector encountering youth squeeze pressures.

Like their national counterparts, older workers in Montachusett are more frequently employed in part-time jobs, and those over 65 are much more likely to be employed part time. Eighty-four percent of Montachusett workers aged 55 to 60 worked full time (thirty-five or more hours per week) compared to around 80 percent nationwide. This proportion falls to 78 percent of those aged 60 to 65 and to 23

150   FLEXIBLE EMPLOYMENT

TABLE 8.2. Comparison of Social and Economic Characteristics among the Montachusett and U.S. Populations, 1980 (in percent)

Characteristic	Montachusett	United States
Age		
Under 18	27.9	27.1
18 to 64	60.7	61.3
Over 64	11.4	11.6
Education		
High school graduates	65.8	65.5
Labor force participation		
55+	35.0	33.0
55–64	62.0	56.0
66–70	16.6	18.5
Over 70	7.0	7.0
Income (1979)		
Median family	$19,677[a]	$19,917
Per capita	6,531	7,298

Source: U.S. Bureau of the Census, *U.S. Census of Population and Housing, 1980.*
[a]Calculated as a weighted average of the median family incomes for all eighteen towns in the Montachusett region.

percent for those aged 66 to 70 and then rises to 31 percent for those over 70. Nationally, the decline in full-time work among people over 65 is much less abrupt, with 45 percent of those aged 66 to 70 (and 35 percent of those over 70) who are working being employed full time.

National studies of the employment behavior of older workers indicate that the nature of their jobs changes substantially as they move from career employment toward retirement. Many workers end their career jobs before retirement and take on bridge jobs, often in different industries and different occupations (chapter 2 and 5 above). The Montachusett economy appears to fit this pattern as well.

Full-time workers in Montachusett who are 55 to 60 years old tend to be concentrated in manufacturing (50 percent), services (16 percent), and wholesale and retail trade (9 percent). The high concentration in manufacturing reflects the industrial mix of the region. Within manufacturing, most older workers are employed in paper, plastics fabrication, furniture, nonelectrical machinery, professional equipment, and the fabricated metal industries. Within services, around 50 percent are employed in the health sector and another 30 percent in education or legal services.

This pattern continues to hold for full-time workers aged 61 to 65, with the percentage in services and trade increasing slightly and the percentage in manufacturing and the distribution of workers among industries within manufacturing remaining constant. After age 65, the percentage employed in manufacturing falls sharply to 24 percent; 41 percent of the workers within manufacturing are in the furniture industry, with the rest spread evenly among a number of different industries. The percentage in trade more than doubles to 28 percent and in services increases to 28 percent.

The pattern of part-time employment for older workers is somewhat different. Only 10 percent of those aged 55 to 60 work in manufacturing, but over 50 percent are employed in services, split evenly across the health, education, and personal and business sectors. Almost 18 percent are employed in the trade sector. Of those aged 61 to 65, 32 percent are employed in manufacturing, and the rest are evenly divided between trade and services. Furniture accounts for almost 30 percent of the part-time manufacturing jobs and paper and food processing almost 20 percent each, with the rest spread evenly among plastics, nonelectrical machinery, and electrical machinery. Employment in manufacturing drops off again for those over 65, accounting for 14 percent of part-time jobs, with trade accounting for 25 percent and services almost half of total employment.

Thus for both full-time and part-time workers, most bridge jobs seem to be concentrated in the service sector even though most workers' career jobs were in manufacturing. The only exception is the furniture industry, which employs substantial numbers of older workers. It is not possible to determine from the data whether these workers have always been in the furniture sector or whether some of them are in bridge jobs leading to retirement.

Identifying Sectors Characterized
by Business Necessity

To obtain a clear-cut set of case studies of employers, we used more stringent criteria than those applied nationally to determine retirement bulge and youth squeeze industries in the region. We chose a cutoff point for inclusion in our retirement bulge group at industries having 20 percent or more of their work force over age 55. This criterion was used because it is 20 percent above the proportion of older workers in Montachusett's employed population. Likewise, industries in which at least 28 percent of the work force consists of people aged 16 to 25 are classified as facing a youth squeeze. This fraction is 20 percent larger than the proportion of 16- to 25-year-olds in the Montachusett labor force.

RETIREMENT BULGE INDUSTRIES

Our analysis of the age distributions in different industries reveals that those most likely to be suffering from retirement bulge pressures are several manufacturing industries—furniture, fabricated metals, nonelectrical machinery industries (such as engines and turbines and metalworking), paper, and apparel—utilities, and household and personal services (see table 8.3). Except for furniture and paper, all these manufacturing industries are classified as retirement bulge industries nationally, as are utility and service industries.

Because the utility sector was so small and the service industries composed largely of proprietorships, we focused our interview efforts on manufacturing. The manufacturing firms facing retirement bulge pressures cover a wide spectrum. Many have had declining employment over the last fifteen years, but some have seen considerable employment growth. Some have highly skilled work forces and generous pay scales and benefits; others offer minimal benefits and poor wages. Some have largely male work forces, while others have more of a mix of male and female workers, and still others are made up predominantly of women. Some offer only full-time work options; others have many part-time and part-year workers.

YOUTH SQUEEZE INDUSTRIES

The industries identified as potentially facing the problem of a youth squeeze are several retail trade industries—eating and drinking establishments, grocery, clothing, hardware, department and variety stores, and lumber outlets—and several manufacturing industries—miscellaneous plastics, miscellaneous pulp and paper products, office and accounting machinery in the nonelectrical machinery sector, and furniture (see table 8.3). Furniture is particularly interesting because it is also classified as a retirement bulge industry.

The manufacturing industries facing youth squeeze pressures offer below-average wages and employ a largely unskilled work force. With the exception of the furniture industry, very few offer much part-time employment. In contrast, the retail establishments offer mostly

TABLE 8.3.   Retirement Bulge and Youth Squeeze Industries in
Montachusett

Industry	Percent of Work Force Aged 55 and Over
Retirement bulge	
Nonelectrical machinery (except high technology)	25.2
Fabricated metals	21.7
Paper	27.0
Furniture	26.0
Apparel	26.7
Utilities	20.0
Household and personal services	20.0
Average	16.7
Youth squeeze	
Retail	42.9
Lumber and hardware	35.7
Department and variety	36.4
Grocery stores	53.9
Apparel and shoes	50.0
Eating and drinking	49.7
Plastics	33.8
Miscellaneous pulp and paper products	29.2
Office and accounting machinery	52.6
Furniture	28.0
Average	23.3

part-time jobs, although the wages are often close to the minimum and allow little room for advancement.

A Glimpse into Workplace Employment Practices

To determine how these key industries were responding to emerging labor market pressures, as well as to assess employers' overall perception of the labor market for older workers, we conducted interviews with almost sixty firms in the Montachusett region. The survey included almost all manufacturing firms with eighty or more employees, a sample of smaller manufacturing firms, and a sample of youth squeeze and retirement bulge firms in the retail and service sectors. The interviews were open-ended to enable us to probe the

TABLE 8.4. Size, Union Classification, and Retirement Program Status of Montachusett Firms Interviewed

Number of Employees	Firms Interviewed	Unionized	Formal Retirement Programs
7,500	6	3	4
200–500	6	3	1
100–200	10	5	0
50–100	11	1	0
Less than 50	25	0	0
Total	58	12	5

perceptions and practices of these firms as they affected older workers (see appendix for an outline of the interview questions). Table 8.4 shows the size breakdown of the firms interviewed, their union status, and whether formal retirement programs were in place.

RESPONSES OF EMPLOYERS IN RETIREMENT BULGE INDUSTRIES

Although many firms were aware of the retirement bulge in their labor forces, most had not experienced critical labor scarcities resulting from mass retirements. For many firms in mature industries, the combination of long-term and cyclical economic decline substantially reduced their need for replacement labor. Some firms had felt labor scarcities briefly in 1980, but these disappeared in the subsequent recession. Other firms were still contracting at the time of our interviews and were using retirement as the means of reducing staff.

A second set of firms had begun to insulate themselves from retirement bulge problems by using older workers to train and upgrade younger employees. Some of these firms were also seeking to secure greater flexibility in the deployment of their workers to alleviate replacement problems in job classifications or departments where pending retirements were concentrated. In some cases, the use of older workers as trainers and greater flexibility in job assignments required negotiating concessions with unions.

Some firms solved their retirement bulge problems by bidding away skilled workers from other industries. These were generally higher-wage firms in nonelectrical machinery, paper, and fabricated metal industries that were able to draw labor from low-wage furniture firms and plastic fabricating firms. The latter firms regularly served as labor supply reservoirs for these higher-paying companies.

Lower-wage firms facing a retirement bulge (furniture, apparel, and the retail establishments) often encouraged older employees to remain at work as a business strategy and typically offered their employees fewer pension incentives for retirement. The clearest example of the continued employment of retirement-age workers in low-wage companies was the furniture industry, which had the highest concentration of workers over 65 among manufacturing industries.

Many of these firms in the furniture industry also had relatively flexible production processes, which resulted in the availability of more part-time jobs than in the higher-wage firms. Although these jobs were staffed by people of all ages, almost all of their workers over age 65 were part-timers. Employers indicated that these workers could work full time but preferred part-time work.

These findings about the availability of temporary or part-time jobs for older workers were confirmed by interviews with temporary help firms. These firms identified a pool of older, predominantly male clients who were easily placed in temporary positions in the local machine or fabricated metal shops. Most of their male clients preferred occasional work to full-time jobs.

Responses of Employers in Youth Squeeze Industries

Employers in youth squeeze industries frequently complained about the difficulty in finding labor for entry-level jobs, and many employers expressed dissatisfaction with the work habits and skill levels of local vocational school graduates. Employers complained of the unstable work histories, high turnover, and frequent absences of their newly hired younger workers. They thought this trend began five years ago and was increasing.

The complaints about the quality of younger workers were often framed as a problem of turnover—roughly two new hires were required to find one stable worker. It was felt that the higher-wage firms were skimming off the top-quality younger workers from the labor pool, leaving the lower-quality group for the low-paying jobs. Recently, these labor shortages had become serious enough that several plastics and furniture employers had been required to turn down orders because they were experiencing reduced production capabilities.

Employers in youth squeeze industries had a highly favorable impression of older workers. Most felt their older workers had better attendance records and were more conscientious on the job than their younger workers. Several managers of retail establishments felt that older workers were more patient in dealing with customers. These employers expressed definite preferences for hiring older workers. In youth squeeze industries such as furniture, which employed many older workers, the managers often hoped to hire older workers as substitutes for younger workers but felt that this labor reserve was limited largely by the work disincentives of Social Security.

Of all the firms we studied, retail establishments had most readily accommodated to youth squeeze pressures. All of them had large files of previous applicants from which to hire and had received many responses to newspaper advertisements and signs in their store windows. Most were already employing some older workers and generally believed their work habits and experience made them preferable to the average younger worker. Almost all indicated that they would like to hire more older workers but were uncertain how to recruit them. Most of these firms paid near the minimum wage, and only firms linked to national chains offered retirement benefits. The fast-food outlets offered wage premiums for part-time jobs during busy periods. None of the firms had been targeting their recruitment efforts toward older workers, nor were any conscious of the likely impact on their hiring pool of the aging of the local work force.

Another group of youth squeeze firms had not sought to adjust their staffing practices to replace younger workers with older ones. One set of such firms employed very few older workers and rarely considered them as a potential labor force. This lack of experience and contact with older workers inhibited their recruitment into such firms. Many of these firms had faced labor supply constraints, but they very seldom received applications from older workers and seldom had older workers referred to them by temporary agencies. They assumed that older persons looking for work wanted higher-paying jobs and better conditions than most of them offered.

Moreover, these same firms often had few part-time work opportunities that would be attractive to older workers. Some employers in the plastics industry indicated that they occasionally employed older workers on their part-time weekend shifts. But these employers were unwilling to introduce more part-time employment during the regular workweek, fearing that part-time workers would not be as attached to the job and that absenteeism would leave some shifts uncovered.

Lack of interest in jobs with these firms among older workers was substantiated in our interviews with temporary help agencies. Very few older people with low skills who were seeking relatively low-wage jobs came to them looking for work. These firms hoped to attract such workers because there was high demand for unskilled labor.

A second set of youth squeeze firms that did not seek to recruit among older workers failed to appreciate the demographic changes affecting their young labor supply. Part of the reason for their ignorance was that Massachusetts was experiencing a very low unemployment rate, and these employers attributed the shortage of younger workers to the many employment options available. They thus perceived their labor shortages as a short-run problem. The solutions they were pursuing involved drawing more extensively from recent immigrants to the region, mostly Puerto Ricans and Cambodians. In addition, attempts were being made in male-dominated industries to hire more women who were entering the labor market for the first time. Finally, many were trying to glamorize existing jobs to make them more attractive to higher-quality young workers and to compete with the higher-wage firms.

RETIREMENT STRATEGIES

When questioned about their policies regarding retirement and strategies for retaining older workers beyond the standard retirement age, none of the firms had any formal programs either to encourage or discourage retirement. Indeed, many firms indicated that most of their workers preferred full retirement because the work was arduous and the pay and pensions were high enough to provide a very comfortable retirement.

Most small and medium-sized firms, however, developed informal arrangements with individual employees. Such "customized" arrangements were not unique to retirement bulge firms in the area but were prevalent in almost all the small and medium-sized firms interviewed. Many firms employed a few workers in their late sixties and early seventies, and most employers wanted to keep these workers as long as they continued to be productive. Moreover, several firms attempted to keep in touch with their retirees through Christmas gifts and annual parties, and several convinced their retirees to return to work on short-term projects.

These findings are in sharp contrast to approaches to retirement found in the few large firms in the area that were part of much larger national corporations. These firms had formal programs designed to facilitate retirement, including providing retirement counseling and offering various "golden handshake" options.

SKILL OBSOLESCENCE

Our interviews also provided an opportunity to assess the extent to which skill obsolescence affected the employability of older workers. In particular, we interviewed several firms in which rapidly changing technology was altering skill requirements. We found that these firms made an important distinction between current older employees and older persons looking for work.

Employers seemed willing to retrain their own older employees but were reluctant to hire older workers who required training. Employers often expressed reservations about the ability of older workers trained by other firms to adapt to new machines. Displaced older workers and older job changers in Montachusett continue to face employment barriers at the workplace that have not been markedly reduced by retirement bulge pressures.

Labor Market Structure and the Older Worker

The interviews with employers provide an idea of how they have responded to the economic necessity of replacing skilled and experienced retirees and the increasing scarcity of younger workers. They also suggest a set of organizational and strategic features of the demand side of the labor market for the older workers that affects the employment prospects of this group. These aspects of the labor market structure have important implications for policy.

Internal Labor Markets

The clustering of older workers in certain jobs and industries arises largely from personnel practices designed to facilitate the development of human resources within the firm and to minimize the costs of labor turnover. Most employers in all sectors prefer to draw upon current employees, whose qualities and reliability are well known, for more skilled and responsible jobs rather than fill vacancies from the external labor market. These employers also rely on on-the-job training rather than formal schooling to teach their workers many of the skills and practices required in their particular businesses.

As a result, staffing practices such as limiting entry-level jobs to the least skilled positions, on-the-job training and promotion from within, and seniority-based job assignments and layoffs are common to most firms in the region, both union and nonunion. These practices result in internal labor markets that award the most skilled, highest-paying, and most secure jobs to older workers already employed in the firm.

The rules of seniority and promotion from within that tend to place older workers in the more secure and better paying jobs also act as barriers to the employment of displaced older workers from outside the firm. These internal labor market practices mean that new employees are confined to the least skilled and lowest-paying jobs and that there are strong organizational barriers to lateral transfers of skilled labor from employer to employer. Learning and employment are seen as long-term processes, and workers who can make long-term job commitments are generally favored over those who cannot. These considerations weigh far more heavily than skill or experience in the hiring decisions of many employers and inhibit the hiring of older workers who are retired or displaced from other companies into jobs of comparable skill and pay.

Because of these internal labor market barriers, older workers seeking alternative employment can rarely attain previous levels of pay and job security. Thus, except for those with highly transferable skills, older workers almost invariably face inferior job prospects when they leave their established jobs.

There is also a larger pattern to employers' staffing practices—rooted in the economics of workplace training, compensation, and job security—that constrains and channels employment opportunities for older workers. Our interviews suggest that because older employees tend to hold the better jobs in the economy and younger workers the less desirable jobs, internal labor markets may also affect employers' perception of what is an appropriate job in terms of skill, compensation, and duties to offer an older worker. They may also affect the older workers' perception of what is an appropriate job to accept, given their skills and previous experience (see chapter 9).

Low-Wage and Youth-Sector Jobs
for Older Workers

Older workers who seek alternative employment to their career jobs are often obliged to enter those low-wage sectors of the labor market that traditionally hire younger workers or those with little skill. These jobs not only tend to pay relatively lower wages, they often have more arduous or unpleasant job content and the poorest working conditions, are in the least attractive shifts, and have the least job security. Further affecting potential workers' decisions are the work disincentives of pension income.

Youth-sector and low-wage employers—retail trade, services, furniture, plastics, and apparel in Montachusett—provide easy access to jobs. Such employers rarely discriminate against older workers. They generally need labor badly because they serve as a feeder or labor pool for higher-paying and more selective firms. Although such jobs almost always pay less than the career jobs held by older workers, they represent the older workers' largest block of employment opportunities.

Apart from the drawbacks of low pay and poor working conditions, there are certain advantages for older workers in low-wage and youth-sector jobs. In those occupations that do not require the physical stamina of youth, high levels of formal education, or recent vocational preparation, older workers often have the stability that many employers in the youth sector favor. At a time when the supply of younger workers is contracting, this youth squeeze translates into growing demand for older workers as an alternative source of labor. Moreover, jobs in retail trade and services are often flexible with respect to part-time and part-year employment. Older workers, particularly females and those receiving pension and Social Security income, often prefer part-time or part-year work.

SKILLED ENTRY JOBS

In addition to jobs in low-wage industries, there is a second group of jobs—much less numerous but much better paying—for which older workers are also the preferred source of labor. In many of the firms surveyed (in industries such as machine tools and metal fabrication, for example) the combination of retirement pressures and fluctuating production requirements frequently created "spot" skill scarcities, typically involving short-term assignments in production work or in a training capacity. Because such jobs require skill and experience, and the need is urgent although of relatively short duration, employers place a greater premium on the rapid availability of productive workers than on availability for a long-term career.

These jobs, however, are unpredictable in their timing and uncertain in duration. They are not reliable as a major source of jobs for older workers and are best suited for those older workers who wish to supplement retirement income with part-time or part-year work.

Potential for Change through
Private and Public Initiatives

The preceding analysis focused on current business practices toward older workers. This section examines the extent to which these practices are likely to change through private sector initiatives or to be affected by current employment and training programs.

BUREAUCRATIC VERSUS FLEXIBLE
EMPLOYMENT PRACTICES

Perhaps the most significant distinction for policy uncovered by this study is the difference in workplace employment practices between bureaucratic and flexible firms. Almost all previous case studies and anecdotal evidence on how employment practices affected older workers came from large firms. Small firms, however, tend to employ a disproportionate number of older workers and to provide relatively fewer retirement incentives.

Nationally, workers aged 65 and over account for more than 3 percent of the total employment in firms with fewer than 100 employees and 2 percent of employment in firms with 100 to 499 workers, compared to only 1 percent of employment in firms with 500 or more workers. This differential is even more pronounced in nondurable manufacturing, where workers aged 65 and over account for more than 2 percent of total employment in firms with fewer than 500 workers but only 0.4 percent of employment in firms with over 500 employees (see chapter 3).

Large firms tend to have relatively rigid retirement policies and pension plans that often encourage permanent, and sometimes early, retirement. In unionized firms, these practices are embodied in collective bargaining agreements and informal practices that are enforceable through grievance procedures and arbitration. The union presence tends to strengthen already rigid job structures and seniority systems. Unions also tend to favor full-time over part-time jobs, thus sometimes reducing options for older workers to extend their retirement on a part-time basis.

Because these practices often have an important business rationale and are beneficial to employees as a group, they are difficult to change. This helps to explain why formal programs based on more flexible retention or reemployment of older workers have tended to arise in nonunion environments and why they are usually seen as experimental. Because these programs are experimental, and because they are usually operated in firms that continue to offer attractive retirement arrangements, most of them have attracted relatively few participants (Paul 1983).

This same pattern characterized the retirement policies of the large firms in Montachusett. Most had relatively rigid rules that favored retirement, strong pension incentives to retirement, and little business necessity that encouraged the retention of older workers.

In contrast, small and medium-sized firms demonstrated a far greater flexibility in providing bridge jobs that would accommodate the work and retirement preferences of older workers—a flexibility often motivated by business necessity. Corroborating evidence of such flexibility has also been found in small firms outside the Montachusett region (Gibbons and Perotta 1981).

These firms did not adopt formal programs, because there were few hard-and-fast personnel procedures that needed to be revised to permit flexibility. Most of these firms were either nonunion or had sufficiently good working relationships with their unions so that collective bargaining rules could be adjusted to accommodate flexible employment.

As with the larger companies, however, relatively small numbers of workers are involved in these extended work programs. Participation is often inhibited by the work disincentives of ample retirement earnings, pensions, and limitations on Social Security benefits. Only in low-wage and limited pension firms, such as in the furniture industry, do relatively large numbers of older workers continue to work beyond age 65.

Although flexible firms are more likely than bureaucratic firms to provide customized employment opportunities for older workers, large firms, particularly large retailing establishments and, increasingly, large banking and financial institutions, sometimes allow for staffing flexibility. There are indications, however, that flexibility in these large firms does not translate as readily into bridge jobs for older workers as it does in small and medium-sized firms (see chapter 6).

WORKPLACE PRACTICES AND THE JOB TRAINING PARTNERSHIP ACT

Further insights into how workplace practices affect older workers and the extent to which reforms in such practices can be stimulated by public policy can be found by looking at programs for older workers organized under the Job Partnership Training Act (JTPA). The JTPA provides an explicit set-aside of 3 percent of all employment and training funds to be devoted to programs for workers 55 or older. The principal restrictions on the use of these funds are that they must be targeted to poor persons and they cannot be used to provide stipends for program participants.

In Massachusetts, the JTPA programs for older workers have operated under a mandate to encourage strong employer involvement and to foster changes in employment practices. These programs are acknowledged to be among the most progressive of the JTPA efforts in the country (*Employment and Training Reporter* 1987). Their experience is, therefore, indicative of the potential for public policies to expand employment opportunities for older workers.

At the time of our field interviews, there was only one JTPA program for older workers operating in the Montachusett region. Programs operating elsewhere in Massachusetts, however, provided a broad enough range of experience to allow us to reach some tentative conclusions about the success of these public policy initiatives.

The Massachusetts programs have operated during a period of very low regional unemployment and widespread staffing difficulties for employers. This climate has encouraged employers to recruit older workers and has made it easier for older workers to find jobs. At the same time, employers see older persons as only one of many potential sources of workers, including youth, women, and immigrants. Changes in workplace practices may be required to accommodate the employment needs of some but not all of these groups. Most older workers could readily find employment but often only in entry jobs paying relatively low wages and in jobs that do not offer preferred work schedules.

The JTPA experience in Massachusetts has been shaped by this employment environment. One result has been that placement activities have dominated training efforts. The state agency responsible for JTPA programs for older workers estimates that between 80 and 90 percent of all grant funds have been devoted to job placement activities, sometimes coupled with employment counseling and work orientation services. Although some employers have provided training, preemployment classroom training has generally been difficult to design for older workers who have immediate needs for income and who can find work without further training. The job placements have paid in the range of $6.36 and $7.62 per hour. This is somewhat above the prevailing low-skilled entry wage in Massachusetts, but obtaining good-quality jobs for disadvantaged older workers has been an elusive goal.

Despite the emphasis on involving employers in the restructuring of job opportunities, most JTPA programs for older workers have provided services to clients rather than to employers. Programs were encouraged to secure hiring commitments from employers, but initially most could obtain only general endorsements of JTPA programmatic efforts and a willingness to consider "qualified" candidates. Although some older workers received training on their new jobs, there was generally little emphasis on training in the private sector workplace under JTPA auspices. Nor has there been much interaction between JTPA programs and subsidized jobs programs for older workers in the public sector.

In an attempt to focus JTPA resources for older workers on work-place adjustment, an Employer Challenge program was established in Massachusetts in 1986 requiring significant employer involvement as a condition for funding. The proposals submitted for challenge grants, however, further confirmed how difficult it is to secure advance commitments from employers to hire older workers or to restructure jobs, even in a tight labor market. In the words of one experienced program operator, "There is a lot of lip service among employers about becoming involved in older worker programs and making job pledges, but few companies really deliver."

Although JTPA programmatic incentives do not seem to result directly in the reorganization of workplace employment practices, there are some signs that a gradual process of educating employers about employment issues of older workers, backed by a strong element of business necessity, can lead to restructuring of employment. The most dramatic examples have occurred among smaller companies, similar to those in Montachusett, that began to hire older workers and then found that a few adjustments in employment practices could result in a much larger flow of productive older employees. One company, for example, reports that it successfully recruited a couple of older workers into hard-to-fill vacancies and within several months had developed a recruiting network that yielded a substantial group of newly hired persons over 55.

Similarly, a number of companies have participated in JTPA-sponsored business roundtables that promote changes in employment practices such as job sharing and flextime through peer-to-peer dialogues about what does and does not work when employing older workers. As employers became more familiar with the potential for employing older workers, job restructuring became more common (Commonwealth of Massachusetts 1987). The most noteworthy successes were in companies that had been experiencing substantial labor turnover, that had not hired older workers previously, and that were not so large as to have developed highly bureaucratic internal labor market arrangements that were difficult to amend.

The general impression that emerges from the JTPA experience is that flexible employment practices are more likely to be adopted because of business necessity than public policy. New options in bridge jobs for older workers are most likely to be introduced when flexibility is easy (as in smaller firms) or business necessity is most intense (as in low-wage service jobs). Among larger companies and those with higher-paying jobs, flexible employment opportunities for older workers appear to emerge much more slowly.

Reforming Employment and Training
Policies for Older Workers

The most significant contribution of this study is the insight it provides into the relationship between business necessity and workplace employment practices that help to explain differences in the job opportunities various firms provide for older workers. The findings of our interviews with employers have allowed us to demonstrate how the private sector approaches the labor market and how employers' decisions shape the employment prospects of older workers.

Montachusett appears to be a relatively flexible labor market for older workers. Our interviews indicate that many of those who wish to remain in the work force are able to stay in their current jobs and that options for part-time bridge jobs are widespread. The flexibility of the Montachusett economy in accommodating older workers is linked to the high concentration of traditional manufacturing industries but is best explained by the prevalence of small and medium-sized companies. This relationship between business structure and the performance of the labor market for older workers suggests that much of the detailed experience with bridge jobs for older workers in Montachusett has more general applicability.

Because they hold more skilled jobs, older workers represent an important productive and experienced resource to their employers. They are also an important element in the training process by which skills are passed on to younger generations of workers. In the companies studied, the skills and experience of the older workers were highly valued, as was their role in training their replacements in anticipation of retirement. As a result, many of the firms that had heavy concentrations of workers at or near retirement age exhibited a desire to find flexible ways to retain workers in bridge jobs beyond the usual retirement age to avoid a sudden depletion of skilled human resources.

Our findings suggest, however, that the potential for employment and training policy is severely constrained by company staffing practices and pension strategies. Public policies to change these practices have met with little success. Exceptions occur when a business need for restructuring employment practices has been identified and exploited. Business necessity will need to be the primary criterion for securing employers' involvement, and program design will need to be more directly driven by an awareness of employers' staffing needs. Some potentially fruitful policy directions suggested by these research findings are briefly summarized below.

CHANGING PERSONNEL PRACTICES

Efforts to encourage the more flexible use of older workers by providing bridge jobs in large companies are likely to be costly and unproductive, except when they are accompanied by a substantial increase in the business necessity to do so.

Although pressures toward greater staffing flexibility in large companies may lead to easier retention and reemployment of older workers, important obstacles are likely to remain (see chapter 6). The most important current obstacles are the bureaucratic personnel management practices that characterize many large businesses. These practices, however, have a compelling business logic. They are designed to move workers in a cost-efficient and administratively orderly way from relatively less-skilled entry jobs (usually filled by younger workers) into relatively higher-skilled, better-paying, secure jobs for more senior workers, and then into retirement. Generally, these rules are designed around the needs of full-time workers, reflecting the work norm in such companies.

For most large companies, such practices are highly satisfactory. These companies recruit workers who generally welcome such arrangements and see them as fair. The companies' positions in the labor market enable them to recruit entry labor easily, and they provide internal training so as to avoid skill scarcities. Many also provide senior workers with sufficient pension income to encourage complete and permanent retirement.

In unionized companies, many of these practices are part of collective bargaining agreements. To the extent that unions improve pension benefits, retirement incentives are further enhanced. Because changes in such rules must be negotiated, collective bargaining may further complicate the introduction of new employment and retirement arrangements.

For all these reasons, personnel practices in large firms are hard to change. Moreover, such firms have generally insulated themselves from the necessity of retaining older workers so that there is little or no cost advantage to more flexible retirement practices, particularly if they disrupt the economic prospects of younger workers. This helps to explain why most formal programs of flexible retirement or reemployment of older workers are often seen as experiments rather than as part of normal business practice.

Bridge Job Opportunities in
Small and Medium-sized Firms

Employment policies for older workers should focus much more on small and medium-sized firms in fashioning remedial programs and in trying to learn about informal "best practice" arrangements that can be extended to other companies.

Small and medium-sized firms have far fewer inhibitions about retaining and reemploying older workers than do many large businesses, and they often face a greater business necessity to do so. Such firms often lack the training capacity and business stability of larger companies and may have recruitment problems because they tend to pay lower salaries. As a result, they have incentives to rely on their older, more skilled workers and can make a variety of ad hoc arrangements to secure their services. At the same time, because such firms often have limited pension plans, their retirees often face economic incentives that encourage returning to work to meet the critical production needs of their companies.

Because small and medium-sized firms are less visible in local economies and can supply far fewer jobs per firm than larger businesses, their employment potential has often been overlooked. These businesses routinely need older workers, however, and often devise effective informal programs to obtain them.

Organizing Temporary Bridge Employment

More efforts should be made to organize older workers into temporary help pools to meet the growing need for high-quality, experienced, short-term workers.

Although most of the small and medium-sized companies studied have been able to develop arrangements to retain or reemploy their older workers, some were unable to meet short-term labor needs from their reserves of retired employees. Such companies had difficulty recruiting part-time skilled labor. Moreover, some large companies also expressed a need for a hiring pool of short-term workers.

These conditions suggest that in many local labor markets with a sufficient pool of skilled older workers interested in part-time work or part-year, full-time work, there may be a large enough group of employers needing such workers to establish some form of clearinghouse for these jobs and workers. In Montachusett, there seemed to be a niche for such a service in industries such as machinery and metalworking.

Such a service would be the skilled labor counterpart of temporary help agencies that refer clerical and unskilled workers to local businesses. Temporary help is being used increasingly throughout the Montachusett economy, as it is elsewhere, and such agencies have become interested in employing older workers to augment existing sources of labor. This experience suggests, more generally, that temporary help agencies may be a useful vehicle for organizing recruitment, training, and placement activities for older workers.

A second model for organizing short-term job opportunities in skilled occupations is the craft union. Although examining the job opportunities for older workers in craft unions was beyond the scope of our study, the craft union labor referral system in the building trades is a good example of a labor market institution that successfully organizes intermittent skilled work.

LOW-WAGE AND SHORT-DURATION BRIDGE JOBS

Employment programs for older workers are most likely to place workers in jobs that routinely employ younger workers—retail trade and low-wage manufacturing.

Although bridge jobs at high pay are likely to be limited to somewhat specialized employment niches in nonbureaucratic firms, placement opportunities are readily available in youth squeeze industries and in declining industries for which the expected duration of employment may be limited. These firms rarely provide high-paying or high-status employment opportunities, but they often are desperate for labor and are willing to accommodate the flexible work schedules that older workers prefer. Thus jobs in these industries offer an accessible work option, particularly for those older workers seeking to augment pension income with part-time employment.

Moreover, firms in these industries are often willing to work with government programs to customize training and recruitment activities to meet their own needs. Many of these firms, however, have little experience with recruiting older workers, and there is an opportunity to develop recruitment and placement programs that concentrate on bringing such jobs to the attention of older workers.

We also found that these firms are often unfamiliar with the supportive services and variety of flexible employment arrangements that would increase their supply of older workers. These firms could benefit from assistance in modifying pension arrangements and health plans to accommodate later retirement and in counseling older employees in the various ways that work and retirement can be intermingled.

Appendix to Chapter 8:
Interview Guidelines

We conducted open-ended interviews with management officials in about sixty firms, following the guidelines outlined below. We began each interview with a general discussion of the business and its labor problems and followed with a flexible sequence of questions that allowed us to follow up on interesting points as they arose during the discussion. The most important aspects of this interview technique are that it prevents the interview from taking on a very narrow focus because of the interviewer's preconceptions, and it permits midcourse corrections in the flow of the interview.

   I. Describe your business and product
      a. Type of product, technology, future demand
      b. Size of business, number of employees, types of skills
      c. Type of business ownership
  II. Performance over last business cycle
      a. Pattern of layoffs and hiring
      b. Sources of labor
 III. Perception of quality of labor force
      a. Skills, attitudes, work ethic, etc.
      b. Shortages of labor in general or for any key jobs
      c. Retraining programs
      d. Perception of older employees and older workers in general labor market
      e. Special problems or strengths of older workers
  IV. Entry-level wages and jobs
      a. Job ladders and pay scales
      b. Comparison with other firms in the area
      c. Types of part-time employment

    d. Areas of part-time employment

    e. Changes in part-time employment over time

    f. Skill, training, and education requirements for entry and part-time jobs

V.   Recruiting policies

    a. Change in last ten to fifteen years

    b. Successes and problems with older workers

VI.   Characterize age profile of work force

    a. If retirement bulge, does skewed profile concern you?

    b. If youth squeeze, discuss demographic projections and determine what plans or forecasts interviewee has made

    c. Strategies considered or implemented

    d. Evaluation of effect of any internal policy changes

VII.   Perceptions of older work force

VIII.   Internal policies toward older workers

    a. Describe retirement options

    b. Other explicit incentives

    c. Try to draw out unanticipated implicit incentives

IX.   Experience with special arrangements to recruit, retain, or flexibly employ older workers

    a. Types of programs

    b. Successes, failures, and their causes

    c. How extensively used

    d. What has been the experience of other employers in your industry and labor market area?

X.   Familiarity with local employment and training programs for older workers

    a. Do you know of special programs for older workers in your area?

    b. What is their reputation?

    c. Do you have any direct experience with these programs?

    d. Under what circumstances would you use these programs?

XI.   Constraints on expanding employment of older workers

    a. What problems do you foresee in increasing the employment of older workers?

    b. Are there special problems of
       training
       attendance

        health
        legal barriers
        insurance or pension issues
        other costs

c. Would any of these options be attractive or difficult for your firm:
        part-time or part-year jobs
        temporary employment
        job sharing
        flexible retirement
        other options (to be described)

PART III

Voices of Older Workers

9

BRIDGES OVER TROUBLED WATER: HOW OLDER WORKERS VIEW THE LABOR MARKET

Kathleen Christensen

I‍T IS COMMONLY BELIEVED that if older Americans are to work after retirement, they will want and need flexible employment opportunities. The evidence for this assumption is rooted in a number of sources. When queried directly by national pollsters, more than 75 percent of workers aged 55 to 64 years stated that they wanted to work part time after retirement (Louis Harris and Associates 1981). Union retirees, as well as older employees of IBM and Travelers, echoed these findings, indicating that they preferred reduced workweeks (Charner et al. 1988; Marquardt and Gold 1981; Kraut 1987). National statistics seem to support this view by showing that the demand for jobs that can serve as bridges to retirement is growing as career jobs end earlier (see chapter 5).

The supply of flexible jobs appears to be increasing as employers search for greater flexibility in their staffing arrangements (see chapters 6 and 8) and as some firms implement flexible retirement programs. Staffing flexibility has been driven by employers' desire to expand, contract, or redeploy staff without incurring massive expansions or layoffs; management wants the elasticity of a just-in-time work force that parallels just-in-time inventories (Plewes 1988). Flexible retirement programs have been implemented by firms such as Polaroid, which allows older workers to rehearse their retirement, and The Travelers Companies, which encourages its retirees to "unretire" and

work in the company's internal temporary pool. Unions have supported these programs only insofar as they are convinced that their
members, including older workers, are not penalized by flexible scheduling arrangements (see chapter 7). From the perspectives of employers and unions, therefore, the demand and supply for flexible job
options seems on the surface to be balancing well. But what about the
worker's perspective?

Evidence from earlier chapters is somewhat pessimistic on this
point. Despite the impression created by the well-known experiences
of firms such as Polaroid and Travelers, national figures indicate that
flexible employment among older workers remains small and that in
some areas, such as part-year employment, it is shrinking (see chapter
3). Furthermore, even if firms continue to offer opportunities for
part-time, temporary, or contract work, older workers face intense
competition from younger workers, specifically mothers and teenagers, for these jobs (see chapter 6). And finally, typical bridges to
retirement entail lower pay and status than career jobs (see chapter
5). This evidence points to the need for a better understanding of
how older workers view their opportunities in the labor market.

This chapter addresses the workers' perspective by examining three
questions: (1) what are older workers looking for in the labor market;
(2) how do the jobs they obtain match their needs and expectations;
and (3) what do they regard as the key issues that should form the
basis of future policy? Answers to these questions will shed light on
the meaning of bridge jobs to older workers. For example, what are
the reactions of older workers to the changes in status characteristic
of most bridge jobs, and are workers voluntarily or involuntarily making those changes?

Focus on Flexibility

Most surveys of older Americans reveal an overwhelming preference
for flexible employment as the way to bridge career jobs and full
retirement. This chapter looks specifically at flexible bridge jobs. Yet
the notion of flexibility should be defined carefully. It has become
clear throughout my research that the meanings of, as well as the
opportunities for, flexible employment for older workers vary widely.
For some, flexibility comes in the form of highly desired, reliable,
dependable part-time or part-year employment with flexible hours;
for others, it has resulted in their marginalization in the work force
as self-employed, temporary, or off-the-books workers who have little
or no job security and limited income reliability. The essential meaning

of flexibility is best captured in what it is not: flexible arrangements are not full time or full year.

Four typical categories of flexible bridge jobs emerged from my research. They are part time; self-employment, including contract work; temporary; and off-the-books work. A fifth category made up of unemployed older workers who are actively seeking work is also included because their experiences provide insight into the possible failure of the labor market to respond to the needs of older workers. I selected these categories because they illustrate the different work patterns that older workers follow in making the eventual transition into retirement. The five categories are defined as follows.

Regular part-time employment: These workers are on their companies' payrolls and are assured of relatively stable, reliable work.

Self-employment: For tax purposes, these workers are self-employed as sole proprietors, sometimes working under independent contracting arrangements. Although self-employment figures typically include incorporated businesses and limited partnerships, none of the people interviewed for this study fell into those groups.

Temporary work: Some of these workers are hired through the temporary industry and are considered employees of that agency. Others receive assignments from a booking service or the firm itself but for tax reasons are listed as self-employed.

Off-the-books work: These workers generally work part time for one employer but are paid off the books and do not report their income for tax purposes. Off-the-books employment is treated as a separate category for several reasons. First, these arrangements are not included in the federal government's figures on employment and income among older workers, indicating that there is an official underreporting of employment and income and thereby preventing a full picture of bridge jobs. Second, off-the-books labor provides further evidence of the irregularity and lack of permanence of employment in the bridge market and needs to be understood on its own terms. Third, it appears that off-the-books jobs are often created at the initiative of the older worker rather than of the market, representing a different mechanism for employment.

Unemployed: These workers meet the federal definition of unemployed insofar as none are gainfully employed and all are actively seeking employment.

Another group of workers was not identified in this study: discouraged older workers, who would take a job if one became available but who, for a variety of reasons, found work to be unavailable and so dropped out of the search. Andrew Sum of Northeastern University estimates that discouraged older workers constitute anywhere from 2 to 15 percent of older Americans (Sum 1988a, b).

The research from which these categories emerged was conducted in the New York City and Philadelphia metropolitan areas in the fall of 1987.

Data Base and Methodology

Although national labor statistics provide an important overview of general employment trends, they cannot, by their very nature, shed much light on the specific motivations, attitudes, or experiences of older workers seeking flexible jobs between their career work and retirement. Such information is best provided by in-depth, focused interviews, the principles of which were originally laid out by Robert Merton et al. (1956). These interviews can be conducted either in group or individual formats. The group interview, often referred to as a focus group, allows for shared meanings and experiences to emerge, while the individual interview provides much greater detail regarding particular life histories. For this study, two groups of ten individuals each were interviewed using the group format, and twenty-six were interviewed in the individual format. (See appendix for further description of the methodology.)

The focus groups and interviews examined the following aspects of the older workers' experiences and attitudes: individual work histories, satisfaction with current job or job last held, meaning of a job, meaning of not having a job, satisfaction with range of job opportunities, and the virtues older workers bring to the workplace.

The sample of older workers interviewed for the study was not designed to be representative of all older workers. It was drawn to be illustrative of the five categories of work situations in which older Americans find themselves: part time, temporary, self-employed, off-the-books work, and unemployment. The participants also had to meet several selection criteria regarding age, household income, and current employment status. All participants had to be between 55 and 80, although most were between 65 and 75 years of age, since that age band conforms to the general conception of postretirement ages. No one could earn more than $25,000 annually so as to focus on workers who are most desirous and in need of finding bridge jobs to retirement. Individuals with incomes above $25,000 would have more resources upon which to draw if the job market did not function efficiently for them.

In this study, there were nineteen self-employed workers, sixteen who worked on temporary or part-time bases, and eleven who were unemployed. Employed workers were likely to be white, and those unemployed were more likely to be black or Hispanic, which appears to parallel recent national trends (see chapter 3). The career jobs of these employed and unemployed workers cut across a variety of occupations but were most likely to have been in skilled or unskilled positions that did not require college education. The earnings cap of $25,000 precluded workers with professional or executive backgrounds from the survey.

The focused interviews provide a basis for assessing the employment conditions under which many older Americans work and for laying out some general propositions regarding how older Americans experience their current opportunities in the labor market.

Older Workers' Experiences with Flexible Bridge Jobs

In this analysis I rely on the actual experiences and perceptions of selected older Americans to illustrate both their employment arrangements and their broader notions about work in America.

Regular Part-Time Employment

Despite repeated calls for part-time employment for older workers (National Commission for Employment Policy 1985; National Alliance of Business 1985; American Association of Retired Persons 1986), my study indicates that the true picture of part-time employment among older workers is less sanguine than it appears. Older workers report that opportunities for reliable, financially satisfying part-time work that is congruent with their career jobs are rare. When they do occur they are often the result of an older worker phasing into retirement on a reduced work load with the old employer. The experiences of Marie and Janet are illustrative of this reality. (To ensure anonymity, names and some characteristics of the workers have been changed.)

Marie. Marie has lived in upper Manhattan in the same building for the last thirty-five years. She has been a widow for the last twelve years and has one grown daughter who also lives in Manhattan. She was married for thirty-one years before her husband died.

Like many women of her generation, Marie went into clerical office work and then retail sales after graduating from high school. When her daughter was younger, Marie worked sporadically for Lord and

Taylor as a salesclerk, usually at holiday time. As her daughter got older, she started working through temporary agencies and did that for the next thirteen years. She was a full-time temporary from September to June.

Temporary work provided her with the jobs she wanted. "I wanted to try office work. I didn't care to do typing or bookkeeping. I wanted diversified work, and somebody advised me to go into temporary work, so I started with an agency. I found it so stimulating, but of course the salary was very low."

She finally decided to get a permanent job because "I realized that I wasn't getting any health benefits. All right, I had my husband, and I was being covered through him; but I wanted to protect myself." Marie found a permanent full-time job with a small Manhattan jewelry business, and she stayed there for about three years. She was laid off and got her second job with a midtown jeweler through a neighbor in her building. The job appealed to her because it provided health benefits and a small profit-sharing plan, even though there was no pension. She stayed with that firm for over fifteen years. "I wasn't making big money because they didn't pay big salaries, but the surroundings were so wonderful and comfortable, and I was my own boss. Nobody bossed me around. And the people were so nice. That was what really kept me there for such a long time." Three years ago, when she was 65, her firm moved to a New Jersey suburb. Rather than quit altogether, she decided to work part time for the business.

For the last three years, she has commuted by bus and works about twenty hours a week pricing gold. She goes in whenever the business needs her, and she is paid on an hourly basis, making about $4 an hour. Her work is on the books, and she is paid by check, making about $4,000 to $5,000 a year. Although her job is not as diversified as it once was, she continues to like it.

Part of the attraction of her job is that it gives her something to do. "I like being occupied. I'm not one to sit around and brood. I mean, I don't want to complain to anybody. Some people could sit and talk about their problems all day, but not me. I'd rather work." If her employer no longer needed her, she would job hunt by working for a temporary agency. "I'd have to look for something else because I couldn't wait around depending on someone else to do something for me. I would look on my own because I'm not ashamed of that. I'm not afraid of that." She would like to continue working. "As long as I can work a few times a week, I'll keep going."

Marie sees several unique virtues of older workers. "Seniors are more reliable. Those who want to work feel proud that they can go on working. They're anxious to work. The younger ones have no patience. A lot of them don't have that much interest in their work." She attributes part of her attitude to her age. "We were glad to have a job years ago because it was the Depression. But today's young people take jobs for granted, and they don't put their whole heart into their work."

Marie receives about $650 a month from Social Security and gets no pension. Her profit-sharing option with the firm terminated when she went part time. She also no longer receives health coverage from her employer. She now pays about $600 a year for Blue Cross/Blue Shield and Medicare coverage, and she also pays $160 a year for a membership in a health maintenance organization. She needs the money she earns at her job, particularly since the recent increases in Social Security have been small.

Janet. "I live in Brooklyn. And I lost my husband two years ago. I have worked at the same small manufacturing company for the last twenty-eight years. I retired at age 65 in 1986, but they rehired me right back to work part time in the supply department. I now work three days a week for about twenty-five hours. I enjoy it. I have many friends there."

Before Janet retired, she usually worked the evening shift from about 3:00 P.M., largely because she did not want to be at home. "To be honest about it, I would say that my job was more or less my home."

After her husband died, she decided to retire because she no longer wanted to work nights. "The only way I could see getting out of my department was to retire. I had a beautiful boss who understood. And I said, 'I'm going to retire,' but I knew I'd be hired right back to work part time." She earns about $6 an hour compared to the $10 an hour she earned before she retired. Because of the Social Security earnings test, which places a limit of $8,160 on what she can earn before she has to pay back some of her Social Security check, Janet has refused pay increases. "I can't take any more money. My boss tried to give me more money, but I turned him down, because I didn't want to mess up my Social Security." Instead, Janet bargained for more flexibility in her schedule. "When I want a day off, I take it. Sometimes I go in an hour later or I leave an hour earlier." Janet's supervisor willingly accepts this arrangement because he values her skills and regrets that she cannot or will not take a pay increase.

Although Janet worked in the production end of the business for most of her career at the firm, she now is responsible for maintaining the firm's inventory. "I do all the ordering of the supplies. It's a lot of paperwork." She continues because she likes the people with whom she works. "I consider myself pretty sociable and friendly, and thank God, up to now, I have a pretty good memory for the names of all the people. Basically, I enjoy the people I work with. And I enjoy doing the job."

The alternative of staying at home does not appeal to her. "I'd get disgusted at home if I didn't have anything to do. I already find the evenings a little rough. I'm getting too attached to the boob tube." She is also concerned about the effect of staying at home on her weight. "I'm always on a diet, it seems, but when you're in the house you keep running to the refrigerator." Even though Janet prefers working, she is now considering full retirement so she can move to Florida to be closer to her nephew and his family. Yet she feels some trepidation about this idea. Before she completely gives up her work, she would like to take an unpaid leave of absence to see how she likes living in Florida.

Janet feels she has been lucky to be able to work on a part-time basis after her first retirement. "I know so many people in my age group who say to me, 'Oh, how I wish I could work three days a week like you.' "

Marie's and Janet's experiences illustrate a trend that emerged from the focused interviews: older workers who worked part time on a regular basis were more likely to have converted to a part-time arrangement from their full-time positions with the same employer than to have been hired from outside the firm on a part-time basis. In other words, these were not people who went out in their sixties or seventies and were able to find satisfying part-time work. This picture does not mesh with the public image of companies actively recruiting older workers.

Much of this public image is premised on the experience or efforts of a few large corporations such as McDonald's or Travelers that are very receptive to hiring older workers. Although their efforts are worth acknowledging, they are limited in terms of the general public's experiences. In fact, Marie believes that if she lost her job and had to go looking, there would be few part-time jobs available to her. If she had to go out on the market, she would try to find a job through temporary agencies; but as the case studies later in the chapter indicate, that may not be a successful strategy. Both Marie and Janet feel grateful for the opportunity to continue working on a reduced work load because they feel it has made their lives more enjoyable. Neither of them is interested in full-time employment.

THE SELF-EMPLOYED

The self-employed in this study typically wanted to maintain an active involvement in their career work but had no opportunity to do so on a regular part-time basis with their previous employers or other employers in the same industry. Most, like the two examples here, made the switch to self-employment because of the lack of adequate job opportunities. A few of the older self-employed had always been self-employed, so their arrangement in their older years was simply an extension of their prior work experiences.

Jean. Jean is a 68-year-old woman from the Northwest, the daughter of a doctor. She was raised as a Mormon but converted to Episcopalianism as an adult and became a nun. In her mid-forties, she left the order, earned a master's degree in teaching, and taught remedial reading for five years in Harlem. "That got just a little too much for me as I got older, so I stopped and got a job in publishing."

Someone from an employment agency had encouraged her to enter publishing, and she was hired by a friend who had become vice-president of a small New York City publishing company. About five years ago, the firm moved out of town and Jean decided to do free-lance editing out of her home.

Her age and eligibility for Social Security influenced her decision. "I was at retirement age, so I knew that I could at least have my Social Security as a backup to pay bills." And she was confident that her old firm would give her jobs because it was in some disarray after the move and needed stable, reliable help.

In many ways she is grateful for being forced out on her own. "I've only had one experience in a corporation, but I didn't like it. There was so much wasted time and so many attitudes that I found hard to take. I didn't like the gossiping and backbiting. It was so dehumanizing. I really don't think that the corporation that I was with was worse than any other. It was just average. Now I really like just being my own boss. I feel very free where I am. I just love to get up in the morning and create my day and organize it in my own way. It's such a luxury."

She has been her own boss, setting her own pace, for the last five years. She works year-round about twenty hours a week, and most of her work comes from word-of-mouth. She is paid by the hour, which is usually $15 an hour, sometimes $20 for a very specialized job. She receives $401 a month from Social Security, and she pays for a supplemental health plan that costs her about $500 a year.

She feels that the Social Security earnings test strongly affects her decision to earn. "I might say that it dictates my thinking, particularly since I have gone over it once or twice. In fact, one time I got into a lot of trouble because I didn't realize that I was going over, and they penalized me $395. I pleaded my case and got out of the penalty. My accountant thought that my self-employment form was sufficient and didn't realize that a second form had to go in to Social Security. As a result, I don't seek out work, and that is certainly dictated by the fact that if I took more I would only be getting paid half. Of course, that is a consideration to me."

She can get by on her free-lancing and her Social Security check, but she receives no pension. "When I taught in the New York public schools I paid into a pension, but I never became eligible for it because I didn't teach long enough. After going to work for the publishing firm, I withdrew my money from the pension fund because it was only getting me 4 1/2 percent interest, and at that time I could get 15 percent from other investments. You might call that money enforced savings. But I have no pension because the years that I worked haven't been continuous."

She says that as she gets older her primary consideration is time. "I'd just rather have the time than the money."

She does volunteer work in a hospital, reads, and loves to listen to good music. "I usually go on one big bang-up trip at least every two years and take smaller trips in between. I go to Europe mostly, and I love music. I spend a lot of money on the opera and concerts during the season. But other than that, I don't need a lot of money. I live simply, and I just don't feel any anxiety at all."

Michael. Michael is a 65-year-old man from Queens who has been married for thirty-one years. He has a 30-year-old daughter who lives in New Jersey and an 18-year-old son who lives with him. He sent his children to parochial schools and wants his son to go to college if he can get a scholarship.

Michael is a high school graduate. For over twenty years he worked for the federal government as a customs officer at the airport. For the last nine of those years, he moonlighted as a driver for car dealerships and individuals who needed to have their cars picked up or delivered.

He fell into this line of work accidentally. "Someone asked me years ago, as a favor, if I could help him out. He needed someone to drive a car for him. I said, 'Do you have plates for this other car?' And he said he'd give me a set of plates, and that's what started it going. By word-of-mouth and meeting different dealers here and there, I started driving cars. Certain people got to know me. They want their cars only handled by Michael Vincenti, and I do it because in all the years that I've been doing this, I've never had an accident."

He had to retire early from the federal government, about ten years ago, because of a bad back. Although he has had two heart attacks since he retired, he has continued to drive cars, on his own terms. "Winters I hardly do anything. I won't drive on those roads with ice and snow. I don't want to take any chances with these cars because I'm liable for them." After two heart attacks, he also wants to slow down. "I don't push myself. I take it easy. As long as I make what I figure I should make, that's fine with me. When you're dead, you're dead a long time. I've got a nice family. I've got two kids, and I want to enjoy them."

When Michael does work, he makes two to three local trips or one out-of-town trip a day. The paid work may be only four hours in a day, but he has to get back home, which may be an additional four unpaid hours. The fee is by the job and is fairly well set: $125 to Boston, $30 to $40 to Brooklyn. He has to pay his own gas and transportation back so he tries to arrange to drive another car back for a fee. His profit from a $75 trip is about $50.

He says it sounds as though he makes a lot of money, but he tries not to push himself. There are no ladders to climb or hills to get to the top of, and he says he has to accept that.

He likes being self-employed because he is his own boss, but he adds that if he did not have his pension to rely on, this would not be a good job. The irregularity of the work bothers him. Sometimes he does not know when he will have a job to do, when he will get back from it, and how he will get home. Often he buys old clunkers to drive back from a job. "There are some places that are really unbelievable, where you have no trains or buses to get out of that town." Buying an old car is the only way he can get home.

On the whole, Michael feels he has been treated very well by the dealerships and has had very little difficulty. Yet there are aspects of his self-employment that he does not like. "I have to keep my own records, and the taxes kill me. There's no employer who is contributing anything at all to my taxes. If I had an employer, then I wouldn't need to keep records, and I would only have to contribute maybe 7 percent or 8 percent to my Social Security. But this way I've got to contribute almost 14 percent." And there are many expenses. "Every single day, I lay out money for tolls, gas, trains, or buses. Sometimes I'll spend $30, $40, $50, $60 for expenses in one day. If I have to fly back, it really gets expensive. I remember when I used to pay $11 for a flight from Boston and they used to give me a cup of coffee with it; now they want $79 or $99 for the same trip." He also pays about $1,300 a year for insurance. Overall, Michael earns $25,000 a year driving cars plus his pension, and his wife makes about $1,200 a year. He has not yet filed for his Social Security benefits because of the earnings test and the limits it places on his earnings. "I don't want any Social Security. It doesn't work to my advantage."

Michael intends to keep working because of financial need and the desire to keep active. "I'm still a workingman no matter what. I'm still part of the proletariat." For Michael, working provides self-esteem and a clear sense of identity.

For both Jean and Michael, self-employment was one of the few options they saw available as a way to bridge their career work and their retirement. For Jean, self-employment was a way to continue to work in publishing after her firm moved out of the city. Unexpectedly, she discovered that self-employment has provided her with a work-style that has been more conducive to her personality and lifestyle than working for a large firm had been. Expectedly, because of her work history, she has needed to work after retirement. Like 80 percent of today's women over 65, she has no pension.

For Michael, self-employment grew out of a moonlighting job he had while he was employed by the government. Unlike Jean, however, self-employment represents a mixed blessing for him. He likes the autonomy but dislikes the increased paperwork and expenses.

It must be stressed that both Jean and Michael possess skills that are in demand in the marketplace. Without those skills or a sense of self-confidence in them, self-employment represents a high-risk, low-gain work arrangement.

Perhaps it is because of the potential insecurity that the rate of self-employment among older workers has been dropping over the last several decades (see chapter 3). The decline in self-employment rates may also be partially tied to the growth of the temporary industry. Older workers, particularly women doing clerical work, can avoid self-employment by finding short-term employment in the temporary help industry, often in the hope of a job there turning into a full-time position.

TEMPORARY WORKERS

The temporary help industry is one of the fastest growing in this country. Some proponents have promoted temporary work as an ideal arrangement for older Americans. The Travelers instituted an internal temporary pool for its retirees. Other firms have created internal pools by hiring retirees, along with students and young mothers. Despite these corporate efforts, the majority of people who work as temporaries tend to work for temporary agencies, and most temporary agencies focus primarily on providing clerically related skilled workers. The result is that older temporary workers are most likely to be women. The question must be asked, How effective is temping for older women? What does it allow them to achieve, and what does it preclude? A look at the experiences of two older women sheds some light on these questions.

Ruth. Ruth is a 67-year-old single woman originally from Iowa. In the 1940s, she was in the Marine Corps for twenty-seven months, during which time she moved to New York City, where she has lived ever since. After she left the service, she worked in a law firm and then went to modeling school and spent a little time modeling.

By 1955, she realized she needed a steadier income than modeling provided and returned to work as a legal secretary. She took a position with the legal counsel in a Fortune 500 firm, which she held for the next fifteen years. "I only resigned there because they relocated out of the city. Then I started over at another Fortune 500 firm because they assured me that they were not moving and that, in fact, they were trying to coordinate all their personnel under one roof."

She reluctantly took a floater position with that firm, which meant that "I worked wherever I was needed. One other girl and I were called senior floaters, so we worked for top management. When there was no demand or call for us, they would move us down the line to a director or a manager."

Despite the lack of a permanent position, she liked her job largely because the people were nice. But contrary to its promise, this firm also decided to move out of the city. "After three or four years, they relocated out of the city and offered me a good job with them if I would go. I said no, again, and was ousted out of the firm."

Ruth was tenacious, as well as qualified, and she took a position with a third Fortune 500 company, once again as a legal secretary. Her position gave her access to the firm's financial records, and she could see that the business was going down. Eventually, it was taken over. The president of the parent company promptly moved the executive office to Dallas. She was made a handsome offer and this time considered it—at least until she went to Dallas for a visit. "It was the hottest place I'd ever been. I realized right away that I just wasn't interested in any part of Dallas."

This time, Ruth did not have an easy time job hunting. It was the early 1980s, and many firms were leaving the city. "It was a time when jobs were almost impossible to find, and people just didn't want to move from New York to take new positions." She also feels that her lack of computer skills put her at a relative disadvantage in the marketplace. "Unfortunately, I've not been introduced to computers in any way. I say I'm willing to learn them, but I'd rather not. But I will if necessary."

For the last several years, Ruth has worked in a series of temporary positions. She finds the average placement firm demeaning. "Well, I think I've proven that I can type accurately fifty words per minute, and yet I still have to take all those tests."

At 68, she would still like to get a full-time position as a legal secretary. At the moment, she is working as a part-time receptionist for a small public relations firm. She constantly responds to want ads and increasingly feels that her age works against her. "Yesterday I called this agency that I've been working with and the guy had three jobs that he told me about. Two of them didn't pay a whole lot and I wasn't interested; but the other one sounded pretty good. But it was clear he wanted a younger person. He's a 35-year-old senior vice-president who travels a lot and wants somebody who can go with him. So when the guy finished telling me about the other job, I said, well, they are looking for a young person. I said, when he says that he's 35 and he wants someone to go with him, it's pretty indicative. I've learned how to translate these things without too much difficulty." Ruth said the messages are generally muted. "Obviously, you don't hear it directly in plain English, but I hear it in other ways at the agencies which don't pass me on to jobs."

Marjorie. Marjorie is a 56-year-old widow with two children. Her husband died twenty years ago. Her son is 26, and her daughter is 24.

She went to college at the age of 18. After graduation, she worked for an ad agency and eventually moved into TV production, where she worked for six years. She then married and left the work force to raise her children. She occasionally did a little part-time work when her son was young and she loved it, but her husband was not supportive and the hours were erratic.

After her husband died, she started temping, but then her daughter got sick so she did not work for three years. When her daughter recovered, she found a job working for a man who designed dresses.

She worked part time, which gradually took up more and more hours. She hated the work, but she did it for about four years. Last July, she started temp work again. She had wanted to return to television but says she does not have any contacts in TV anymore and does not want to start at the bottom again—she feels she has paid her dues. As a temp, she has worked in ad agencies, real estate offices, banks, and brokerage houses.

She works as a temp three to four days a week, depending on what is available. She works primarily as a receptionist. She needs the money but would prefer a permanent job. She hopes that as people get to know her, she can find something permanent. She gets paid $6 to $7 an hour and works about thirty hours a week.

"It's kind of fun, floating in and out of offices—the challenge of piecing it all together. . . . It's not terribly taxing or hard." But she does not like the pay arrangement. "I find it very hard to do anything on an hourly wage. Although I know I'm only going to be paid until 5:00, I can't put it down and walk out if it's not finished. I will stay even if it's another 15 to 20 minutes and I don't get paid for it. The only merit is being asked back."

Marjorie is not sanguine about her career options. "I find it very scary. I really don't know where I'm going to end up, and I find that very frightening. I really don't have anything to fall back on. There will come a time, I guess, when they won't want to hire me."

She thinks that the political cross-currents of the last two decades have disadvantaged older women like herself. "What gets me very angry, and has for quite a while, is when the women's movement started to say that staying at home with your children was a waste of time. They degraded that. Then the other camp said women belong at home. Well, if women are so great and we belong there, then why hasn't there been some kind of backup system for us when times change? I guess now I'm just really full of resentment. I've spent my whole life out of step. When I was young and wanted a career, everyone told me I was nuts. Now, I really don't want a career, but I need one and can't get one. I should have gotten a teaching degree."

In retrospect, she thinks she would have done things differently. "I don't think that I would have stopped working as easily as I did. I would have continued something on a free-lance or part-time basis, and I certainly would have kept my hand in it. I also would have made sure that things were better taken care of financially. I would have made sure that we had safeguards for the kids and for me."

She does not feel she is alone but that she and other women like her are largely ignored. "I don't know how to get it organized, but I

would imagine that there are a lot of widows who are in the same
position and if we could all get together and get group rates for
insurance or better training, it would help. . . . I think businesses and
schools should come up with some scholarship programs. I think a
great pool of talent is being lost." She has specific proposals. "If there
were agencies that worked only with older people or people returning
to the work force after twenty years, that might be a way of making
people aware that there is all this pool of talent. You've got to get it
out as a public service announcement on radio, TV, ads. One-shot
ads would never sell it."

She gets no health benefits from the temporary agencies. She had
to pick up on her husband's medical plan, and she pays "a fortune"
for it—over $2,400 a year. She is not yet eligible for Social Security
because of her age.

Although Ruth and Marjorie have different life histories, they have
found themselves in similar economic situations as they age. Ruth has
never married and always supported herself. As she has gotten older,
and as economic times have made corporate careers more precarious,
she has found it increasingly difficult to support herself. In addition,
because of her sequence of relatively short-term positions, she has
very little to show in the way of a pension. Ruth still seeks a full-time
position such as she had throughout her career.

Marjorie's situation is typical of one faced by many older divorced and widowed women. Educated and with some career experience, she dropped out of the work force for almost fifteen
years to raise her children. Now that her financial circumstances
have changed, she must support herself but finds her opportunities for entrance and advancement limited by her age and work
history. Although she is in her late fifties, she would like the opportunity to build a career that would provide her the income and
satisfaction she seeks.

Marjorie's experience sheds some doubt on the appropriateness of
the notion of bridge jobs to describe all older women's experiences
in the labor market. The notion of bridge jobs implies a transition
from career work to retirement. Yet Marjorie has never had a career
from which she could retire. Instead she still wants to work full time
and to develop her career.

Furthermore, the experiences of both these women can quickly
disabuse one from believing that temporary jobs are an effective tactic
for achieving a permanent full-time position. Temporary jobs leave

some women in relatively precarious financial circumstances because of the unreliability of the income and the failure of some agencies for which they work to provide health benefits.

Temporary agencies provide an important mechanism for older workers, but as the case studies indicate, they do not serve as a panacea for all older working women.

WORKING OFF THE BOOKS

Throughout the course of the interviews and focus groups, it was clear that a large number of older workers took jobs that paid off the books. Although their motivations for so doing will be illustrated in the following examples and explained in more detail later, it is important to note that most saw nothing morally or legally wrong in working off the books and not paying taxes. For them it was a practical decision.

Joe.   Joe is a 65-year-old Catholic who has been married for nearly forty years. Both he and his wife are high school graduates. They own a house in Philadelphia that they bought for $6,000 and that is now worth about $87,000. They have a son living in California who is 39 years old and divorced and a 38-year-old married daughter with two children who lives nearby.

Joe's wife works full time for the sanitation department as a data processing coordinator. Previously she worked for a private firm for twenty-one years, and she receives a pension from that firm. They receive $41 a month from Joe's Social Security account and $650 a month from her pension.

Joe's entire work history has been centered around the police force. He joined the force in 1939 and stayed there for the next ten years. "Then I did what they called in those days 'shelfing your pension.' Any time I wanted to come back, I could be reinstated." He decided he wanted to try something different while he was young. "I went into auto repair work. I could fix anything." He owned his own company for several years and then went back to the security of the police department. "I had shopped around for employment, and there was nothing there for me to do in those years, nothing. That was in the late 1940s. So I went back in, and I put in another twenty-one years, and I was given the full pension."

He retired last year at the age of 64 because "I figured I couldn't wait much longer to retire because nobody would hire me pretty soon. ... They all want you under 65." He dislikes that attitude because he feels his reflexes are as good now as ever, but he feels that the attitude of many employers is "what good can a man be at 65?"

He retired a year ago and stayed home for a month, and "it drove me up the walls." He started to job hunt then—in his own way. First, he decided how much money he needed to meet the family's monthly expenses. He figured out they needed $105 a week.

He went to a local bank and proposed that it hire him as a night security guard for $35 a day, eight hours a day, three days a week—in cash. "I told them that I'd take the contract, providing they pay me off the books. I didn't want to make X amount of dollars and then have to turn around at the end of the year and say to Social Security, well, here's half of my money because I earned too much." He works cheaper than most guards because he is paid off the books and, in addition, he knew that he could make extra money through kickbacks from delivery boys or repairmen.

He gets no health benefits from the bank, but he is covered under his wife's plan and his own retirement plan. He expects to make about $5,000 this year as a security guard. His pension, which he began receiving in January 1988, averages about $12,000 a year.

Sylvia. Sylvia is a black 73-year-old New Yorker, born in Brooklyn, who has lived in subsidized housing there for the last ten years. She rents her apartment for $95 a month. She has one daughter who is a dancer and one son who works for a real estate firm. The daughter has three children; the son has four, and some of these grandchildren have children. Both of Sylvia's children went to college, as have most of their children. Sylvia has been married twice: once divorced, once widowed.

At the end of high school, she went to business school at night. When she graduated, she and her sister started typing menus for Brooklyn restaurants—carrying their typewriters to different restaurants and typing that day's menus for breakfast, lunch, and dinner. "We'd go to the restaurant and the chef or boss would bring us the menu and we'd sit at a table outside and just type it out. We were like the mailmen, you know. Snow, sleet, rain, we had to get out there. If one of us took sick, the other one had double work."

They had several portable typewriters. If one broke, they had another one ready to go. They would walk over a territory that covered fifty square blocks, carrying their typewriters. "We did so many on a block that we rarely got to sit. We had to type fast, and we had to do it right, you know?" People used to come to watch them type, as though they were playing the piano. She particularly remembers the first time Joe Louis came to watch.

Sylvia finally decided to quit the business, partly because of the walking but mostly because she began to plan financially for her future. "I was about 37 and I knew about pensions, and that made me say I better get a job where I can get some security."

She decided to look for a job in a local municipal hospital. "I knew some girls who worked there, but they weren't doing secretarial work. They were in practical nursing. But I said, well, let me try. So I went down, and I didn't even expect them to call me because in those days, I don't want to say it, but they didn't care too much for blacks, especially in the office. But I went into the hospital and told them what I wanted. I went home, they looked at my application, and the very next day they called me to work in the nursing office."

She started out transcribing medical reports from the dictaphone. "I was there about a month, and the next thing, they wanted me to be the assistant to the supervisor. I worked in that capacity for about ten years, and the next thing, they asked me to be the supervisor because the supervisor had to leave. So, of course, I took her place. And there I was for the next eighteen years."

Sylvia finally decided to retire nearly eleven years ago, when she was 62 years old. She was reluctant. "I didn't want to retire. I kept on putting it off. Then my daughter said, 'Ma, you know, getting up so early in the morning is hard on you.' " So she retired, but with regret, because the people she had worked with had become like family. As she says, "I wanted to retire but I didn't want to leave my job."

She has very warm memories of her job. "I went from home to home. When you like your job, it's home to home." After she retired, she was in no hurry to take another job. She had her Social Security check and pension. But in 1980, she started to baby-sit in her apartment. "I started because I had pity. Some mothers knocked on my door and they said they had to go to work and needed someone to watch their kids. I know how it is when you need a job, and you need someone you can rely on. So I said okay. Then one mother saw how nice I was to the children and she asked me to watch hers, and I have had some children ever since. But I don't even consider this like a job."

Sylvia sees what she does more as a favor to help out working mothers. She now baby-sits for one of her great-grandchildren and two of her neighbor's children. She will take no more than three children. "I like just to have enough so that I can watch them, and help them, and I can still do what I want to do." She helps them with their homework and sings songs that her Caribbean mother used to sing to her when she was a child.

Her day typically starts at 8:00 A.M. when her first child arrives and ends at 5:30 P.M. She charges $6 a day for the child who has been with her the longest and $10 to $12 a day for each of the other children. She makes about $125 a week—about $500 a month, ten months a year.

Sylvia plans to continue baby-sitting, but at times she would like to be free of the responsibility and time obligations. Although she likes working because it keeps her mind active and because she is needed, she loves to travel and would like to do more of it. She would also like to be able to spend more time at the local senior citizens center. Yet her memories will probably prompt her to continue baby-sitting as long as she can. "I remember when I used to need help with my little ones, and I feel so good to know that I'm able to help someone so they don't have to worry, and they can go to work and not have to worry about what's happening."

No one knows the exact number of Americans, young or old, who work off the books. As is clear from these stories, their motivations for doing so are varied. Some, such as Joe, do it as a way to earn a specific amount of money; others, like Sylvia, do it because they do not think of their work as a job that needs to be reported. But clearly the quality of the work, in status and pay, does not predispose these people to report their income. More important, the earnings test of the Social Security system is a justification for not reporting it. In some cases, the Social Security restriction is not understood, and in other cases it is understood all too well in the form of a penalty.

As long as the jobs that are available to older workers tend to be of a low-skilled or low-paying nature, we can expect many older Americans to do them off the books. But even if the job quality is enhanced, there will probably always be some workers who want to earn that extra little amount and not report it.

Unemployed

Relative to other age groups, unemployment is low for older workers, either because they do not want paid work or because they do but have become discouraged in their search and ceased looking. But some groups, particularly those who are black or Hispanic, are relatively vulnerable in the labor market (see chapter 3). Research has indicated that older workers with health problems also face difficulties in finding appropriate jobs as they get older (National Commission for Employment Policy 1985). The case studies below illustrate some of the issues.

José. José is a 71-year-old Hispanic man who is divorced and lives with his son outside Philadelphia. He is from Colombia and first came to the United States in 1974. He has moved since then from Massachusetts to Florida, back to Colombia, to California, and then to New York. Most of his moves have been precipitated by job searches. He has a daughter who is married and living in California, a brother and sister in Oregon, two sisters in New York, and another in Massachusetts.

When he moved to the United States, he held a Colombia license as a civil engineer but quickly discovered that it was not valid here. As a result, he took any job he could find, leading to a varied work history. He has made blueprints and cables for microwaves, worked in a gas station, supervised construction work for swimming pools, and worked in warehouses and in factories making tables and washing machines. While living in Florida, he worked for a consulting firm that moved him back to Colombia, but the firm had financial problems and he returned to the United States. He has not worked here since his return in the fall of 1987, largely because he lost his green card. "The consulate told me that I could go home or I could stay here like a tourist; so I went to California like a tourist. I asked the consulate for a duplicate of my green card, but they told me that I needed to make a new application. I made a new application, and I suppose that I will get a new card by next week."

He has resumed his job hunt and says, "I'm looking for any job, anything at all. I need work; I must work." At the time of the interview, he had applied for work as a quality control inspector. The job would pay $4 an hour. He had also received a minimum wage offer from a community center to bring Spanish-speaking older people to the center. He is willing to take minimum wage jobs even though he is a licensed engineer in South America because "in this country, I'm nothing." Yet he prides himself on his work ethic. "All the time I work very well. They all the time increased my salary. They were very happy with my job. Wherever I worked, at all times, in all the companies I worked for, I did a good job, a good job."

He does not think it is necessarily harder to get a job when one is older, "depending on what kind of job you're looking for." But he realizes he needs training. "I would like to get training, but for my age, maybe, who would give me training? I would love to get any training.... I am in condition to learn."

Charley. Charley is a 68-year-old World War II veteran who was born and raised in New York City. Although basically in good health, he has arthritis in one knee, which causes him to limp. He currently lives in a high-rise apartment building in New York City with his 69-year-old wife, who is retired. She recently had a serious bout with cancer, and after she got out of the hospital, they spent much of their savings to have a good time while they still could.

He has been a chef for nearly fifty years and has often worked for hotel chains. He started in the business after service in the army by working in his father's delicatessen. He then worked in a small restaurant for a couple of years, then at a restaurant-bar. Later, he opened up his own restaurant with a partner, but it proved to be unsuccessful. About ten years ago, the owner of a high-rise building gave him space rent-free, maintenance-free, and utility-free to run a restaurant. All five previous managers had gone broke. After seven years, a new owner took over, and Charley could not afford the rent that was being charged so he left. He then worked at a convention hotel as a supervisor for a couple of years. Since then he has worked whenever he could—weekends here and there.

He works when called for special jobs or to fill in. He is paid off the books, but he has had few calls in the last year. This past year he has been looking for a steady job. He says his name must be in a hundred different places. He looks through the papers or fills out applications. "They'll show you courtesy in the interview, and that's as far as it goes. Then they'll say to you, 'How come you're looking for a job? At your age, you should be enjoying yourself.' "

He has friends in the deli business, but their staffs are filled and he does not want to work for somebody he knows. "You lose your friends that way. I feel it's demeaning, and I don't need it that bad." He needs work primarily for financial reasons, though he says that he also needs to keep busy. He cannot depend on his Social Security check of $503 because it barely covers the rent, and he has no pension.

He says he has the ability to work as a chef, but people do not want him because of his age, physical condition, and pay demands. They think he should be sitting around in Florida. "They'll take someone in their early forties, but they'll never take anybody in their sixties. Why don't they use some of the capabilities of a man like me who can cook in five different ways, knows how to save a dollar, has good relationships with the other employees? They just don't want to use us—they say we're too old." Employers are also often reluctant to hire someone with a health problem. One prospective employer remarked about his limp: "You might fall, and up goes my insurance."

He is frustrated. "There are a lot of us around who may be a little handicapped, but we still have a brain. We still have two hands and two eyes. Find somebody who wants to use us." In addition, no one wants to pay what he would like. "I want $15 an hour for my mind and ability . . . they almost want to faint in front of you. They say they can get somebody for $6 or $7 an hour or even $4.50 an hour. I'd much rather not work. I think anybody who has the ability should be paid for it. I think I have ability . . . and I'm not going to give it away for nothing. Maybe I'm selfish, but I've been banged around too much and treated like nothing . . . maybe I'm angry, angry at the world. I still got a lot of life in me. Just because you're old doesn't mean you can't be successful."

Charley feels that the public must be made aware that the population of this country is getting older. "The people who do not care now are going to be the ones who will suffer later. Somewhere later on in their life these people are going to hurt. They've got to take care of the problems now."

The problems faced by older unemployed workers are frequently invisible, probably because the unemployed constitute a small percentage of older Americans. But for those older people who are seeking jobs, the obstacles are real and often insurmountable: they find their options are limited, particularly if they are women with sporadic work histories, members of racial or ethnic minorities, or people with health problems. José is penalized because of his minority status; although he is a well-educated man from South America, he has not been able to find a comparable position in the United States. Charley feels he is confronted with obstacles because of his age and slight physical handicap. But he also feels that his unwillingness to take a low-skilled job for minimum wage puts him at a distinct disadvantage in the work force.

As José and Charley illustrate, certain jobs are available to older unemployed workers, but they are often below the skill and compensation levels of the workers' previous jobs. To be gainfully employed at a certain age workers may have to change their attitudes toward work. This brings us to the broader issue of how older workers feel the marketplace treats them.

What Do Older Workers Want
from the Labor Market?
What Are They Getting?

When asked what they want, older workers are clear: satisfying work, pay commensurate with what they earned in their career jobs, and respect. What they get in the labor market seems much different. Many feel they are treated very badly. These older workers recognize and resist the characteristics of the bridge jobs that Ruhm has identified (see chapter 5): they dislike the changes in status brought about by their postretirement jobs, as well as the drop in income. Few feel, however, that if they need to work they have any choice except to take these jobs. As a result, a sense of alienation pervades the experiences of older workers in today's labor market.

TREATMENT OF OLDER WORKERS
IN THE MARKETPLACE

Older workers feel that they have a unique work ethic that was forged during the Depression. It is an ethic that values reliability, punctuality, pride in one's work, and giving a full day's work for a day's pay. The notion of career choice is an enigma to most because they were forced to take whatever jobs were available to pay the rent and put food on the table. Now that they are in their sixties and seventies, they want to be appreciated for their lifetime of hard work and the knowledge and experience gained through it.

Many express disappointment and frustration that the marketplace does not sufficiently value the work ethic, skills, and knowledge they are capable of bringing to a job. Older workers who do not have the option of reducing their full-time jobs to part time often find an inhospitable marketplace when they look for jobs. Many of the respondents report that although postretirement part-time jobs are available, they are generally inferior in status and pay to those they held before retirement. For example, a retired district sanitation supervisor switched to driving a car for a taxi service two to three days a week. A machinist with twenty years of experience with the railroad now supervises the installation of storm windows. A retired assistant office manager currently provides home care for an elderly woman and her disabled daughter. A woman with thirty years of experience in retail sales, but no pension, stocks shelves in a local pharmacy. The only people who were able to continue in their lifelong work were those who, like Marie and Janet, phased into retirement, gradually reducing the hours worked, and those like Jean and Michael, who went into business for themselves. The women who thought temporary work would provide an avenue to permanent employment have not succeeded so far.

McDonald's advertising campaign about employing older workers illustrates the situation in which most of the participants in the study find themselves: as productive members of the work force, they must now take jobs below their skill and experience levels. Although most appreciate the ads for portraying older workers as valuable, productive, and congenial members of the labor force, none expressed any interest in such a job unless he or she was desperate.

Fast-food employment was unappealing because of the perceived status of the work and the assumption that it paid minimum wage. Relatively low-wage work upsets unionized and nonunionized workers, like Charley, who spent their lives trying to raise their standard of living. As a 67-year-old unemployed woman who worked in quality control in the pharmaceutical industry for thirty-five years said, "A lot [of employers] want to pay you only $3.75; you know that knocks senior citizens down. They've been used to making good money. They've worked all their lives for it. They've come up, come up, come up, and now they've got their status. Do you realize how it affects your brain when you got to come back down to $3 an hour?"

The issue of pay is tied to a number of concerns that older workers have. Obviously, they want to be fairly compensated for a lifetime of skilled work, but the pay scale also symbolizes status and appreciation. At minimum wage, they feel they have little status and are not being treated with the respect and appreciation they deserve.

Older workers' opinions on their treatment in the labor market are tied to their views on several other issues.

MEANING OF A JOB

A job has a variety of meanings for older workers. As they say, "a job's your life; it's your life." "It's security." "I need it to pay the bills." "It keeps older people alive." "Without a job there's nothing to look forward to." "I didn't realize I liked my job so much until I left it." "I looked forward to it every morning. It was a routine."

A job generates needed income and provides a way to organize the day. Yet older workers want jobs in which they feel they are appreciated and are accorded status and respect. Some feel that they are taken advantage of because employers see senior citizens as a cheap and relatively disposable pool of labor.

MOTIVATION TO WORK:
TARGETED EARNINGS

Many of the older workers indicated that they are very targeted in their earnings. The logic of targeted earnings is that an older worker supplies his or her labor until enough income has been earned and then withdraws from the work force. Targeted earners cut across all employment arrangements so the ways they accomplish their target figures vary. Some, although national figures indicate increasingly fewer, workers accomplish this by working part year. Others do so by working on a part-time or temporary basis. Some report their income; some do not.

An interesting aspect of the notion of targeted earnings is that there is probably little that could be done to entice older workers with this mind-set to work longer hours or to be more closely attached to the labor market than they currently are. They decide precisely how much money they either need or want to earn each month and have no interest in earning more. In some cases, the figure represents the amount needed to cover their expenses; in other cases, it represents discretionary income.

ATTITUDE TOWARD UNREPORTED INCOME

A surprisingly large number of the respondents in this study work at jobs that pay off the books. Most do it simply to earn extra money; they see the job as providing pocket money to supplement their Social Security or pension checks. Most of them do not want to risk losing any of their Social Security payments by reporting the income. Yet most would not be in any jeopardy because they typically earn less than $5,000 off the books—well below the earnings test set by the Social Security system.

There appear to be several other reasons they feel it is all right to cheat the system. Most feel that they are in marginal jobs and claim that if they were being paid enough money then they would report it. Others are angry at the Social Security system, which they feel penalizes them for having been born during the "notch years" or having been widowed. During the Carter administration the Social Security earnings of Americans born between 1917 and 1921 were reduced, and many feel that they have been unfairly penalized as a result. The people in the focus groups who are affected by this policy estimate that they lose between $110 and $150 a month. Several widows were angry because they are not allowed to collect Social Security monies from their deceased spouses' accounts as well as their own. They feel that the prohibition against "double dipping" unfairly robs them of money that both of them contributed to their individual accounts.

Interestingly, no one seemed to experience any dissonance between the work ethic that they so highly value and taking money off the books. Most accepted this practice as the norm.

GENDER DIFFERENCES

The major gender differences seem to be those bred by the intersection of occupation and work history. Older women who took low-paying clerical or retail clerk jobs or moved in and out of the labor force for family reasons find themselves particularly disadvantaged. Often the only work they can get is on a temporary basis, with low pay and minimal security, off the books or on a self-employed basis. This general picture corresponds to the bleak picture of the economic insecurity of older American women (Kahne 1985–86).

The picture is somewhat better for women with consistent and stable work histories but depends largely on whether they are eligible for pension coverage. Most of the women in the focus groups and interviews either had no pensions or were poorly recompensed from their pensions.

ATTITUDE TOWARD UNEMPLOYMENT

For workers with satisfying lifelong work experiences, not having a job proves difficult. After one man retired, he felt as though he hit a brick wall. Another said he felt he was left out of society. For many, a paycheck is a measure of self-worth. A very small minority feel that not having a job is a great opportunity to find themselves and to define their lives.

The unemployed express no interest in a training program unless they are guaranteed a job at its conclusion. They do not want to waste time or energy.

ATTITUDE TOWARD YOUNGER WORKERS

The older people feel that the "younger generation," which they define as being approximately 35 years old and younger, has never known what it is like to be hungry or desperate. As a result, this generation has a strong sense of entitlement and a relatively lazy work ethic. Younger workers are seen as not giving a dollar's work for a dollar's pay: they show up late for work; they have high absenteeism; and they generally take their jobs for granted.

Older workers feel that, in contrast, they have never felt entitled to a job and that they have gotten through life by working hard. They recognize that their own attitudes toward work were shaped to a great extent by Depression-era scarcities and that the younger generation, having grown up in a relatively affluent era, escaped those conditions. Nonetheless, it irritates some older workers to be passed over in hiring or compensation by someone younger whom they see as less dedicated, reliable, and productive.

Job Discrimination

Unemployed older people feel that they face discriminatory attitudes that make it difficult for them to get jobs other than low-level ones. Despite Charley's nearly forty years of experience as a cook and chef, he can only find minimum wage work in fast food. A former administrator of a drug treatment center can find no job. Ruth, who has worked as an executive secretary for over thirty years with Fortune 500 companies, finds that the only work she can get is as a temporary receptionist.

Unemployed blacks feel that they encounter double discrimination—race and age. They talk about the evasions that employers use to avoid hiring older workers as being similar to the evasions once used to avoid hiring blacks. An unemployed black woman illustrates statements expressed by other minorities when she says, "Getting back into the job market is nerve-racking (like putting a cat in a box of fleas). They can't say 'no' to a retiree, but they use codes—the same codes as years ago when a black woman couldn't get a white girl's job. 'Sorry, we can't hire you today,' or 'we'll look over your application, but we have many others.' 'Don't call us—we'll call you.' " These minorities have experienced a lifetime of discrimination.

The critical question is whether these older workers face employment problems because they are relatively unqualified, as certain economic theories would lead us to believe, or because they are being discriminated against for certain jobs because of their age.

What Are the Policy Issues?

Based on the attitudes and experiences of older workers in the labor market, there are several important policy issues that the private and public sectors should recognize and address.

OLDER WORKERS ARE NOT FUNGIBLE
WITH TEENAGED WORKERS

Government and business should be cautious about treating older workers as they do teenaged workers. Although the fast-food and child care industries have turned to older workers to offset the severe labor shortages caused by the shrinking cohort of young workers, any large-scale effort to substitute older workers for teenaged ones should not be promoted unless several conditions are met. Older workers want respect, dignity, and appreciation for a lifetime of work. They do not want to be seen as just bodies. A teenager may take a job to fill time, but an older worker uses a job to organize time. Older workers want to be appreciated for the time they spend. The extent to which they might trade off earnings for appreciation is not entirely clear. At least in this sample, however, there was little interest in volunteer work, largely because most needed additional income to supplement Social Security or pension checks.

CAREER-CONTINUOUS JOBS ARE NEEDED

If one aim is to respond to the needs and desires of older workers, employers should provide jobs that involve continuity with preretirement employment and earnings. This effort would counteract the prevailing trend toward lower-status, lower-pay bridge jobs that differ in occupation from that pursued during one's career job. Ideally, these enhanced job opportunities would promote autonomy and challenge. There are several alternatives that employers might consider: part-time jobs that are consonant with career experiences; job sharing that divides one full-time position into two jobs; temporary pools within individual firms that would provide options for permanent employment; and redesign of jobs to match physical skills.

How realistic are these options? In the short term, the climate is less than entirely positive for a restructuring of jobs to meet the needs of older workers. There are several reasons for this less than responsive climate: the recent large-scale reductions in the work force in many firms; the ready availability of a work force for most jobs (see chapter 6); and the reticence of unions, until recently, to push for these options (see chapter 7). But these conditions may change. If the U.S. Department of Labor projections are correct, shortages of skilled labor may prompt employers to look for pools of currently untapped labor. Clearly, the fast-food and child care industries illustrate this trend. In addition, firms such as The Travelers, which operate in relatively tight labor markets, also have turned to creative approaches regarding returnees. But if these industries or firms see older workers as simply fungible with the shrinking cohort of teen workers, they are likely to face serious difficulties in recruitment.

Today's older Americans are financially secure and unlikely to be motivated to return to the labor force unless the conditions are right. They are more likely to take short-term jobs, off the books, to earn a little extra money and so as not to jeopardize their Social Security payments or to turn to self-employment to maintain continuity with their career work. Ironically, it appears that the policies of today's employers are pushing older Americans away from employment rather than enticing them toward it. Yet there remain certain older Americans such as women with intermittent work histories, members of minorities, and those with health problems who continue to want to work but find neither the opportunities nor the right conditions.

NEED FOR PENSION PORTABILITY

The pension coverage for older American women is abysmal. According to the Census Bureau in 1986, only one out of every five women over the age of 65 receives an income from a pension, whether that pension is private or public or garnered as a spouse or a returned worker. The picture is better for younger women but far from ideal. According to the Current Population Survey of all employed women in 1983, only three out of eight received pension coverage. In addition, women's earnings from pensions are substantially lower than men's. Women's monthly average earnings from pensions was $233, while men's were $484.

There are several reasons women's coverage is so poor, and evidence indicates that these reasons are not changing dramatically for younger women (Porter 1988).

1. Many employers do not provide pensions, particularly smaller employers, who hire a relatively large percentage of women.

2. Employers exclude many categories of workers from pension plans, and these are often the categories in which women predominate. These include clerks, part-time workers, hourly workers, and workers taking a job near retirement age.

3. The time required to earn a pension (to become vested) is typically ten years. This is difficult for many women to achieve, particularly those born before 1933 who are now aged 57 years or older, since they are not likely to have such an earnings history.

4. Credits toward a pension are lost when a worker moves from one job to another or has a break in service with the same employer.

For all of these reasons, the federal government should move quickly in considering portable pensions as a way to safeguard the financial well-being of older Americans, particularly women.

Need for Public Awareness

A number of the older workers surveyed argued for a strong public service campaign to highlight the virtues of older workers. They believe one major obstacle is the attitudes among employers toward the appropriateness of older workers for certain high-profile or high-status jobs. It is unclear whether the prejudices some older workers have encountered will be offset by the changing demographic structure of the work force.

Need for Choice in the Marketplace

Although all forty-six of the people interviewed for this study were motivated to work, the majority still wanted a choice in whether or not to work and in what jobs to take. Their desire for choice may be compounded because this Depression-era generation feels they have had little choice all their lives.

If it is to respond to their message, the federal government should not institute financial disincentives for older Americans who want to retire completely. But if it seems that the economy would be well served by more active participation by older workers, it is incumbent on both the public and private sectors to provide more opportunities for older persons to work under the conditions that suit their financial and psychological needs.

Because this study included only older Americans who work or want to work, it is not representative of the majority of older Americans who neither work nor seek to work. Nonetheless, the findings raise provocative questions regarding what might motivate nonworking older Americans to rejoin the work force. Are there certain conditions under which they would want to work? Are these conditions tied to tangible arrangements such as scheduling alternatives, payment arrangements, or compensation incentives or to the intangibles of status and appreciation? What trade-offs might be made?

If American business and government want to provide increased opportunities for the employment of older workers, they would be well served to understand the needs and desires of older Americans.

Appendix to Chapter 9:
Focus Groups versus
Individual Interviews

Although focus groups and individual interviews share many points in common, each format has unique strengths.

Focus groups are intended to bring to light the "felt," subjective, experiential side of social phenomena. This method does not intend, nor is it capable of yielding, what social scientists would consider statistically representative findings. In addition to their primary aim, which is to identify the issues that are the most salient or critical to individual participants, focus groups reveal the language respondents use to address or characterize these issues. They also provide an interpretive framework for understanding particular attitudes on the issues. For example, the focus groups in this study revealed the significance of the Depression as an organizing experience that affects the work ethic of older individuals and their perception of choice in their work lives. Finally, by letting participants speak for themselves, focus groups can sometimes disabuse a researcher of biases he or she is unlikely to be aware of and can thus bring a richer understanding to the issues at hand.

Focus groups have traditionally been used in proprietary market research to test consumers' reactions to new products or advertising campaigns. Recently, social scientists have employed them in a variety of applied research settings, including the selection of juries for criminal trials.

Each of the focus groups in this study consisted of ten participants who were recruited by a New York City market research firm. Participants were seated around a conference table with microphones in the ceiling. They were told that the discussion was being taped and were afforded the opportunity to leave if they found it disconcerting.

Focus groups have a distinctive advantage over individual personal interviews because the focus group generates interaction among participants and allows for a variety of opinions on a topic. In effect, a focus group reveals the different edges of meaning, sometimes permitting consensus to build, sometimes indicating unbridgeable differences.

Individual personal interviews have a unique strength insofar as they allow for in-depth probing of individual life histories. Such interviews provide insights into critical life junctions or key decision points. When interview transcriptions are analyzed collectively, it is possible to discern patterns in people's lives. Whereas a focus group allows all participants to react to each other, individual interviews do not. The art of weaving and interweaving becomes much more the responsibility of the researcher.

The New York City personal interviews were arranged by the same market research firm contracted to recruit the focus group participants, and the interviews were conducted in the author's office at the Graduate School and University Center, City University of New York. The Philadelphia interviews with the unemployed were arranged by the Mayor's Commission on Aging and were conducted at its offices. All respondents were paid for their participation.

REFERENCES

Abt Associates, Inc.
  1985 *A Proposal to Conduct Research to Improve Services for Dislocated Workers.*
       Cambridge, Mass.

AFL-CIO
  1985 "Draft Resolution on Part Time Work." Washington, D.C.: AFL-
       CIO Convention.
  1988 "Statements Adopted by the AFL-CIO Executive Council." Wash-
       ington, D.C.

Akerlof, George, and Brian Main
  1981 "An Experience-Weighted Measure of Employment and Unem-
       ployment Durations." *American Economic Review* 71:1003–11.

American Association of Retired Persons
  1986 *Managing a Changing Workforce.* Washington, D.C.

Anderson, Kathryn, and Richard Burkhauser
  1985 "The Retirement-Health Nexus: A New Measure of an Old Puzzle."
       Journal of Human Resources 20(3):315–30.

Anderson, Kathryn, Richard Burkhauser, and Joseph Quinn
  1986 "Do Retirement Dreams Come True? The Effect of Unanticipated
       Events on Retirement Plans." *Industrial and Labor Relations Review*
       39(4):518–26.

Appelbaum, Eileen
  1987 "Restructuring Work: Temporary, Part-Time and At-Home Em-
       ployment." In *Computer Chips and Paper Clips*, vol. 2, ed. Heidi Hart-
       mann, 268–310. Washington, D.C.: National Academy Press.

Barzel, Yoram
  1973 "The Determination of Daily Hours and Wages." *Quarterly Journal
       of Economics* 87(2):220–38.

Bazzoli, Gloria
  1985 "The Early Retirement Decision: New Empirical Evidence on the Influence of Health." *Journal of Human Resources* 20(2):214–34.

Becker, Eugene H.
  1984 "Self-Employed Workers: An Update to 1983." *Monthly Labor Review* 107 (July):14–18.

Bednarzik, Robert W., and Richard M. Devens, Jr.
  1980 *Using the Current Population Survey as a Longitudinal Data Base.* Washington, D.C.: Bureau of Labor Statistics, Report 608.

Bell, Daniel, and William Marclay
  1987 "Trends in Retirement Eligibility and Pension Benefits." *Monthly Labor Review* 110 (April):18–25.

Belous, Richard S.
  1984 *Wage Restraints in the 1980s: A Turning Point in U.S. Labor Markets?* Washington, D.C.: Congressional Research Service.
  1987 "Flexibility and American Labour Markets: The Evidence and Implications." Geneva: International Labour Office, Working Paper No. 14.
  1989 *The Contingent Economy: The Growth of Part-Time Temporary and Subcontracted Workforce.* Washington, D.C.: National Planning Association.

Blank, Rebecca M.
  1987 "Part-Time Work and Wages among Adult Women." In *Proceedings of the Thirty-Ninth Annual Meeting of the Industrial Relations Research Association,* 479–86. Madison, Wisc.: Industrial Relations Research Association.

Blinder, Alan, Roger Gordon, and David Wise
  1980 "Reconsidering the Disincentive Effects of Social Security." *National Tax Journal* 33:431–42.

Boskin, Michael J.
  1977 "Social Security and Retirement Decisions." *Economic Inquiry* 15:1–25.

Boskin, Michael J., and Michael D. Hurd
  1978 "Effect of Social Security on Early Retirement." *Journal of Public Economics* 10:361–77.
  1984 "The Effect of Social Security on Retirement in the Early 1970s." *Quarterly Journal of Economics* 99(4):767–90.

Bould, Sally
  1980 "Unemployment as a Factor in Early Retirement Decisions." *American Journal of Economics and Sociology* 39(2):123–26.

Bureau of National Affairs
    1987 *Bulletin to Management* (August 13).
    1988 "Flexible Staffing." *BNA Employee Relations Weekly.* Cited in *Working at the Margins.* Cleveland, Ohio: 9 to 5, National Association of Working Women.

Burkhauser, Richard
    1979 "The Pension Acceptance Decision of Older Workers." *Journal of Human Resources* 14(1):63–75.
    1980 "The Early Acceptance of Social Security: An Asset Maximization Approach." *Industrial and Labor Relations Review* 33(4):484–92.

Burkhauser, Richard, and Joseph Quinn
    1983 "Is Mandatory Retirement Overrated? Evidence from the 1970's." *Journal of Human Resources* 18(3):337–58.

Burkhauser, Richard, and John Turner
    1982 "Labor-Market Experiences of the Almost Old and Implications for Income Support." *American Economic Review* 72:304–8.

Burtless, Gary
    1986 "Social Security, Unanticipated Benefit Increases, and the Timing of Retirement." *Review of Economic Studies* 53:781–805.

Burtless, Gary, and Robert Moffitt
    1984 "The Effects of Social Security Benefits on the Labor Supply of the Aged." In *Retirement and Economic Behavior,* ed. Henry Aaron and Gary Burtless. Washington D.C.: Brookings Institution.
    1985 "The Joint Choice of Retirement Age and Postretirement Hours of Work." *Journal of Labor Economics* 3(2):209–36.

Butler, J., Richard Burkhauser, Jean Mitchel, and Theodore Pincus
    1987 "Measurement Error in Self-Reported Health Variables." *Review of Economics and Statistics* 9:644–50.

Charner, Ivan, Shirley Fox, and Lester Trachtman
    1988 *Union Retirees: Enriching Their Lives—Enhancing Their Contributions.* Washington, D.C.: National Institute for Work and Learning.

Christensen, Kathleen
    1987 "Women and Contingent Work." *Social Policy* 17(4):15–18.

Collins, Glenn
    1987 "Wanted: Child Care Workers, Age 55 and Up." *New York Times,* December 15, Al.

Commonwealth Fund Commission on Elderly People Living Alone
    N.d. *Old, Alone, and Poor: A Plan for Reducing Poverty among Elderly People Living Alone.* New York.

Commonwealth of Massachusetts, Office of Training and Employment Policy
   1987   "Policy Statement to the Third National Older Worker Conference."
         Washington, D.C.

Cooper, Cary L., and D. P. Torrington
   1981   *After Forty: The Time for Achievement?* Chichester, England: Wiley.

Costello, Cynthia
   1984   "On the Front: Class, Gender and Conflict in the Insurance Work-
         place." Ph.D. dissertation. University of Wisconsin, Madison.

Cyert, Richard M., and David C. Mowery
   1987   *Technology and Employment.* Washington, D.C.: National Academy
         Press.

Danziger, Sheldon H., Robert H. Haveman, and Robert D. Plotnick
   1986   "Antipoverty Policy: Effects on the Poor and the Nonpoor." In *Fight-
         ing Poverty: What Works and What Doesn't,* ed. Sheldon H. Danziger
         and Daniel H. Weinberg, 50–77. Cambridge, Mass.: Harvard Uni-
         versity Press.

Day, Jeff S.
   1987   "Employee Leasing." Paper presented at conference, "The Contin-
         gent Workplace: New Directions for Work in the Year 2000," co-
         sponsored by the Graduate Center of the City University of New
         York and the Women's Bureau of the U.S. Department of Labor.

Devens, Richard M.
   1986   "Displaced Workers: One Year Later." *Monthly Labor Review* 109
         (July):40–43.

Diamond, Peter, and Jerry Hausman
   1984   "The Retirement and Unemployment Behavior of Older Men." In
         Retirement and Economic Behavior, ed. Henry Aaron and Gary Burtless,
         97–134. Washington, D.C.: Brookings Institution.

Doeringer, Peter B., and Andrew Sum
   1984   "Job Markets and Human Resource Programs for Older Workers in
         New England." Report prepared for the New England Board of
         Higher Education, Boston.

Easterlin, Richard A.
   1980   *Birth and Fortune: The Impact of Numbers on Personal Welfare.* New
         York: Basic Books.

Edelman, Marian Wright
   1986   *Families in Peril: An Agenda for Social Change.* Cambridge, Mass.: Har-
         vard University Press.

Ehrenberg, Ronald G., Pamela Rosenberg, and Jeanne Li
  1986 "Part-Time Employment in the United States." Paper presented at
       a conference, "Employment, Unemployment, and Hours of Work,"
       Berlin, Germany.

Eisdorfer, Carl, and Donna Cohen
  1983 "Health and Retirement, Retirement and Health: Background and
       Future Directions." In *Policy Issues in Work and Retirement,* ed. Herbert
       S. Parnes, 57–73. Kalamazoo, Mich.: W. E. Upjohn Institute for
       Employment Research.

Employment and Training Reporter (Bureau of National Affairs)
  1987 November.

Fields, Gary, and Olivia Mitchell
  1984 *Retirement, Pensions, and Social Security.* Cambridge, Mass.: MIT Press.
  1986 "Earlier Retirement in the United States." Mimeo, Cornell Uni-
       versity.

Finegan, T. Aldrich
  1978a "Improving Our Information on Discouraged Workers." *Monthly
       Labor Review* 101 (September):15–25.
  1978b *The Measurement, Behavior, and Classification of Discouraged Workers.*
       Background Paper No. 12. Washington, D.C.: National Commission
       on Employment and Unemployment Statistics.

Flaim, Paul O.
  1973 "Discouraged Workers and Changes in Unemployment." *Monthly
       Labor Review* 96 (March):8–16.

Flaim, Paul O., and Ellen Sehgal
  1985 "Displaced Workers of 1979–83: How Well Have They Fared?"
       Monthly Labor Review 108 (June):3–16.

Flynn, Patricia M.
  1987 *Facilitating Technological Change.* Cambridge, Mass.: Ballinger.

Freedman, Audrey
  1982 "A Fundamental Change in Wage Bargaining." *Challenge* (July–
       August):15–17.
  1985 *The New Look in Wage Policy and Employee Relations.* New York: Con-
       ference Board.

Fullerton, Howard N.
  1987 "Labor Force Projections: 1986 to 2000." *Monthly Labor Review* 110
       (September):19–29.

Fullerton, Howard N., and John Tschetter
  1984 "The 1995 Labor Force: A Second Look." In *Employment Projections
       for 1995*, BLS Bulletin 2197, 1–8. Washington, D.C.: U.S. Govern-
       ment Printing Office.

Gastwirth, Joseph L.
  1973 "Estimating the Number of Hidden Unemployed." *Monthly Labor Review* 96 (March):17–26.

Gibbons, J. A., and M. L. Perotta
  1981 "Employment Opportunities for Older Workers." New York Chamber of Commerce and Industry, Human Resource Department.

Ginzberg, Eli
  1977 "The Job Problem." *Scientific American* 237(5):43–51.

Gordon, Roger, and Alan Blinder
  1980 "Market Wages, Reservation Wages and Retirement Decisions." *Journal of Public Economics* 14:277–308.

Gregory, Judith
  1983 "Electronic Office Homework from the Perspective of a Clerical Workers' Organization." Paper presented at National Executive Forum: Office Work Stations in the Home, National Academy of Sciences, Washington, D.C. An edited version appears in *Office Work Stations in the Home*. Washington, D.C.: National Academy Press.

Gustman, Alan, and Thomas Steinmeier
  1983 "Minimum Hours Constraints and Retirement Behavior." *Contemporary Policy Issues, A Supplement to Economic Inquiry* 3:77–91.
  1984 "Partial Retirement and the Analysis of Retirement Behavior." *Industrial and Labor Relations Review* 37(3):403–15.
  1985 "The 1983 Social Security Reforms and Labor Supply Adjustments of Older Individuals in the Long-Run." *Journal of Labor Economics* 3(2):237–53.

Haber, Carole
  1985 *Beyond Sixty-Five: The Dilemma of Old Age in America's Past.* New York: Cambridge University Press.

Hall, Robert E.
  1982 "The Importance of Lifetime Jobs in the U.S. Economy." *American Economic Review* 72:716–24.

Halpern, Janice
  1978 "Raising the Mandatory Retirement Age: Its Effect on the Employment of Older Workers." *New England Economic Review* (May–June):23–35.

Hanoch, Giora, and Marjorie Honig
  1983 "Retirement Wages and Labor Supply of the Elderly." *Journal of Labor Economics* 1(2):131–51.

Louis Harris and Associates, Inc.
  1981 "Aging in the Eighties: America in Transition." Survey conducted for the National Council on the Aging.

1986 *Problems Facing Elderly Americans Living Alone.* New York: Commonwealth Fund Commission on Elderly People Living Alone.

Harrison, Bennett, and Barry Bluestone
1988 *The Great U-Turn: Corporate Restructuring and the Polarizing of America.* New York: Basic Books.

Hayghe, Howard
1979 "The Effect of Unemployment on Family Income in 1977." *Monthly Labor Review* 102 (December):42–44.

Hedges, Janice, and Stephen J. Gallogly
1977 "Full and Part-Time: A Review of Definitions." *Monthly Labor Review* 100 (March):21–28.

Honig, Marjorie
1985 "Partial Retirement among Women." *Journal of Human Resources* 20(4):613–21.

Honig, Marjorie, and Giora Hanoch
1985 "Partial Retirement as a Separate Mode of Retirement Behavior." *Journal of Human Resources* 20(1):21–46.

Horvath, Francis W.
1987 "The Pulse of Economic Change: Displaced Workers of 1981–85." *Monthly Labor Review* 110 (June):3–12.

ICF
1988 "Strategies for Increasing the Employment Levels of Older Workers." Paper prepared for the Commonwealth Fund Commission on Elderly People Living Alone. Washington, D.C.

Ichniowski, Bernard E., and Anne Preston
1986 "New Trends in Part-Time Employment." In *Proceedings of the Thirty-Eighth Annual Meeting of the Industrial Relations Research Association,* 60–67. Madison, Wisc.: Industrial Relations Research Association.

Kahne, Hilda
1985 *Reconceiving Part-Time Work.* Totowa, N.J.: Rowman and Allanheld.
1985 "Not Yet Equal: Employment Experience of Older Women and
–86 Older Men." *International Journal on Aging and Human Development* 22(1):1–13.

Kennedy, Kim
1980 *Part-Time Employment Desires of Older Workers: The Findings of a Survey of Persons Aged 55 and Over.* Boston: Policy and Evaluation Division, Massachusetts Department of Manpower Development.

Kieffer, Jarold A.
1984 "Longer Worklives: A Strategic Policy Reversal Needed." *Public Administration Review* 44:434–38.

Kingson, Jennifer
  1988 "Golden Years Spent under Golden Arches." *New York Times,* March
        6, E26.

Klein, Deborah Pisetzner
  1983 "Trends in Employment and Unemployment in Families." *Monthly
        Labor Review* 106 (December):21–25.

Kochan, Thomas A., Harry C. Katz, and Robert B. McKersie
  1986 *The Transformation of American Industrial Relations.* New York: Basic
        Books.

Kotlikoff, Laurence, and Daniel Smith
  1983 *Pensions and the American Economy.* Chicago: University of Chicago
        Press.

Kotlikoff, Laurence, and David Wise
  1987 "The Nature and Incentive Effects of Private Pension Accruals and
        Their Impact on Retirement." Mimeo, National Bureau of Economic
        Research.
  1989 "Employee Retirement and a Firm's Pension Plan." In *The Economics
        of Aging,* ed. David Wise, 279–330. Chicago: University of Chicago
        Press.

Kraut, Allen
  1987 "Retirees: A New Resource for American Industries." *Personnel Ad-
        ministrator* (August).

Lapidus, June
  1988 "An Empirical Analysis of the Supply Side of the Temporary Help
        Services Industry." Mimeo, University of Massachusetts, Amherst.

Lasden, Martin
  1984 "Growing Old in DP." *Computer Decisions* 16 (November):126–81.

Lazear, Edward
  1986 "Retirement from the Labor Force." In *Handbook of Labor Economics,*
        vol. 1, ed. Orley Ashenfelter and Richard Layard, 305–55. New
        York: Elsevier Science Publishers.

Levitan, Sar A., and Elizabeth A. Conway
  1988 "Part-Timers: Living on Half-Rations." *Challenge* (May–June):9–16.

Levitan, Sar A., and Frank Gallo
  1988 *A Second Chance: Training for Jobs.* Kalamazoo, Mich.: W. E. Upjohn
        Institute for Employment Research.

Levitan, Sar A., and Isaac Shapiro
  1987a *The Working Poor: A Missing Element in Welfare Reform.* Washington,
        D.C.: Center for Social Policy Studies, George Washington
        University.

1987b *Working but Poor: America's Contradiction.* Baltimore: Johns Hopkins University Press.

Loveman, Gary, Michael Piore, and Werner Sengenberger
1990 "The Evolving Role of Small Business in Industrialized Economies and Some Implications for Employment and Training." In *New Developments in the Labor Market,* ed. Katherine Abraham and Robert McKersie. Cambridge, Mass.: MIT Press.

McCarthy, Maureen E., Gail S. Rosenberg, and Gary Lefkowitz
1981 *Work Sharing: Case Studies.* Kalamazoo, Mich.: W. E. Upjohn Institute for Employment Research.

McMahon, P. J.
1986 "An International Comparison of Labor Force Participation." *Monthly Labor Review* 109 (May):3–12.

Marcus, Alan J., James Jondrow, and Frank Brechling
1987 "Older Workers and Part-Time Work." In *Proceedings of the Thirty-Ninth Annual Meeting of the Industrial Relations Research Association,* 471–78. Madison, Wisc.: Industrial Relations Research Association.

Marquardt, L., and Alice Gold
1981 *The Travelers Pre-Retirement Opinion Survey: Report of Results.* Hartford, Conn.: Travelers Life Insurance Company.

Merton, R., M. Fiske, and P. Kendall
1956 *The Focused Interview: A Manual of Problems and Procedures.* Glencoe, Ill.: Free Press.

Mincer, Jacob
1973 "Determining the Number of Hidden Unemployed." *Monthly Labor Review* 96 (March):27–30.

Mintz, Steven, and Susan Kellogg
1988 *Domestic Revolutions: A Social History of American Life.* New York: Free Press.

Mirkin, Barry
1987 "Early Retirement as a Labor Force Policy: An International Overview." *Monthly Labor Review* 110 (March):19–33.

Mitchell, Olivia, and Gary Fields
1984 "The Economics of Retirement Behavior." *Journal of Labor Economics* 2(1):84–105.

Monthly Labor Review
1986 "Union Membership of Employed Wage and Salary Workers, 1985." *Monthly Labor Review* 109 (May):44–46.

Morrison, Catherine, E. Patrick McGuire, and Maryann Clarke
1988 *Keys to Competitiveness.* New York: Conference Board.

Morrison, Malcolm H.
  1983 "The Aging of the U.S. Population: Human Resource Implications."
        Monthly Labor Review 106 (May):13–19.

Mott, Frank L., and R. Jean Haurin
  1981 "The Impact of Health Problems and Mortality on Family Well-
        Being." In *Work and Retirement,* ed. Herbert S. Parnes, 198–253.
        Cambridge, Mass.: MIT Press.

Moynihan, Daniel P.
  1986a *Family and Nation.* New York: Harcourt Brace Jovanovich.
  1986b "We Can't Avoid Family Policy Much Longer." *Challenge* (Septem-
        ber–October):9–17.

Nardone, Thomas J.
  1986 "Part-Time Workers: Who Are They?" *Monthly Labor Review* 109
        (February):13–19.

National Alliance of Business
  1985 *Invest in Experience: New Directions for an Aging Workforce.* Washington,
        D.C.: NAB Clearinghouse.

National Commission for Employment Policy
  1985 *Older Workers: Prospects, Problems and Policies.* Ninth Annual Report.
        Washington, D.C.: National Commission for Employment Policy.

National Commission on Employment and Unemployment Statistics
  1979 *Counting the Labor Force.* Washington, D.C.: U.S. Government Print-
        ing Office.

National Federation of Independent Business
  1985 *Small Business Employee Benefits.* Washington, D.C.: National Feder-
        ation of Independent Business, Research and Education Foundation.

New York City Coalition of Labor Union Women
  1985 *Bargaining for Child Care: Contract Language for Union Parents.* New
        York: New York City CLUW Child Care Committee.

9 to 5, National Association of Working Women
  1986 *Working at the Margins: Part-Time and Temporary Workers in the United
        States.* Cleveland: 9 to 5.
  1987 *Social Insecurity: The Economic Marginalization of Older Workers.* Cleve-
        land: 9 to 5.

Nussbaum, Karen, and Deborah Meyer
  1987 "Marginal Work Means Trouble for Workers, Economy." Cited in
        Bureau of National Affairs, *The Changing Workplace: New Directions
        in Scheduling and Staffing.* Washington, D.C.: Bureau of National
        Affairs.

OECD
  1986 *Flexibility in the Labour Market.* Paris: OECD.

Olmstead, Barney
   1983   "Changing Times: The Use of Reduced Time Options in the United States." *International Labor Review* 122:479–92.

Parnes, Herbert S.
   1981   *Work and Retirement: A Longitudinal Study of Men.* Cambridge, Mass.: MIT Press.
   1982   *Unemployment Experiences of Individuals over a Decade: Variation by Sex, Race, and Age.* Kalamazoo, Mich.: W. E. Upjohn Institute for Employment Research.
   1983   "Introduction and Overview." In *Policy Issues in Work and Retirement*, 1–27. Kalamazoo, Mich.: W. E. Upjohn Institute for Employment Research.

Parnes, Herbert S., Mary G. Gagen, and Randall H. King
   1981   "Job Loss among Long-Service Workers." In *Work and Retirement*, ed. Herbert S. Parnes, 66–92. Cambridge, Mass.: MIT Press.

Parnes, Herbert S., and Lawrence J. Less
   1985   "Shunning Retirement: The Experience of Full-Time Workers." In *Retirement among American Men*, ed. Herbert S. Parnes et al., 175–208. Lexington, Mass.: D. C. Heath.

Parnes, Herbert S., and G. Nestle
   1975   "Early Retirement." In Herbert S. Parnes et al., *The Pre-Retirement Years*, vol. 4. Washington D.C.: U.S. Government Printing Office.

Parnes, Herbert S., et al.
   1968   *The Pre-Retirement Years: A Longitudinal Study of the Labor Market Experience of the Cohort of Men 45–59 Years of Age*, vol. 1. Columbus: Center for Human Resource Research, Ohio State University.
   1975   *The Pre-Retirement Years: A Longitudinal Study of the Labor Market Experience of Men.* Manpower R & D Monograph 15. Vol. 4. Washington, D.C.: U.S. Government Printing Office.
   1985   *Retirement among American Men.* Lexington, Mass.: D. C. Heath.

Parsons, Donald O.
   1981   "Black-White Differences in Labor Force Participation of Older Males." In *Work and Retirement: A Longitudinal Study of Men*, ed. Herbert S. Parnes, 132–54. Cambridge, Mass.: MIT Press.
   1982   "The Labor Force Participation Decision: Reported Health and Economic Incentives." *Economica* 49:81–91.

Paul, Carolyn E.
   1983   "A Human Resource Management Perspective on Work Alternatives for Older Americans." Mimeo, National Commission on Employment Policy.
   1988   "Work Options—A Challenge to the Decision to Retire." *ILR Report* 25(2):18–21.

220 REFERENCES

Pellechio, Anthony
  1979 "Social Security Financing and Retirement Behavior." *American Economic Review* 69:284–87.

Personick, Valerie A.
  1987 "Industry Output and Employment through the End of the Century." *Monthly Labor Review* 110 (September):30–45.

Plath, David W.
  1988 "The Eighty-Year System: Japan's Debate over Lifetime Employment in an Aging Society." *The World and I* 3 (May):464–71.

Plewes, Thomas J.
  1988 "Understanding the Data on Part-Time and Temporary Workers." In *Flexible Workstyles: A Look at Contingent Labor*. Washington, D.C.: U.S. Department of Labor, Women's Bureau.

Podgursky, Michael, and Paul Swaim
  1987 "Job Displacement and Earnings Loss: Evidence from the Displaced Worker Survey." *Industrial and Labor Relations Review* 41(1):17–29

Porter, Sylvia
  1988 "Pensions Go to Work for Women—Finally." *Daily News*, March 26, 38.

Poterba, James, and Lawrence H. Summers
  1987 "Public Policy Implications of Declining Old-Age Mortality." In *Work, Health, and Income among the Elderly*, ed. Gary Burtless, 19–58. Washington D.C.: Brookings Institution.

Preston, Samuel H.
  1984 "Children and the Elderly: Divergent Paths for America's Dependents." *Demography* 21(4):435–57.

Program Analysis Staff
  1982 "Mortality and Early Retirement." *Social Security Bulletin* 45 (December).

Pursell, Donald E., and William D. Torrence
  1979 "Age and the Job-Hunting Methods of the Unemployed." *Monthly Labor Review* 102 (January):68–69.

Quinn, Joseph
  1977 "Microeconomic Determinants of Early Retirement: A Cross-Sectional View of White Married Men." *Journal of Human Resources* 12(3):329–46.

Rones, Phillip L.
  1983 "The Labor Market Problems of Older Workers." *Monthly Labor Review* 106 (May):3–12.

1985 "Using the CPS to Track Retirement Trends among Older Men." *Monthly Labor Review* 108 (February):46–49.

Rosen, Harvey S.
1980 "What Is Labor Supply and Do Taxes Affect It?" *American Economic Review. Papers and Proceedings* 70(2):171–75.

Rosen, Sherwin
1985 "Implicit Contracts." *Journal of Economic Literature* (September): 1144–75.

Ruhm, Christopher
1988a "From Job Shopping to Job Stopping: Career Employment and Retirement in the United States." Department of Economics Working Paper 157, Boston University.
1988b "Health and Female Labor Supply." Department of Economics Working Paper 173, Boston University.
1989 "Why Older Americans Stop Working." *Gerontologist* 29(3):294–99.

Ruhm, Christopher, and Andrew Sum
1989 "Job Stopping: The Changing Employment Patterns of Older Workers." In *Proceedings of the Winter 1988 Industrial Relations Research Association Meetings,* 21–28. Madison, Wisc.: Industrial Relations Research Association.

Sanderson, Susan R., and Lawrence Schein
1986 "Sizing up the Down-Sizing Era." *Across the Board* (November): 14–23.

Senior Community Service Employment Program
1987 "Senior Community Service Employment Program—National Summary." Mimeo.

Shank, Susan E.
1986 "Preferred Hours of Work and Corresponding Earnings." *Monthly Labor Review* 109 (November):40–44.

Shaw, Lois B.
1983 *Retirement Plans of Middle-Aged Married Women.* Columbus: Center for Human Resource Research, Ohio State University.

Silvestri, George T., and John M. Lukasiewicz
1987 "A Look at Occupational Employment Trends to the Year 2000." *Monthly Labor Review* 110 (September):46–63.

Slade, Frederick
1987 "Retirement Status and State Dependence: A Longitudinal Study of Older Men." *Journal of Labor Economics* 5(1):90–105.

Spencer, Gregory
1989 *Projections of the Population of the United States, by Age, Sex, and Race:*

1988 to 2080. U.S. Bureau of the Census, Current Population Reports, Series P–25, No. 1018. Washington, D.C.: U.S. Government Printing Office.

Sproat, Kezia
   1983   "How Do Families Fare When the Breadwinner Retires?" *Monthly Labor Review* 106 (December):40–44.

Sum, Andrew
   1977   "Why Female Labor Force Projections Have Been Too Low." *Monthly Labor Review* 97 (July):18–24.
   1988a *Estimating Potential Labor Force Participants among the Older Population: Findings of Previous Research and Their Implications for the Design of Future Surveys.* Center for Labor Market Studies, Northeastern University and Center for Applied Social Science, Boston University.
   1988b "Do Older Workers Want to Work More?" Unpublished research paper. Boston: Center for Labor Market Studies, Northeastern University.

Sum, Andrew, Neal Fogg, and Neeta Parekh
   1988   "Family Income and Poverty Problems of Young Families and Their Children." Paper presented at the Children's Defense Fund Annual Conference, Washington, D.C.

Summers, Lawrence H.
   1986   "Why Is the Unemployment Rate So Very High Near Full Employment?" *Brookings Papers on Economic Activity* 2:339–83.

Terry, Sylvia Lazos
   1982   "Unemployment and Its Effect on Family Income in 1980." *Monthly Labor Review* 105 (April):35–43.

Tschetter, John
   1987   "Producer Services: Why Are They Growing So Rapidly?" *Monthly Labor Review* 110 (December):31–40.

Uchitelle, Louis
   1988   "Reliance on Temporary Jobs Hints at Economics Fragility." *New York Times,* March 16, A1.

Ulmer, Mark G., and Wayne J. Howe
   1988   "Job Gains Strong in 1987: Unemployment Rate Declines." *Monthly Labor Review* 111 (February):57–67.

Upp, Melinda
   1983   "Relative Importance of Various Income Sources of the Aged, 1980." *Social Security Bulletin* 46(1):3–10.

U.S. Bureau of the Census
   1980   *U.S. Census of Population and Housing, 1980.* Washington, D.C.: U.S. Government Printing Office.

1987a "Money Income and Poverty Status of Persons and Families in the United States." Current Population Reports, Series P–60, No. 157. Washington, D.C.: U.S. Government Printing Office.

1987b *Technical Documentation CPS Survey.* Washington, D.C.: U.S. Government Printing Office.

U.S. Department of Labor, Bureau of Labor Statistics

1982a *BLS Handbook of Methods.* Vol. 1, Bulletin 2134–1. Washington, D.C.: U.S. Government Printing Office.

1982b *Labor Force Statistics from the Current Population Survey.* Bulletin 2020. Washington, D.C.: U.S. Government Printing Office.

1984a *Employment Projections for 1995.* Bulletin 2197. Washington, D.C.: U.S. Government Printing Office.

1984b *BLS Reports on Displaced Workers.* Washington, D.C.: U.S. Government Printing Office.

1985 *Handbook of Labor Statistics.* Washington, D.C.: U.S. Government Printing Office.

1986 *Reemployment Increases among Displaced Workers.* Washington, D.C.: U.S. Government Printing Office.

1987a *Employment and Earnings.* January.

1987b "More Than 125 Million Persons Had Some Work Experience during 1986, Up 2.3 Million from 1985." News release.

1987c "Notes on Current Labor Statistics." *Monthly Labor Review* 110 (June):63–64.

1988a *Projections 2000.* Bulletin 2302. Washington, D.C.: U.S. Government Printing Office.

1988b *Employment and Earnings.* January.

1988c *Employment and Earnings.* February.

1988d *BLS Reports on Worker Displacement.* Washington, D.C.: U.S. Government Printing Office.

1989 *Employment and Earnings.* January.

U.S. General Accounting Office

1986 *Dislocated Workers: Extent of Business Closures, Layoffs, and the Public and Private Response.* Washington, D.C.

U.S. President

1986 *The State of Small Business. Report of the President.* Washington, D.C.: U.S. Government Printing Office.

U.S. Small Business Administration, Office of Advocacy

1988 *Small Business in the American Economy.* Washington, D.C.: U.S. Government Printing Office.

CONTRIBUTORS

EILEEN APPELBAUM received a Ph.D. in economics from the University of Pennsylvania in 1973 and is now a professor of economics at Temple University. She has served as a consultant to the Office of Technology Assessment of the U.S. Congress on the effects of factory and office automation on employment and on the employment effects of trade in services. Appelbaum's research has focused on the effects on employment of such major changes in the U.S. economy as the increased economic role of women, the diffusion of information and computation technologies, the growth of part-time and other contingent work arrangements, and the shift toward service jobs. She has published numerous articles on these topics and is the author of four books, including *Back to Work* and *Job Saving Strategies: Worker Ownership*.

RICHARD S. BELOUS is vice-president of international affairs and a senior economist at the National Planning Association (NPA). He is also North American director of the British–North American Committee, of which NPA is the U.S. sponsoring organization. Before joining NPA, Belous served as a senior research associate with the Conference Board and as an economist with the Congressional Research Service. He has been an adviser to several presidential commissions and has written four books and numerous articles in the fields of international economics and human resources. Belous earned a Ph.D. in economics from George Washington University, where he is an adjunct lecturer.

KATHLEEN CHRISTENSEN is an associate professor of environmental psychology at the Graduate School and University Center, City University of New York. She specializes in issues of women's employment and contingent work and is the author of *Women and Home-Based Work: The Unspoken Contract* and editor of *The New Era of Home-Based Work: Directions and Policies* and *Flexible Workstyles: A Look at Contingent Labor*. She is currently directing a national survey on alternative work arrangements and recently wrote *A Look at Flexible Scheduling and Staffing in U.S. Corporations.* She holds a Ph.D. in geography from Pennsylvania State University.

PETER B. DOERINGER joined the faculty of Boston University in 1974 as a professor of economics and served as director of the Institute for Employment Policy until 1987. He has also taught labor economics at Harvard University and been a lecturer at the London School of Economics. Doeringer's research specialties include labor markets, industrial policy, and economic development. He contributes regularly to professional journals and has published seven books, including *Internal Labor Markets and Manpower Analysis* and *Invisible Factors in Local Economic Development.* He has served frequently as a consultant and adviser on employment and industrial policies to government agencies and chaired the Task Force on Older Workers in the Commonwealth of Massachusetts. Doeringer, who holds a Ph.D. in economics from Harvard University, is also a practicing labor arbitrator and a member of the National Academy of Arbitrators.

W. NEAL FOGG is a research associate at the Center for Labor Market Studies at Northeastern University. His research work has focused on the changing employment patterns and problems of young male adults, the employment problems of older workers, and the economic and social conditions of families in the United States. His research publications include *Withered Dreams: The Declining Economic Fortunes of America's Non-College Bound Male Adults, The Massachusetts Construction Boom: Implications for Employment and Training Programs,* and *Welfare Impacts of Full Employment in Massachusetts.* He holds a master's degree in economics from Northeastern University.

JUDITH GREGORY is in the Ph.D. program of the Department of Communication at the University of California, San Diego. Previously she was a research associate with the Department for Professional Employees of the AFL-CIO and was research director for 9 to 5, National Association of Working Women. Gregory's research interests focus on women's issues in white-collar employment, and she co-edited the book *Office Automation: Jekyll or Hyde?* on office work and new technologies. She also served as a member of the advisory panel of the U.S. Congress Office of Technological Assessment Study on Computer Technology in the American Economic Transition.

CHRISTOPHER J. RUHM is an assistant professor of economics and a research associate at the Center for Applied Social Science at Boston University and a postdoctoral research fellow at the Florence Heller Graduate School for Advanced Studies in Social Welfare at Brandeis University. He received his Ph.D. in economics from the University of California, Berkeley. In addition to his studies on older workers, Ruhm has conducted extensive research into the causes and impact of labor displacement in the United States, the mechanisms by which income inequality might persist over time, and the effects of health problems on labor force participation.

ANDREW M. SUM is a professor of economics and the director of the Center for Labor Market Studies at Northeastern University. His research interests have been in the fields of labor market analysis, human resource program planning and evaluation, and youth employment problems and programs. His recent publications include *Vanishing Dreams: The Growing Economic Plight of America's Young Families, Toward a More Perfect Union: Basic Skills, Poor Families and Our Economic Future,* and *Cracking the Labor Market: Human Resource Planning in the 1980s.* He holds a master's degree in economics from the Massachusetts Institute of Technology.

DAVID G. TERKLA is an assistant professor of economics at the University of Massachusetts, Boston, and a senior research associate at the Center for Applied Social Science at Boston University. In addition to his research on the labor market for older workers, he has published in the areas of local economic development, fishery economics, and environmental economics. His recent books include *The New England Fishing Economy: Jobs, Income, and Kinship* and *Invisible Factors in Local Economic Development.* He holds a Ph.D. in economics from the University of California, Berkeley.

INDEX

Abt Associates, 46
AFL-CIO, 137, 139
Aging of population, effect on
work force, 147
Akerlof, George, 96n6
American Association of Retired
Persons (AARP), 12, 123, 146,
179
American Federation of State,
County and Municipal Work-
ers, 137, 144
Anderson, Kathryn, 24
Appelbaum, Eileen, 131
Asians. *See* Minorities, Asian
Assets, 29
Autonomy, desire for, among
older workers, 203

Barzel, Yoram, 4, 146
Bazzoli, Gloria, 24, 27, 29
Bell, Daniel, 133
Belous, Richard S., 112, 114, 117,
121
Blacks. *See* Minorities, nonwhite
Blank, Rebecca M., 56
Blinder, Alan, 24, 27, 29
Boskin, Michael J., 4, 24, 27, 29,
31, 146
Bould, Sally, 70
Brechling, Frank, 53
Bridge jobs, 5–7, 11–12,
13–14, 33, 46–47, 49–50,

63, 79, 89–91, 92, 98, 99,
100, 106, 107, 111, 112, 120,
132, 134–35, 147–48,
150–51, 160–62, 164–68,
175
appropriateness of concept for
women, 190
and flexible employment,
176–77
older workers' attitudes toward,
198–99
Bureau of Labor Statistics. *See*
U.S. Department of
Labor, Bureau of Labor
Statistics
Bureau of National Affairs, 123,
125
Bureaucratic firms, 160, 162, 164,
166
Burkhauser, Richard, 4, 24, 25,
27, 29, 146
Burtless, Gary, 24, 27, 29, 30,
102n12
Business necessity, 146–47, 151,
161, 164–67
Butler, J., 24

Career continuity, desire for,
203–4
Career jobs. *See* Employment,
career
Carter administration, 200